THE CHILDREN ACT 1989:
PUTTING IT INTO PRACTICE

To Archie and my children
Daniel, Max and Euan

The Children Act 1989: Putting it into Practice

Mary Ryan

Published by
Arena
Ashgate Publishing Limited
Gower House
Croft Road
Aldershot
Hants GU11 3HR
England

Ashgate Publishing Company
Old Post Road
Brookfield
Vermont 05036
USA

British Library Cataloguing in Publication Data

Ryan, Mary
  Children Act 1989: Putting it
  into Practice
  I. Title
  362.7

ISBN 1 85742 192 2 (Hardback)
ISBN 1 85742 193 0 (Paperback)

Typeset in 10 point Palatino by Photoprint, Torquay, Devon and printed in Great Britain at the University Press, Cambridge

Contents

Acknowledgements

In many ways this book is a collective effort because so much of the practical information contained in it arises from my involvement in the advice, training and policy work of the Family Rights Group over the last eleven years.

I would like to thank all my colleagues, past and present, but in particular Jo Tunnard and Celia Atherton for their continuing support, careful reading of the text, helpful comments and criticisms, and direct input, particularly in the chapter on child protection. In addition I would like to thank Liz Dornan for typing all the drafts.

Note on references and terms listed

In this book when the term 'care' is used in relation to pre-1989 legislation it refers to children in both compulsory and voluntary care, which would now be care or accommodation.

References to section numbers or paragraphs from schedules are from the Children Act 1989. References to schedules combined with a section or paragraph number, or standing alone, are to schedules of the Children Act 1989. References to schedules following a Regulation are to the schedules of those particular Regulations. Where a reference is made to other legislation the relevant Act is included in the reference. Initials are used as follows:

FLRA 1987   Family Law Reform Act 1987
CYPA 1969   Children and Young Persons Act 1969
PACE 1984   Police and Criminal Evidence Act 1984

There are two relevant sets of court rules:

- the Family Proceedings Court (Children Act) Rules 1991, referred to as FPC 1991, which apply to the family proceedings courts,

- the Family Proceedings Rules 1991, which apply in the county court care centres and the High Court, referred to as FP 1991.

The rule numbers are mainly the same and we have used the FPC 1991 rules throughout, except where there is a difference between them, which is indicated in the text.

1 Setting the scene

Introduction

This book concentrates on those parts of the Children Act 1989 that relate to the provision of services by local authorities to children and families; the powers and duties of local authorities in such circumstances; care and supervision proceedings, and child protection issues. There is some consideration of the private law in so far as it relates to child care matters, and to the court system and the principles which govern it.

The book is intended for use by key frontline workers and managers involved in child care work, especially social workers, guardians *ad litem*, education welfare officers, teachers, probation officers, senior nursing officers, doctors, health visitors, and police officers working in juvenile bureaux or special assessment teams. It is also relevant for child care solicitors based in a local authority or private practice.

The Children Act is important, not just because it is such a comprehensive piece of legislation, but because it is also the end product of a substantial amount of debate about law and practice, and philosophy and principle.

History

In 1984 the House of Commons Social Services Committee produced a report on children in care. The report (known as the Short Report) did not doubt the good intentions of workers and agencies but it was critical of the lack of resources and skills made available to promote the well-being of children in the community and in care. The committee considered child

1

care law to be in urgent need of reform. It stated that the aim of the review of child care law that they proposed should be

'the production of a simplified and coherent body of law comprehensible not only to those operating it but also to those affected by its operation. It is not just to make life easier for practitioners that the law must be sorted out; it is for the sake of justice that the legal framework of the child care system must be rationalised.' (House of Commons 1984)

The Government responded by setting up an inter-departmental working party which, between July 1984 and September 1985, carried out a detailed consultation exercise on all aspects of child care law. Their report made 223 recommendations for improving, clarifying and consolidating both child care law and health and welfare legislation relating to children (DHSS 1985(1)).

This was followed in January 1987 by the publication of a White Paper which set out proposals for a new legislative framework largely based on the recommendations of the review (DHSS 1987(1)).

At the same time, between 1985 and 1988, the Law Commission was issuing consultation papers on the law relating to children involved in custody, guardianship and wardship proceedings. Their final report (Law Commission 1988), issued shortly after the Cleveland Inquiry Report (DHSS 1987(2)), contained a draft bill which formed the basis of the Children Bill introduced into Parliament in November 1988.

There were other important influences on the Act. First, there were research studies into the circumstances of children in care. Nine separate studies looking at the child care service in 49 local authorities and covering some 2,000 children had been produced, and their findings brought together and published by the DHSS in 1985. These studies painted a sober picture of current practice, and concluded that 'the gap between aims and achievements in the child care service is still distressingly wide' (DHSS 1985(2), p.22).

Second, there were enquiries into policy and practice in different local authority areas – Cleveland, Brent, Lambeth and Greenwich – in response to a particular case or set of cases. These attracted considerable public interest, and all made specific proposals for changes in practice and in legislation.

Third, important court cases in the 1980s established principles which were to find their way into the legislation. The Gillick case (*Gillick* v. *West Norfolk Health Authority* (1986) AC 112) established that parental rights, now replaced with parental responsibility, diminished as children grew in age and understanding, and that a child under 16 of sufficient understanding could give or withhold consent to medical treatment. A number of cases in the European Court successfully challenged the legal position in the UK on access to children in care, and emphasised that parents should be able to participate in planning and decision making concerning their children (*O, H, W, B and R* v. *United Kingdom*, case nos. 2/1986/100/148 to 6/1986/104/152, (1987) *The Times*, 9 July).

Key principles and philosophy

Many of the key principles underlying the Act emerged clearly from the findings of research and the process of consultation described above. Some of them were spelt out in the Government's review paper and the resulting White Paper. More recently, the Department of Health (DOH) completed and published a comprehensive list of the principles governing social work with children and families which underpin the Act (DOH 1989(1)). The following list highlights the key principles, drawn from the above documents and from the Act itself, which are particularly relevant to the issues covered in this book:

- The primary responsibility for the upbringing of children rests with families, and for most children their interests will be served best by enabling them to grow up within their own families. Where children are separated from their families they should be enabled to maintain contact with them. The way the Act is drafted, with a number of specific references to 'parents, relatives and friends', clarifies that, within this principle, there is a recognition that 'family' means the wider extended family and includes close family friends.
- Race, culture, language and religion are crucially important when either the courts or local authorities are making decisions about children. The Act re-emphasises the requirements of the Race Relations Act in relation to service delivery, and specifically encourages the development of anti-racist family and child care practice.
- When children are receiving services from the local authority – whether living at home, or when being provided with accommo-dation, or when in care – the relationship between those children and their families and the local authority should be one based, wherever possible, on partnership and participation. Partnership and partici-pation involve empowering children and families, providing infor-mation, encouraging active involvement in decision making and providing a system for resolving disagreements.
- Children should be involved as fully as possible in actions and decisions about themselves. This is emphasised in the requirements on courts and professionals to consult children and to take their

wishes and views into consideration, in giving children themselves the right to apply for court orders, and in the recognition of their right to refuse consent to medical or psychiatric examinations or treatment, or other assessments. Regrettably this last principle has been undermined by court decisions since the implementation of the Act, most notably *Re W (A Minor) (Consent to Medical Treatment)* [1993] 1 FLR 1 (see page 85).

- The provision of substitute care should be seen as a service for children and families to help avoid long-term family breakdown. The provision of accommodation by a local authority on a voluntary basis should be seen as just one of the family support services available, and should be viewed positively rather than negatively. If, in order to protect them, children need to live away from their families, this should be arranged, wherever possible, on a voluntary rather than a compulsory basis.

- The approach to the provision of services to children and families by the local authority should be a corporate one, with the local authority as a whole having clear policies about service provision under the Act. The Act also recognises the importance of multi-agency, multi-disciplinary work, and co-operation between different agencies and authorities and different professions.

- There should be only one route for the state to intervene in family life: through the courts, and only on the basis that the child is suffering, or is likely to suffer, significant harm. Court procedures should be fair.

- There should be a rationalisation of the legal framework, including the bringing together for the first time of private and public law relating to children.

These principles will be examined in more detail in Chapter 2. The central underlying theme is that of partnership.

Partnership – the central theme

The word 'partnership' does not appear in the legislation and regulations, but it does occur many times in Government guidance on the Act and in the DOH list of principles that should underpin practice (DOH 1989(1)):

'One of the key principles of the Children Act is that responsible authorities should work in partnership with the parents of the child who is being looked after and also with the child himself, where he is of sufficient understanding, provided that this approach will not jeopardise his welfare. A second, closely related principle, is that parents and children should participate actively in the decision-making process . . .

Planning and review of a child's case, with the involvement of parents, will provide the basis of partnership between the responsible authorities and parents and child. The development of a successful working partnership between the responsible authorities and the parents and the child, where he is of sufficient understanding, should enable the placement to proceed positively so that the child's welfare is safeguarded and promoted . . .

Although genuine partnership will be easier to achieve in the absence of compulsory measures, the same kind of approach should be taken in cases where a child is in the care of the local authority as a result of a court order. This will be achieved by:

(a) Consulting and notifying the parents about decisions affecting the child;
(b) Promoting contact between the child and his parents and family where it is reasonably practicable and consistent with the child's welfare; and
(c) By seeking to work with the parents to achieve a safe and stable environment for the child to return to (where this is judged feasible) or by finding a satisfactory alternative placement for the child.'

(DOH 1991(3), Vol. 3, paras. 2.10–2.12)

It has been argued that the term 'partnership' is an inappropriate one to use when talking about relationships between powerful agencies and the children and families in whose lives they intervene and to whom they provide services. A commitment to working in partnership with children and families is, however, one of the main principles underlying the Act. It is, therefore, crucially important that practitioners are prepared to shift and challenge attitudes and old ways of working so that partnerships are able to develop despite the unequal balance of power.

'Partnership' can be defined as working together towards a mutually agreed goal. Partners may have different amounts of power, but partnership will involve a genuine commitment to open negotiation with clients about how best to promote and safeguard the welfare of children. Clients need to be empowered to engage in this negotiation by having easy access to clear information about services and about ways in which services can be delivered.

2 Some general legal principles and the forum for cases

Introduction

This chapter comments first on the bringing together of private and public law. It then explores the principles which guide all courts in making decisions under the Children Act 1989, explains the principle of 'parental responsibility', and describes the private law orders available and how they link with the public law. The final section is about the new court structure.

Public and private law

The private law governs relations between different individuals. Public law governs the powers and duties of local authorities and other organisations towards children and families, and it controls the extent of state intervention in family life. For the first time the public and private law relating to children is now brought together in a single piece of legislation. Moreover, the Act now incorporates into child care law certain aspects of health and public welfare law, relating primarily to children with disabilities. The Children Act also represents a final break away from the Children and Young Persons Act 1969 principle of grouping together delinquent and deprived children. The failure to implement CYPA 1969 fully meant that this principle has never been properly tested, and the way the legislation operated in practice pending implementation was found to be unsatisfactory for both groups of children. The Children Act now makes a clear distinction between civil and criminal matters concerning children.

Principles which guide the courts

The following principles apply to all proceedings concerning the upbringing of children brought under the Act, whether they are private or public law proceedings.

Welfare principle

In 1987 the Government's White Paper on child care law (DHSS 1987(1)) noted that: 'The lack of clarity is perhaps the most striking defect in the present law . . . An essential part of clarification is to rationalise and where possible simplify existing legislation' (para. 7, p.2). Part of that simplification process is the introduction by this Act of a single welfare principle to apply in all cases concerning the upbringing of a child; the principle is that 'the child's welfare shall be the court's paramount consideration' (s.1(1)). It applies only to decision making by courts, and there are still some proceedings where another principle applies instead. For example, in adoption proceedings under the Adoption Act 1976 the child's welfare is the 'first' consideration.

Decisions based on the welfare of the child are ultimately value judgements, albeit based on some current influential theories about child rearing. In an attempt to introduce some uniformity in the courts' approach to decision making under the Children Act a checklist has been attached to the welfare principle. The checklist sets out specific matters that must be considered when a decision is being made (s.1(3)). The list is short and general and, in the Law Commission's view, designed not only to help the courts in their considerations but also to help the parties, their legal advisers, welfare officers and guardians *ad litem* when preparing relevant evidence for the hearing (Law Commission 1988). The checklist applies in contested private law cases and in all care and supervision cases. The factors listed are:

'(a) the ascertainable wishes and feelings of the child concerned (considered in the light of his age and understanding);
(b) his physical, emotional and educational needs;
(c) the likely effect on him of any change in his circumstances;
(d) his age, sex, background and any characteristics of his which the court considers relevant;
(e) any harm which he has suffered or is at risk of suffering;
(f) how capable each of his parents, and any other person in relation to whom the court considers the question to be relevant, is of meeting his needs;
(g) the range of powers available to the court under this Act in the proceedings in question.' (s.1(3))

It is a matter of regret that the checklist does not refer specifically to the importance of considering a child's racial origin, religious persuasion and cultural and linguistic background. The Act requires local authorities and other agencies to take these factors into consideration when making any decision about a child they are looking after or proposing to look after. Those involved in cases concerning children should raise these issues under part (e) of the checklist.

Principle of non-intervention

The second principle governing the courts is the principle of non-intervention, also known as the efficacy principle:

> 'Where a court is considering whether or not to make one or more orders under this Act with respect to a child, it shall not make the order or any of the orders unless it considers that doing so would be better for the child than making no order at all.' (s.1(5))

Again, this principle applies in all proceedings concerning children, including care and supervision proceedings. In relation to the private law it arises from the desire to encourage and enable parents, if their relationship breaks down, to make their own arrangements for their children without the necessity of always obtaining a court order. In relation to the public law it arises from the concern that there was a tendency for courts to make care or supervision orders under previous legislation simply because the grounds had been made out, without proper consideration being given to what the order would achieve. Now the court must be satisfied that the order will be *better* for the child than any other order or no order. There are a variety of reasons why it may be better to make an order, even where all the parties are in agreement, for example in order to give a relative parental responsibility for the child living with them (*B* v. *B (A Minor) (Residence Order)* [1992] 2 FLR 327).

Delay

The third principle governing court proceedings is that 'any delay in determining the question [of the child's upbringing] is likely to prejudice the welfare of the child' (s.1(2)).

The court has specific powers in both private and public law cases to set a timetable within which cases must be heard, and there is provision for court rules to require certain steps to be taken within certain time-limits (ss.11 and 32). It is important that the legislation recognises specifically the damaging effect on children of delay, but it remains to be seen whether these provisions will – without an increase in resources such as available courts, adjudicators and guardians *ad litem* – ensure that cases are heard as quickly as possible. It must also be remembered that in some cases delay in having a hearing can actually be helpful. Perhaps 'constructive delay' would be an appropriate term for those cases where work is going on to resolve the dispute or problem, and the delay in having a hearing enables arrangements to be made by agreement, rather than through a heavily contested court case. In some cases a delay for the purpose of ascertaining the result of an assessment is a proper delay and to be encouraged (*Re C (A Minor) (Care Proceedings)* [1992] 2 FCR 341).

Parental responsibility

The Act has replaced parental rights and duties with parental responsibility. Although the definition of parental responsibility (s.3(1)) is very similar to the definition of parental rights, the change is more than just a semantic one. It marks an important ideological shift away from the notion of children as possessions over whom parents have 'rights' – albeit diminishing rights, as established in the Gillick case – to a position where parents and others looking after children are seen to have responsibilities towards those children. Where a family is receiving services from the local authority, or have a child who is being looked after by the authority, the recognition that parents have continuing responsibility for their children should help professionals working with those families to see their role as helping people to meet their responsibilities. The term 'person with parental responsibility' appears throughout the Act, sometimes together with, and sometimes in place of, the term 'parent', from which it must be distinguished. It is important to be clear who is a parent and who has parental responsibility, and whether or not any court or local authority restrictions have been placed on the exercise of parental responsibility.

Who is a parent?

As this Act came into force after the Family Law Reform Act 1987, any reference to 'parents' includes non-married fathers, whether or not they have obtained parental responsibility (s.1, FLRA 1987).

Who has parental responsibility?

- Mothers and *married* fathers will always have parental responsibility. They will never lose parental responsibility unless an adoption order is made, but their exercise of their responsibility may be limited or curtailed by a particular statutory provision, or by the existence of an order made under this Act (s.2(1), and see below).

Other people can acquire parental responsibility:

- Non-married fathers can acquire parental responsibility either by agreement with the mother or by a court order called a 'parental responsibility' order (s.4). The agreement has to be made out on a special form available from the court. In addition, if a residence order (s.8, and see page 12) is made in favour of an non-married father, the court will also make a parental responsibility order in his favour (s.12(1)). A non-married father who acquires parental responsibility, either by agreement or by a court order, can lose it only if a court subsequently discharges the order or agreement (s.4(3)).
- Any other person in whose favour a residence order is made acquires parental responsibility for so long as the residence order lasts. Parental responsibility is lost if the residence order is discharged (s.12(2)).
- A person appointed as guardian, on the death of a parent, will have parental responsibility (s.5(6)).
- Local authorities acquire parental responsibility when an emergency protection order or an interim or final care order is made in relation to a child (ss.33(3) and 44(4)).

Limits on parental responsibility

Several people can have parental responsibility for the same child at the same time. Usually this would be two parents, but if other people have acquired parental responsibility there may be three or more people who have it (ss.2(5) and (6)). Generally, each person with parental responsibility may act independently of the others (s.2(7)), but some limitations apply:

- Where a particular piece of legislation requires consent for an action. For example, both parents with parental responsibility need to give their consent or have their consent dispensed with in adoption cases (s.16, Adoption Act 1976).
- Where an order is in force under the Act, exercise of parental responsibility should not be incompatible with the order. For example, if a residence order has been made on divorce in favour of the mother, then the father, although retaining parental responsibility, should not do anything that will undermine that residence order.
- When any person who is *not* a non-married father acquires parental responsibility as a result of a residence order being made in their favour they cannot:
  - consent to an application for freeing for adoption

  – consent to the making of an adoption order
  – appoint a guardian for the child (s.12(3)).

- When a residence order is in force no one can remove the child from the UK for more than a month, nor can they change the child's surname without either the written consent of everyone with parental responsibility or the leave of the court (s.13).
- When a care order is in force the local authority can determine the extent to which a parent or guardian may meet their parental responsibility for the child, providing that is necessary in order to safeguard or promote the child's welfare (s.33(3), see page 119).

Private law orders

Most private law orders are contained in section 8 of the Act. They are:

A residence order

This is an order settling the arrangements about where a child should live. It replaces custody and custodianship orders. It can be made in favour of more than one person, and could, for example, order that a child spend part of the week with one person and part of the week with another. Conditions can be attached to the order. For example, a condition could be attached that the person with the residence order should not move address, or that the children should not be removed from where they are living. If a residence order is made in favour of someone who is not the child's parent or guardian, they will have parental responsibility (limited, as mentioned above) for as long as the order remains in force. The existence of a residence order affects the exercise of parental responsibility (see above).

A contact order

This is an order requiring the person with whom the child lives to allow the child to visit or stay with the person named in the order, or some other sort of contact to take place. It replaces an access order, and covers more than just visits and overnight or longer stays. It would be possible, for example, to order that someone could phone a child every so often and exchange letters with them, even if they were not seeing them. Guidance on the Act states that a contact order is a permissive order, and cannot be used to stop contact taking place. If this is what is desired, a prohibited steps order (see following page) should be applied for (DOH 1991(3), Vol. 1, para. 2.30).

However, a judgement in the High Court and Court of Appeal has contradicted this guidance (*Nottinghamshire CC* v. *P* [1993] 1 FLR 514, and [1993] 2 FLR 134; see also page 142).

A specific issue order

Both this order and a prohibited steps order (see below) have been developed from the flexible orders that are available in wardship proceedings. The specific issue order is designed to resolve specific questions or disputes that arise in connection with any aspect of parental responsibility for a child. This could be a dispute between parents, or parents and others, over medical treatment or the education or religion of the child. It would be possible for a local authority to apply for a specific issue order (providing they were granted leave, see below) to require a parent to take a child to a clinic or nursery.

A prohibited steps order

This is an order preventing *any person* from taking any step in relation to a child which could be taken by a parent in meeting their parental responsibilities. It can be used to prevent the child's removal from a particular place, or to prevent a change of school, or to stop someone having contact with a child. It cannot be used to prevent parents from having contact with each other (*Croydon LBC* v. *A* (no. 1) [1992] 2 FLR 341). As this order can be made against any person, it could be made against someone who is not a party to the proceedings.

Enforcement of section 8 orders

If a section 8 order is made and one of the parties involved then fails to abide by the order – for example by failing to return a child after a visit, or by threatening to remove the child from the country – they can be taken back to court. In the High Court and county court the person who is in breach of the order is in contempt of court, and the court has the power to make an order sending them to prison. In the family proceedings court, an application can be made to enforce the order, and the court has the power to fine or imprison the person who is in breach of the order (s.63(3), Magistrates' Courts Act 1980). In family cases, sending someone to prison for breach of an order should only be used as a last resort (*Ansah* v. *Ansah* [1977] Fam. Law 138; *Churchard* v. *Churchard* [1984] FLR 635).

The courts also have powers to order a person whom they believe knows the child's whereabouts to disclose that information to the court, and to authorise the police or an officer of the court to search for a child, entering premises and using force if necessary, in order to find the child and return them to their proper carer (ss.33 and 34, Family Law Act 1986). When using this process to get a child returned it would be sensible also to apply for a prohibited steps order to prevent the child's removal (see pages 82–3 on enforcing public law orders).

If a child is taken out of the United Kingdom or there is a threat to do this – whether in breach of an order or not – the provisions in relation to child abduction will apply (Child Abduction Act 1984; Child Abduction and Custody Act 1985).

Injunctions

In the High Court and county court, injunctions to protect children and their carers from violence or molestation can be made in Children Act proceedings against a party to those proceedings. The High Court has an inherent power to make such injunctions, and the county court has the power through legislation (s.38, County Courts Act 1984). In the family proceedings court such orders can only be made if the case concerns a married couple and one of them has also started proceedings under the Domestic Proceedings and Magistrates' Court Act 1978. If it is a case where an injunction is necessary, the proceedings should start in the county court or High Court.

Emergencies

In an emergency injunctions can be applied for without giving notice to the other party – an *ex parte* application. *Ex parte* applications can also be made for prohibited steps and specific issue orders (rule 4(4)). A case decided by the Court of Appeal soon after implementation established that an *ex parte* application for a residence order could be made (*Re B (A Minor) (Residence Order: Ex Parte)* [1992] 2 FLR 1). Subsequently, the court rules were amended to clarify that both residence and contact orders could be applied for *ex parte* (FPC (Miscellaneous Amendments) Rules 1992, SI 92/2068; FP (Amendment no. 2) Rules 1992, SI 92/2067).

Other orders

Other private law orders that are available are a parental responsibility order (s.4(1)), which can be applied for only by a child's non-married father, a guardianship order (s.5), which deals with the appointment of legal guardians for children whose parents have died, and a family assistance order (s.16), which replaces the matrimonial supervision order. It can be made in any family proceedings where the court has the power to make a section 8 order, regardless of whether it makes such an order; where there are exceptional circumstances, and where all the adults involved agree to the order being made. The order can last for only six months and is designed to provide focused work with a family suffering disruption or conflict as a result of family breakdown. It is likely to be particularly useful where there are problems over contact arrangements, although it remains to be seen what circumstances the courts will consider as 'exceptional' and thus justifying an order being made. In a case decided since the implementation of the Act, the court said a local authority could not be required to supervise contact by way of a condition attached to a residence order, instead a family assistance order should be made (*Leeds City Council* v. C [1993] 1 FCR 585). Either a probation officer or an 'officer of the local authority' will be appointed to work with the family under this order. Usually this will be a social worker, particularly if one is involved already with the family, but it would be open to the court to appoint, for example, a welfare rights officer if the local authority had one, and if debt was the family's main problem.

Who can apply?

One of the important changes introduced by the Act is the 'open door' policy about applications concerning children. Anyone can apply for a section 8 order in relation to a child, though there is a distinction between people particularly close to the child – who are *entitled* to apply – and other people who have to seek the court's permission, or 'leave', to make the application. The new legislation thus gives children's relatives and friends far greater access to legal remedies than before. In addition, and also an important innovation, children of 'sufficient understanding' are given the right to seek leave to make their own applications for orders.

Parents, guardians (under s.5), and people with a residence order are entitled to apply for *any* section 8 order (s.10(4)).

The following people are entitled to apply for a *residence* or *contact order* only (they would have to seek leave to apply for any other section 8 order):

(i)   step-parents (in relation to their stepchildren)
(ii) any person with whom the child has lived for at least three years
(iii) any person who has the consent of:

- (where there is a residence order in force) all those with the residence order in their favour;
- (where the child is in care) the local authority;
- (in any other case) all those with parental responsibility. (s.10(5))

Those who have to seek leave first are:

- Children, who may seek leave to make any section 8 application. The court may grant leave only if satisfied that the child has sufficient understanding to make the application (s.10(8)).
- Anyone else not listed above must seek leave to make any section 8 application. When they seek leave the court must consider:

  (i)   the nature of the proposed application
  (ii)   the applicant's connection with the child
  (iii) the possible risk of the child being harmed by disruption to her/ his life by the application being made.

- In addition, if children are being looked after by a local authority the court must consider:

  (i)   the authority's plans for the child's future
  (ii)   the wishes and feelings of the child's parents (s.10(9)).

Section 8 orders can be made in the course of any family proceedings (s.8(3) and (4)), which includes care and supervision and adoption proceedings. The court is able to make any section 8 order, even if no one has specifically applied for it. In addition, applications can be made for section 8 orders even if no other proceedings are going on (s.10(1)).

Restrictions

There are some restrictions on the making of section 8 orders:

- If a child is under a care order the only section 8 order that can be made is a residence order. If a residence order is made, that discharges the care order (ss.9(1) and 91(1)).
- A local authority cannot apply for, or have made in its favour, a residence or contact order. This is to ensure that a local authority obtains control over a child only by establishing the conditions for a care or supervision order (s.9(2)).
- A local authority is able to seek leave of the court to apply for a specific issue or prohibited steps order in relation to a child, providing the aim of the application is not designed to give power to the *local authority* to make decisions that control the exercise of parental responsibility for the child (ss.9(5) and 10(1) and (2)). The order can be made if the court is to refer the matter to another person, such as a doctor, or is to make the decision itself.
- Local authority foster carers who are not relatives of the child concerned and who have not had the child living with them for three years must obtain the consent of the local authority before seeking leave to apply for a section 8 order if the child concerned is or was in

accommodation and is not in care (s.9(3) and (4)). If the child is in care and the foster carers obtain the local authority's consent to make an application they then become entitled to make the application rather than having to seek the court's leave (s.10(5)(c)(ii)).

Court structure

One further aspect of the clarification and simplification process of this legislation is the introduction of concurrent jurisdiction. For many of those involved in child care work the Act was disappointing in that it failed to devise and introduce a proper family court structure. The changes that have been introduced have removed some of the worst complexities and anomalies of the old system, but it is to be hoped that change will not stop here and that the current position is merely a step on the way to a proper family court system.

Concurrent jurisdiction

The relevant courts for cases under this Act are the magistrates' courts, the county courts and the High Court. Concurrent jurisdiction means that all these courts have the same powers to deal with cases concerning children under the Act, and that cases can be transferred, either to a higher court or to another court at the same level.

At the magistrates' court level it will be the family proceedings court that deals with all cases under the Act, whether they are private or public law cases. At county court level not all courts will be able to hear children's cases. One hundred courts have been designated as 'family hearing centres' able to deal with private law applications under the Act and with other family proceedings concerning children. Fifty of these centres are also 'care centres', and these are the only county courts able to hear public law cases as well (article 2 and schedules 1 and 2, The Children (Allocation of Proceedings) Order 1991).

Care and supervision and other public law applications, including applications for emergency protection orders, must normally be made to the family proceedings court (article 3). However, if the public law proceedings arise out of the High Court or county court directing a local authority to investigate the case of a particular child under section 37 (see page 98), they should be started in the court that directed the investigation. Similarly, if other *public* law proceedings concerning the same child are continuing in another court, then the application should be made to that court (article 3(2) and (3)).

Cases can be transferred between different family proceedings courts if this will help the case to be dealt with sooner, or if other proceedings concerning the same family are going on in that other court (article 6). Cases can be transferred to the relevant county court care centre (article 18(3)) where:

- The case is of exceptional gravity, importance or complexity. For example, there might be complicated or conflicting evidence, or a multiplicity of parties and cross-applications, or an important point of law or public policy to be raised.
- There is a need to consolidate with other proceedings. For example, other proceedings involving the same child or the same family might be continuing in another court.
- A transfer would 'significantly . . . accelerate' the hearing, no other method of speeding up the proceedings – including transfer to another family proceedings court – is appropriate, and delay would seriously prejudice the interests of the child. Given the overall principle that delay in hearing a case is detrimental to children's welfare, it would be necessary to show that there was a need for special urgency in this particular case (article 7(1)).

In order for any case to be transferred to the High Court, other than for the purpose of consolidation, it must be established that the proceedings are 'appropriate' for determination in that court, and that transfer would be in the interests of the child (article 12). Cases cannot go direct from the family proceedings court to the High Court, unless for consolidation. However, once the county court is considering whether to transfer a case, or has a case transferred to it, it must also consider whether the case should go up to the High Court (articles 9 and 12).

Care centres can transfer cases to another care centre, and the High Court can transfer cases down to the county court, on the basis that this would be in the interests of the child concerned (articles 10 and 13). The order governing transfer of proceedings under the Act applies also to adoption and freeing for adoption proceedings (article 5).

A number of early cases dealt with allocation and transfer under the Act. They have indicated that:

- Where a case is likely to be lengthy (defined in one case as anything over three days) it will probably not be appropriate for it to be dealt with in the family proceedings court, and it should be transferred to the county or High Court (*L* v. *Berkshire CC* [1992] 1 FCR 481; *Essex CC* v. *L (Minors)* (1992) *The Times*, 18 December).
- Where a child is seeking leave to make an application under the Children Act or is making an application the application should be

made to the High Court or transferred there immediately (*Re AD (A Minor)* [1993] Fam. Law 43, January, and *Practice Direction* [1993] 1 FLR 668).

- If the effect of making the order applied for would be to vary an earlier order or direction of a court made before the Act came into force, the application should be made to the court which made the earlier order (*Sunderland BC* v. *A*, unreported, 15 May 1992).
- Where cases have an international dimension they should be dealt with in the High Court (*Re L (A Minor)*, unreported, 28 September 1992).

Procedure for transfer

Any party to proceedings can request that the case be transferred to a higher court, and the family proceedings court can decide of its own accord to transfer the case. Any request must be in writing. It will be considered by a justices' clerk, a single justice, or the family proceedings court. The request will be either granted or refused.

If the request is refused, the person making the application must be given a certificate by the justices' clerk (rule 6, FPC 1991) and they are then able, within two days of receiving the certificate, to make an application for transfer direct to the county court (article 9). The other parties to the proceedings must be notified of this application, and they have two days to file written representations with the court. Four days from the filing of the application the county court can either grant or refuse the application on the basis of the written representations, or they can set a date for a hearing of the matter, giving one day's notice of the hearing to all the parties (rule 4.6, FP 1991).

All these tight time-limits on applications for transfer are designed to reduce the possibility of applications causing unnecessary delay in the hearing of a case.

Justices and judges

In the family proceedings court all Children Act cases and other family proceedings will be heard by justices from the court's Family Panel. A court should consist of three justices, with at least one man and one woman. Justices outside Inner London elect some of their existing members to sit on the Family Panel. In Inner London justices are appointed to the Family Panel by the Lord Chancellor. Justices who sit on the Family Panel must have served as a justice for a minimum of one year, must be willing to be on the panel, and must be suitable to serve as a panel member. 'Suitable to serve' is not defined further. Court rules also provide for the Lord

Chancellor to remove someone who is 'unsuitable to serve' on a Family Panel. The aim, no doubt, is to encourage the election and appointment of justices who are interested in, and sympathetic to, cases concerning children and family problems. It remains to be seen whether this criterion of 'suitable to serve' will achieve this aim.

A similar point can be made about the Lord Chancellor nominating special circuit judges to hear cases concerning children. These will be judges who 'by reason of their experience and training are specialists in family work.' (*Hansard*, 9 July 1990). There are three types of circuit judge nominated to deal with family proceedings in the county court. These are:

- *Designated* family judges, who are based at care centres and have full powers to deal with private and public law cases, and who chair the local committees set up to monitor the working of the Act;
- *Nominated* care judges, also based at care centres, with full jurisdiction to hear private and public law cases;
- *Circuit* family judges, who can deal with private law cases only.

In addition, district judges (formerly registrars) who sit in the county courts, are able to deal with a limited range of public law matters, similar to the powers of a single justice or justices' clerk. District judges in the Principal Registry of the Family Division (High Court) have wider powers (Family Proceedings (Allocation to Judiciary) Directions 1993 and see pages 109–10).

Specialist training has been, and will continue to be, provided for magistrates and judges dealing with children's cases.

There are two sorts of committees set up to monitor the Act:

- *Family court business committees*, whose work is to monitor how the process of transfer of proceedings and the appointment of guardians *ad litem* are working, and to try to achieve 'administrative consistency' between the magistrates' courts and the county courts. Committee membership is limited to representatives from the local authority legal department, social services, the two courts involved and the guardian *ad litem* panel.
- *Family courts services committees* are there to promote co-operation between all the different professions and agencies involved in family proceedings; to look at any particular issues that arise in relation to the involvement of the different professions in family proceedings, and to identify how the service could be improved. This committee has a much wider membership, including representation from private practice lawyers, the police and the medical profession, as well as magistrates, judges, guardians *ad litem*, local authority

lawyers and the social services department. It is suggested in government guidance that voluntary organisations are also invited to be represented (DOH, 1991(3), Vol. 7, Annex J). The committees are administered by the court administrators.

Legal Aid

All parties to proceedings under the Children Act will be able to apply to the Legal Aid Board for civil Legal Aid.

Children, parents, and other people with parental responsibility have an automatic entitlement to Legal Aid in care, supervision, child assessment and emergency protection proceedings. This means there will be neither a means test nor a merits test, just a very short form to complete. If any of these people wish to appeal in any of these particular proceedings they will have to satisfy a merits test, but not a means test.

Anyone else who either applies to be joined, or is joined, as a party to these particular proceedings will have to pass a means test, but not a merits test. This is likely to have a particular effect on grandparents wishing to become parties, as they frequently fall outside either the income (or, more usually, the savings) limit for Legal Aid. In all other proceedings both the means test and the merits test are applied (s.15 and schedule 2, Legal Aid Act 1988, as amended; the Civil Legal Aid (General) Regulations 1989, as amended).

In an emergency the Legal Aid Board will deal with applications immediately, by telephone if necessary (see also page 107).

3 Family support services

Introduction

This chapter looks at the background to, and the main principles underlying, the provisions relating to family support services in part III and schedule 2 of the Children Act 1989. It sets out the relevant duties and powers of local authorities. It then explains and comments on the provisions about charging for services and about contributions to the cost of children being looked after by the local authority. The term 'looked after' has a specific legal meaning and refers to those children who are in care and those who are provided with accommodation on a voluntary basis for a continuous period of more than 24 hours (s.22(1) and (2); see also page 151).

Background

The term 'family support' was used in the Government's Review of Child Care Law (DHSS 1985(1)) to describe one of the main aims of local authority powers and duties in relation to children living with their families: to help parents bring up their children. The report distinguished 'family support' from the other main aim: a narrower, more specific one of seeking to prevent children being taken into care. The term 'family support' is generally taken to refer to the range of services available for children and their families to help prevent long-term family breakdown. This is the meaning attached to it in this book.

Until 1963 local authorities did not have a specific statutory duty to provide services to prevent the need for children to come into care or stay in care, although a Home Office circular issued after the Children Act 1948 did stress the advantages of improving a home so that it would be unnecessary to remove the children from their parents and so that children who had been removed could be returned home. The circular went on to say:'To keep the family together must be the first aim, and the separation of the child from its parents can only be justified when there is no possibility of securing adequate care for a child in his own home' (Home Office 1948).

In 1960 the Ingleby Report (House of Commons 1960) recommended that local authorities be placed under a general duty to prevent children suffering neglect, and that to facilitate this local authorities should have the powers to carry out preventive casework and provide practical and material assistance. Interestingly, it also recommended that these powers be given to local authorities as a whole, and not to separate departments, to ensure co-ordination of services.

What eventually became law in section 1 of the Children and Young Persons Act 1963, later to become section 1 of the Child Care Act 1980, was the duty to prevent children coming into or staying in care, and the power to provide assistance in kind and, in 'exceptional circumstances', in cash. The focus had shifted from preventing neglect in the home to preventing children coming into care, and insufficient attention was now paid to a corporate approach to providing services.

It was clear from the evidence presented in 1982 and 1983 to the House of Commons Select Committee on children in care, from research findings at that time, and from information culled during the consultation period preceding the Children Act 1989, that there were a number of serious concerns about 'preventive work':

- The Short Report noted: 'One major theme emerged from the evidence of prevention gathered by the Committee – the crying need for improved liaison between the many statutory agencies involved' (House of Commons 1984, para. 27). The corporate approach recommended by the Ingleby Committee had not emerged. In particular, housing, education, health and social service agencies and authorities were not working well together.
- The existence of many different statutory provisions dealing with services for children did not help to encourage a corporate approach, and did not help social workers to be clear about, or familiar with, the statutory basis for preventive work. Social workers were usually most familiar with section 1 of the Child Care Act 1980, but only in relation to the power to provide cash help (Gardner 1992).
- The lack of a clear legislative basis for family support work may also have been instrumental in the declining status of such work and the

lack of skills and resources put into it. On this point the Short Report stated 'if half the funds and the intellectual effort which has gone towards developing strategies for finding alternative families had been put into what we can only lamely call preventive work, there would be unquestionable advantage to all concerned' (House of Commons 1984, para. 30).

- The way section 1 of the Child Care Act 1980 had been framed led to the very narrow view of prevention meaning keeping children out of care, and contributed to a negative image of care. Research showed how family requests for voluntary care were being refused persistently, sometimes to the point where a later crisis then led to emergency and compulsory intervention. There seemed little recognition that an earlier, planned, short-term provision of care might play a part in preventing long-term family breakdown (Fruin & Vernon 1985; Packman et al. 1986). This narrow view of prevention also encouraged a 'tariff' approach – if preventive work failed the child came into care. This was perceived as a failure, and continued attempts at preventive work and the provision of support services for the family often came to an end at that point.

Family support services under the Act

It is clear that the new provisions for family support were influenced by the concerns listed above, and by earlier recommendations and principles dating back to the Ingleby Report and the Home Office circular of 1948:

- The duty to provide family support is phrased positively, and has moved away from the negative, narrow duty of promoting children's welfare by preventing their being received or taken into care.
- The legislation relating to services to children with disabilities has been incorporated into this Act (s.17(10), schedule 2, paras. 2, 3 and 6), as have all duties and powers in relation to the provision of day care and the registration of day care facilities (ss.18, 19, 71–79 and schedule 9).
- There is now a specific legal requirement that different authorities and agencies work together to provide family support services (s.27). This marks a clear attempt to promote better liaison and a corporate approach to the provision of services.
- While the narrow duty to prevent children from coming into care is retained (para. 7, schedule 2) it is now phrased as a duty to prevent compulsory proceedings for care or supervision orders being taken in relation to children. There is no duty to prevent children from being

accommodated by a local authority. This is intended to encourage the use of accommodation as a service (DOH 1991(3), Vol. 2, para. 7.13). It should also help to ensure that support services continue to be offered to the family while the child is in accommodation.

*   The legislative framework for family support is much clearer, with a general overriding duty backed up by a number of specific duties and powers.

General duty

Local authorities now have a general duty:

'(a)   To safeguard and promote the welfare of children within their area who are in need; and
(b)   So far as is consistent with that duty, to promote the upbringing of such children by their families,

by providing a range and level of services appropriate to those children's needs.'
(s.17(1))

This general duty embodies two important principles underlying the Act: first, the desire to have legislation that positively promotes family support work, and second, the belief that the welfare of the majority of children will be safeguarded best by enabling them to grow up within their own family. So, 'The Act rests on the belief that children are generally best looked after within the family with both parents playing a full part without resort to legal proceedings' (DOH 1989(2), p.1), and 'there are unique advantages for children in experiencing normal family life in their own birth family and every effort should be made to preserve the child's home and family links' (DOH 1989(1), p.8).

The legislation builds on these general principles by providing a list of specific duties and powers, 'for the purpose principally of facilitating the discharge of [the local authority's] general duty under this section . . .' (s.17(2) and schedule 2).

Other relevant duties

The Act places local authorities under certain specific duties which underpin the broad general duty to safeguard the welfare of children and promote their upbringing by their families.

1.   Facilitating provision of services by others (s.17(5))   Local authorities are under a duty to facilitate other agencies in providing family support and other part III services, such as after-care. 'Other agencies' refers specifically to voluntary organisations. Details of the services provided by others may be published alongside details of the services provided by the local authority (para. 1, schedule 2). A combination of services provided by the statutory and voluntary sectors can ensure a wider choice of options for children and families, and greater flexibility in meeting the needs of individual children. Voluntary organisations might provide services in relation to welfare rights, housing, education, befriending schemes, day care and play facilities, as well as specialist services such as counselling, parentcraft training, family centres, residential provision for whole families, or the provision of both short- and long-term accommodation.

2. *Identification of need* (para. 1, schedule 2)

Local authorities are under a duty to identify the extent to which there are children in need within their area. In order to carry out this task local authorities need to have a clear interpretation of the definition of 'in need' and work with other agencies – both statutory and voluntary – in collecting information about the local area. It is also good practice to involve the local community in this process, so that, from the outset, service users are involved in establishing the different sorts of needs that exist locally. The process of consultation and identification of the extent to which there are children 'in need' within the area will have an impact on the interpretation of 'in need'. It is important for local authorities to be flexible and to consider whether specific children or groups of children should be identified as being 'in need' in their area, even if the local authority had not previously identified such children as likely to come within the definition.

There is no requirement on local authorities to carry out the process of identification on a regular basis, but, clearly, it will need to be done at recurring intervals, so that authorities are able to re-appraise the services they provide and monitor how effective they are at meeting the needs of children in their area.

Similarly, there is no duty on local authorities to publish either the extent of children 'in need' within the area or their interpretation of 'in need'. Yet publication of this information may be one useful way of ensuring that the community and other agencies understand the basis on which the authority has made decisions about service provision. In addition, where the gap between the extent of children 'in need' and the services provided is wide, it may help authorities to negotiate for greater resources.

3. *Anti-racist practice* (ss.22(5), 61(3), 64(3), 74(6), and paras. 8 and 11, schedule 2)

The Act makes a positive contribution to promoting children's welfare by building on the Race Relations Act and requiring all local authorities, voluntary agencies and private children's homes – in relation to children they are looking after or proposing to look after – to consider the child's religious persuasion, racial origin and cultural and linguistic background when making any decision about the child. Unfortunately, there is no similar requirement to take these matters into account when providing *services* for the child and/or the child's family. Guidance recognises that these matters should be considered when assessing which services to provide for children and families in individual cases and, in addition, requires authorities to provide a range of services which reflect, both in scale and type, the needs of children and families from ethnic minority groups (DOH 1991(3), Vol. 2, paras. 2.8–2.9 and 2.12).

Local authorities *are* under a duty to have regard to the different racial groups within their area when recruiting day carers or foster carers (para. 11, schedule 2). This duty is designed to ensure that day carers and foster carers are recruited from those ethnic groups, and this will obviously involve local authorities in being clear about the number and extent of different racial groups within the area. Local authorities will need to develop effective ethnic monitoring so that they are equipped to check how well they are fulfilling their duties.

Local authorities must also ensure that day care provision meets those additional needs of children that arise from their racial origin or cultural and linguistic background (s.74(6)). In addition, local authorities are duty-bound to provide relevant cultural activities as part of their family support services (para. 8, schedule 2).

All these provisions about race and culture constitute a major landmark for work with children and families.

The duties in the Children Act highlight and complement existing duties in the Race Relations Act 1976. For example, section 71 of the Race Relations Act places a duty on local authorities to make appropriate arrangements to eliminate unlawful racial discrimination and to *promote* equality of opportunity and good relations between persons of different racial groups. Section 20 of the Race Relations Act requires those who provide goods, facilities and services to the public or sections of the public to ensure that they do not *discriminate* between people of different races or cultures in the provision of access to those goods, facilities or services. What is particularly welcome about the Children Act is that it requires agencies to take positive action to promote the welfare of black children; it requires that something be *done*, whereas the Race Relations Act requires that something be *avoided*.

Regrettably, the research studies which informed so much of the Children Act failed to take specific account of the needs and experiences of black children and their families. More recent research is, however, beginning to provide at least a clearer pattern of admissions and discharges of children from different minority ethnic groups to and from care or accommodation, although there is still very little research evidence on the experiences of these children while in care, and the outcomes of their various placements. These are some of the findings:

- Black children were over-represented in admissions to care in the six authorities studied by Rowe et al. (1989) but there were wide differences between different minority groups. So, for example: Asian children were under-represented in all age groups; African and Afro-Caribbean children were over-represented in the pre-school and 5–10 age groups; African teenagers were over-represented, but Afro-Caribbean teenagers were not.
- Fewer black than white children are admitted for long-term care (including accommodation).
- Many more African and Afro-Caribbean children are admitted for short-term care (including accommodation).
- There are fewer compulsory admissions of black children.
- There are only minor differences in length of stay in care, but black adolescents are more likely to stay longer than white adolescents.
- Children of mixed parentage are grossly over-represented in admissions, more likely to have multiple admissions, and more likely to experience placement breakdown.

(DOH 1991(1); Barn 1990; Bebbington & Miles 1989; Bonnerjea 1990; Rowe et al. 1989)

The Act has, however, been influenced by professional opinion, by examples of good practice, and by the glaring realities and inferior experiences of many children and families who come into contact with social services departments. The provisions are, furthermore, an acknowledgement that Britain is a multi-racial, multi-cultural society in which the welfare of every child – regardless of background or current circumstances – will be given equal importance.

4. Inter-agency working (ss.19, 27, 28, 85 and 86) The Act has responded to the call in the Ingleby Report nearly 30 years earlier that the duty to provide family support services should be a corporate one. As Government guidance points out:

> 'Although responsibility for implementation rests mainly with the Social Services Committee and its officers, the Act is directed at the local authority as a whole and cannot succeed without effective inter-departmental collaboration at all levels. The local authority as a whole should therefore have agreed an approved policy on family support services for children and their families and day care and educational provision for children under statutory school age.'
> (DOH 1991(3), Vol. 2, para. 1.8)

Apart from the legislative *requirement* to work together agencies are *urged* by the Government to go even further: 'The various departments of a local authority (for example health, housing, education and social services) should co-operate to provide an integrated service and range of resources even when such co-operation is not specifically required by law' (DOH 1989(1), p.12). In addition, the legislation has responded to the criticisms in the Short Report of the lack of liaison between agencies; it specifically requires different authorities and agencies to work together in providing family support and other services under part III. Where a local authority thinks that another authority (such as housing, health or education) could help it carry out its duties or powers under part III, the local authority can ask for help from that other authority, and can specify the help required. The authority or person whose help is requested '*shall comply*' with the request, providing that it is compatible with their own statutory duty and does not 'unduly prejudice the discharge of any of their functions'.

The authorities that have to co-operate in this way are:

'(a)   Any local authority
 (b)   Any local education authority
 (c)   Any local housing authority
 (d)   Any health authority or National Health Service Trust
 (e)   Any person authorised by the Secretary of State for the purposes of this section.' [This refers to the NSPCC.] (s.27)

A case decided in 1993 has clarified that when a family has been refused accommodation under the Housing Act 1985, on the grounds that they were intentionally homeless, the housing authority is nevertheless obliged to consider providing a home if that becomes necessary under the Children Act 1989. Children in need should not remain unassisted because of the interaction between the two statutory codes. Thus a county council was entitled to request a district council to help with housing a family, and it would not be inconsistent for that district council to conclude that the family should be housed, despite being intentionally homeless. If the district council decided on valid grounds that it could not comply with the request for help under section 27, there was still a duty on the county council to provide help. If children in need did not command protection under one code they would command it under the other (*R* v. *Northavon DC ex p. Smith* (1993) *The Guardian*, 6 August).

There are other, more specific, requirements on authorities to consult, inform each other and work together in providing services:

• There is a duty on a health authority or local education authority (LEA) or any person carrying on a registered care, nursing or mental nursing home to inform their local authority if they have provided, or intend to provide, accommodation for a child for a continuous period of three months. The local authority then has to take such steps as are reasonably practicable to find out if the child's welfare is adequately safeguarded and promoted. In addition the local authority must consider whether they need to take any other action in relation to the child (ss.85 and 86).

- Where a local authority are looking after a child and want to place that child in a residential placement which provides education they must first consult the LEA, and then notify the LEA when the placement starts and when it comes to an end (s.28).
- Local authorities must assist LEAs to provide services for children with special educational needs (s.27).
- The review of day care provision is to be carried out by the local authority and the LEA (s.19).

The review should be undertaken every three years. The review is of all the day care services in the area – those run by the local authority or local education authority, those in the independent sector, and childminding – and the two authorities also have to take account of the nursery and primary education facilities and of any day care services provided in institutions exempt from the requirement to register.

In carrying out the review the two authorities must have regard to any representations made to them by any health authority and 'any other relevant person'. Current and potential service users are likely to want to comment on provision of day care services in the area. Guidance recommends that

> 'the review should be an open process and early involvement is recommended with health authorities, voluntary bodies such as local PPA groups, childmind-ing interests, community groups, lone-parent organisations and ethnic minority groups, with the private day care sector, employers and parents. The model of an under-fives forum with members drawn from a wide range of organisations, which some local authorities have developed, is an effective way of consulting and involving outside interests.' (DOH 1991(3), Vol. 2, para. 9.7)

The local authority and the LEA must publish the results of each review, with any proposals they have in relation to this service. The review report should be 'accessible to a wide audience', and this may involve making sure it is produced in languages other than English (DOH 1991(3), Vol. 2, para. 9.16).

The report should aim to:

- increase interest among the population as a whole in services for young children, and
- encourage debate about local services and about how their development can produce benefits.

Some of the matters to be covered in the report are these:

- Basic information on services in the area.
- Map of the area, showing the location of facilities.
- Policies on day care and early years' education, on children in need, on services for children with special educational needs, and on equal opportunity issues – including race, gender and disability – with comment on how these have been developed and monitored.
- Known problems – such as the gap between supply and demand, difficulties in staff recruitment, shortage of childminders, or difficulties in the operation of the registration system.
- The range of other family support services, such as toy libraries, home visiting schemes, parent/toddler groups, and information services.
- Changes in provision, and plans for the future.

(DOH 1991(3), Vol. 2, paras. 9.17–9.19)

There are many other areas where inter-agency working will be necessary if the Act is to be implemented successfully:

- The inclusion of children with disabilities within the scope of the Act will involve local authorities in joint work with health and education authorities and voluntary organisations.
- The provision of day care and out-of-school care (s.18) will involve liaison and joint planning between social services departments, local education authorities, recreation and leisure departments, and the voluntary sector.
- Preventing children from coming before the courts (para. 7, schedule 2) will require liaison between social services departments, recreation and leisure, local education authorities, the voluntary sector, the probation service, the police, and the community as a whole.
- Provision of accommodation for 16- and 17-year-olds, and after-care services for young people leaving accommodation or care (ss.20 and 24), will require liaison between social services departments, housing departments, local education authorities, and the voluntary sector.

It is important that clear policies and frameworks exist for such interagency work so that all those involved in providing services to children and their families know how to request help, and to respond to requests, from another agency. 'A corporate policy and clear departmental procedures in respect of inter-departmental collaboration will ensure good cooperation at all levels' (DOH 1991(3), Vol. 2, para. 1.13). Agencies will need to work together so that they have an agreed interpretation of the definition of 'in need' for their area. They will also need to work together to plan the services to be provided.

5. Information about services (para. 1, schedule 2) Local authorities have a duty to publish information about the family support services they provide. They may also publish information about relevant services provided by others. The Act states that local authorities should take reasonable steps 'to ensure that those who might benefit from the services receive the information relevant to them' (para. 1, schedule 2). Clearly, this information will be most useful to potential consumers if it is widely available, not only at social services offices but in hospitals, community centres, GP surgery waiting rooms, community health clinics, social security offices, libraries, post offices and Citizens' Advice Bureaux and other local advice agencies. The information could be helpfully disseminated in the form of posters, leaflets and booklets.

The guidance stresses the importance of ensuring that information is translated into different languages, is sensitive to cultural needs, and is made accessible to those with a sensory disability (DOH 1991(3), Vol. 2, para. 2.36). Again, it would be helpful if information could be provided in forms other than writing, such as audio or visual tapes, and in braille. It will be helpful if information contains, in addition to details about services, some explanation of the interpretation of the definition of 'in need', details about the way in which families and children will be assessed, and information about any charging policies.

6. Duties towards children with disabilities (ss.17(1), (10) and (11); paras. 2, 3, 6, schedule 2; s.23(8)) The combining of health and welfare legislation with child care legislation means that the provision of services to children with disabilities is brought within the framework of the Children Act. Since many children with disabilities will be children 'in need' (see page 38) the broad duty of promoting their welfare and, where appropriate, their upbringing by their families, will apply. In addition, there are some specific general duties that apply to children with disabilities.

Services Local authorities are placed under a clear general duty to provide services designed:

'(a) To minimise the effect on disabled children within their area of their disabilities; and
(b) To give such children the opportunity to lead lives which are as normal as possible.' (para. 6, schedule 2)

When placing a child with disabilities whom they are looking after, the local authority has a duty to ensure that the accommodation provided 'is not unsuitable to his particular needs' (s.23(8)).

Register   In order to identify the extent and level of services required to comply with their general duty towards children with disabilities, local authorities are required to maintain a register of disabled children within their area. Government guidance stresses, sensibly, the importance of inter-agency work in compiling this information, and the importance of explaining carefully to parents and young people *why* the register is required.

Registration is voluntary, and the provision of services is not dependent on whether or not the child is registered, but the guidance stresses the importance of publicising why registration is helpful – primarily to ensure that the relevant agencies plan the right level and mix of local services (DOH 1991(3), Vol. 2, para. 2.19).

Guidance recommends that local authorities, local education authorities and health authorities draw up one common register rather than keeping separate ones. Identifying the extent to which there are children with disabilities in the area links, of course, with the identification generally of the extent of children 'in need' and, as the guidance says, this will help local authorities, local education authorities and district health authorities to plan both short- and long-term services (DOH 1991(3), Vol. 2, para. 2.19). It will also be important for the local authority to discuss with the education and health authorities how best to keep the register updated, and how best to establish clear criteria for definitions of disability if they wish to be more flexible than the legal definition requires when registering children (DOH 1991(3), Vol. 6, para. 4.3).

Registration, as with the identification of need generally, should be seen as an opportunity to involve service users early on in the process, and to take into account their views about the services needed. This process, together with the publication of the services available (see above), should ensure that parents of children with disabilities will be better informed than at present. An Office of Populations and Census Surveys report in 1989 on the lives of children with disabilities indicated that 64 per cent of parents had never heard of respite care and 38 per cent were unaware of a relevant voluntary organisation that might have helped them (OPCS 1989).

Government guidance on working with children with disabilities sets out a helpful list of the principles upon which all work with such children should be based:

- The welfare of the child should be safeguarded and promoted by those providing services;

- A primary aim should be to promote access for all children to the same range of services;
- Children with disabilities are children first;
- Recognition of the importance of parents and families in children's lives;
- Partnership between parents and local authorities and other agencies; and
- The views of children and parents should be sought and taken into account.

(DOH 1991(3), Vol. 6, para. 1.6)

In working with black children and children from minority ethnic groups who have disabilities it will be important to incorporate anti-racist practice so that the additional needs of black children with disabilities, arising from their racial origin and cultural and linguistic background, are not ignored. These issues should be addressed in both the provision of services and in the way assessments are carried out:

'The needs of black and minority ethnic children with disabilities are the same as the needs of other children. The additional dimension of disability and race, however, necessitates a different response or creates additional requirements. It is crucial that at the centre of all policy and practice initiatives the needs of black and minority ethnic children with disabilities are considered in terms of both race and disability.' (Macdonald 1991)

Joint assessments   The Act provides for joint assessments of the needs of children, and refers here specifically to assessments made under the Chronically Sick and Disabled Persons Act 1970, the Education Act 1981 and the Disabled Persons (Services, Consultation and Representation) Act 1986 (para. 3, schedule 2). The guidance points out that combined assessments should prevent children being subjected to 'a confusing variety of assessment procedures' and should ensure that authorities 'see children "in the round" whether their particular needs are for educational or health or social care'. Inter-agency work will obviously be important, not only for doing assessments but also for providing services. As the guidance points out, 'Assessment should be less an administrative process for a single department and more an opportunity for a local authority to co-ordinate all services effectively' (DOH 1991(3), Vol. 2. para. 2.21).

7.   *Duty to prevent neglect and abuse* (para. 4, schedule 2)   Besides the general duty on local authorities to safeguard and promote the welfare of children 'in need' there is also a specific duty to 'take reasonable steps' to prevent children in the area suffering neglect or abuse, by providing family support services for them. This links with the specific powers and duties in

relation to child protection in part V of the Act (see Chapter 4), and emphasises the important part played by family support services in child protection work. The duty is owed to all children in the area, not just those in need.

Linked with the above is the specific duty requiring a local authority to notify another local authority where a child thought likely to be at risk of harm is about to move into the other local authority's area, or has moved already. Clearly this applies to children on the child protection register, but it is to be hoped that local authorities will not set up new lists of children 'likely to suffer harm' which contain children who are not on the child protection register. If that were to happen local authorities should question why a child thought 'likely to suffer harm' is *not* on the register. In addition, local authorities would need to ensure that all the natural justice issues that have arisen in relation to child protection procedures – such as informing families, consulting them, and having clear procedures and an appeals process – are dealt with adequately.

8.   *Duty to prevent compulsory proceedings* (para. 7, schedule 2)

Local authorities are under a duty to 'take reasonable steps' to 'reduce the need' to bring care or supervision proceedings in relation to children. This is a specific duty focused on preventing compulsory intervention. It ties in with the general duty to promote children's upbringing by their families (s.17), the specific duty to prevent abuse and neglect by the provision of services (para. 4, schedule 2), and the requirement on the courts to be satisfied that making an order for the child is better than making no order at all (s.1(5)). Legislation and guidance encourage the use of family support services wherever possible – including the provision of accommodation – even in circumstances where the threshold conditions for a care or supervision order might be established.

In addition to this preventive duty, local authorities are also placed under a duty to take reasonable steps:

- to reduce the need to bring criminal proceedings against children, and to encourage children in the area not to commit criminal offences

   and

- to avoid the need for children in the area to be placed in secure accommodation.

All this reflects a general concern to try and stop children coming before the courts and losing their liberty.

In relation to the duty to encourage children not to commit criminal offences it will clearly be important for local authorities to work with other statutory and voluntary agencies and with the community to provide services for children and young people. It is often the case that children who are truanting from school become involved in criminal activities. It is also true that children become involved in delinquent behaviour after school hours and during school holidays. Joint approaches by the social services department, education, recreation and leisure services may help to divert children from crime. In addition, programmes to divert young offenders from care or custody will also be important, and will require co-operative work between social services, the police, probation, intermediate treatment schemes and voluntary youth organisations.

9.   Duties to promote contact with and return to family and friends (s.23(6) and paras. 15 and 10, schedule 2)   The Act places a duty on local authorities to promote contact between children and their families and friends when children are living apart from them (paras 10 and 15, schedule 2). In addition, local authorities are under a duty to try to enable those children to be reunited with their families, providing that is in their interests (s.23(6) and para. 10, schedule 2). These specific duties reinforce the general duty to promote the upbringing of children by their families. The duties in relation to 'looked-after' children will be looked at more closely in Chapters 7 and 9. It is important to note that local authorities also have these duties in relation to children 'in need' whom they are *not* looking after. These children could be living apart from their families for a variety of reasons – because they are fostered privately, or are in a nursing home or other health establishment, or are refugees, or have parents in prison.

Which children and families will receive family support services?

The general duty in section 17 is owed to children in the local authority area who are 'in need'. In relation to specific family support services, *duties* to provide services arise when children are 'in need', but local authorities have the *power* to provide some services such as day care (s.18), family centres (para. 9, schedule 2), and accommodation (s.20) to children who are not 'in need'.

The legislation makes it clear that, providing that the aim is to safeguard or promote the welfare of the child, services can be provided not only for the child in need but also for the child's family or any member of the family (s.17(3)). The definition of 'family' includes any person with parental responsibility for the child and any other person with whom the child has been living (s.17(10)). This is important because it recognises that for many children family is more than mother, father, brothers and sisters; because it makes clear that children should not be looked at in isolation, but as members of their family; and because it recognises that parents and carers are individuals with their own needs, and that meeting those needs frequently benefits the children concerned.

Definition of 'in need'

The term 'in need' is defined in the legislation (s.17(10)). There are three elements to the definition:

(1)   The child is unlikely to achieve or maintain, or to have the opportunity of achieving or maintaining, a reasonable standard of health or development without the provision for the child of services by a local authority under this part of the Act; or
(2)   The child's health or development is likely to be significantly impaired, or further impaired, without provision for the child of such services; or
(3)   The child is disabled.

Part (3) of the definition is what brings services to children with disabilities within the scope of the Children Act. Legislation such as the National Assistance Act 1948 and the Chronically Sick and Disabled Persons Act 1970 has now been amended to relate only to people aged 18 or over, but the link with that legislation remains in the Children Act's definition of disability: 'A child is disabled if he is blind, deaf or dumb or suffers from mental disorder from any kind or is substantially and permanently handicapped by illness, injury or congenital deformity or such other disability as may be prescribed' (s.17(11)). This wording will strike many people as insensitive and unhelpfully narrow. It is the same wording as in the National Assistance Act, under which many children with disabilities will then receive services once they reach adulthood. Local authorities will need to explain to children and their families that this is why the same definition has been used in the Children Act.

   The definition does not include *all* children with disabilities. It excludes, for example, those who are partially sighted, hard of hearing, or suffering from a temporary disability, perhaps as the result of an accident, but such children could well come within the definition of children who are unlikely to achieve or have the opportunity of achieving or maintaining a reasonable standard of health or development without the provision of services. They may, of course, also come within the definition of children whose health or development will be significantly impaired without the provision of services.

In relation to parts (1) and (2) of the definition, health or development is defined widely to cover physical, intellectual, emotional, social or behavioural development and physical or mental health. In part (2) of the definition there is a clear link with the threshold conditions for a care or supervision order and the duty to carry out an investigation under section 47. Children coming within this category are children at risk of abuse or neglect; they are likely, therefore, to be children subject to child protection procedures or on the child protection register, or children where the threshold conditions for a compulsory order could have been established but where the authority is working on a voluntary basis with the family. Sometimes, but not always, it will cover children subject to an investigation ordered by the court under section 37. In addition, all children in care and some children in accommodation will come within this part of the definition.

Part (1) extends the definition to cover a much wider range of children than those referred to above and guidance has made it clear that it would 'not be acceptable' for local authorities to interpret this definition as applying only to children at risk of significant harm (DOH 1991(3), Vol. 2, para. 2.4)). Given that the legislation is also trying to promote a greater focus on family support services and is attempting to de-stigmatise help received from social services departments, it would also be against the spirit of the Act to limit family support services only to those children who are found to be at risk of harm. Many local authorities do, at present, restrict access to family support services because of anxiety about the lack of resources available to fund an adequate provision of services. While lack of resources is undeniably frustrating, it may not necessarily continue into the future, and it is important that a proper framework for family support services is put in place now.

There will doubtless be differences in how local authorities interpret part (1) of the definition, as much will hinge on what is regarded as a reasonable standard of health or development. The definition refers also to children having 'the opportunity' of achieving or maintaining a reasonable standard of health or development, and there are likely to be differences of opinion about future predictions for such children.

The following groups of children might come within this definition:

Children living in poverty Not all children at risk or in accommodation or care come from poor families, and by no means all children of poor families are the subject of state intervention, but it is hard to disagree with the statement in the Short Report that: 'There is a well-established link between deprivation and children coming into care. Put crudely the majority of children in care are the children of the poor' (House of Commons 1984, para. 36). Small-scale local studies confirm that children being 'looked after' by local authorities come predominantly from poor families (Becker & MacPherson 1986). Surprisingly few authorities have sufficient data about family income at the point of entry to accommodation or care, but the evidence that does exist suggests that over 70 per cent of the 70,000 or so children concerned have parents who depend on welfare benefits.

In a study of 2,500 children admitted to care (before 1989) Bebbington and Miles (1989) found that before admission:

- almost three-quarters of their families received income support;
- only one in five lived in owner-occupied buildings;
- over half were living in poor neighbourhoods;
- only a quarter were living with both parents.

The researchers commented, 'Deprivation is a common factor among all types of children who enter care.' These findings are particularly stark when they compare the probability of admission to care of two children of the same age, but living in different circumstances:

Child A	**Child B**
Aged 5 to 9	Aged 5 to 9
No dependence on social security benefits	Household head receives income support
Two-parent family	Single-adult household
Three or four children	Four or more children
White	Mixed ethnic origin
Owner-occupied home	Privately rented home
More rooms than people	One or more persons per room
Odds are 1 in 7,000	**Odds are 1 in 10**

Bradshaw's recent study of child poverty and deprivation in the UK concluded that during the 1980s 'more children had been living in low income families and the number of children living in poverty has doubled. Inequalities have also become wider' (Bradshaw 1990).

We know, for example, that between 1979 and 1987 the proportion of children living in households with incomes below 50 per cent of the average income more than doubled from 12.2 per cent to 25.7 per cent (Oppenheim 1990). Although it is difficult to establish the overall effect on children of this increase in poverty, Bradshaw's study concluded, among other things, that it was probable that children's diets had got worse, that there was evidence to show that children in unemployed families or with lone parents had an inadequate clothing stock, and that there were clear indications of an increase in children's homelessness, childhood morbidity, and drug abuse by children.

Children who are homeless or living in unsuitable housing conditions
Despite guidance to the contrary, children have continued to come into accommodation or care because of homelessness. In the year ending 31 March 1990, 255 children were admitted to care in England because of homelessness and a total of 268 were in care for this reason on that date (DOH 1990). In the figures for Wales for the subsequent year, ending 31 March 1991, the figures were 20 children entering care because of homelessness and 19 in care for that reason on that date (Welsh Office 1992). In 1992 the number of homeless households in England and Wales was 152,370 (DOE 1992; Welsh Office 1992). Studies have shown that the health and development of children in homeless families placed in bed and breakfast accommodation is almost always impaired – the accommodation lacks play space, or indeed any space, often has inadequate or no facilities for cooking, access to health care is very difficult, and children frequently either don't attend school or have to change schools (Conway 1988).

Poor housing conditions also affect the health and development of children. Damp or mildew have adverse affects on health, especially child health, and children living in poor housing conditions often suffer from a lack of play space, either in the home or outside.

Children suffering from the effects of racism   Children subject to racial attacks are bound to suffer an impairment of health or development, or fail to achieve a reasonable standard of health or development, because having a positive sense of identity is crucial to healthy development. Institutional racism is also likely to affect the health and development of children by making it difficult for their families to have access to employment or good housing, and in the way it affects the treatment of children within the education system. The challenge here is for local authorities to devise strategies and services, or to assist in the provision of services, which will help to counter the effects of racism. Local authorities should use their powers under section 27 to co-ordinate multi-agency strategies, for example, setting up a freephone helpline. Some Area Child Protection Committees have recognised that part of their role is to prevent racist attacks by ensuring multi-agency co-ordination to develop individual protection plans for children at risk of such attacks (see also Complaints to the Ombudsman 91/A/1759, 1760, 1762 and 1791).

Children with disabilities not coming within the statutory definition of 'disabled'   Some children with temporary or partial disabilities may not come within the statutory definition of disabled (see page 38). They would come, instead, within this part of the definition and local authorities should discuss with other agencies such as education and health how such children can best be assessed.

Children with caring responsibilities   Children who look after their parents may well not achieve a reasonable standard of health or development without the provision of services for the relevant member of the family. It could be that the parent has a disability, or suffers from mental illness or alcohol or drug dependency, or is HIV-positive or has AIDS. Section 17 provides explicitly for services to be provided for another member of the family, and such service provision may well help promote the child's welfare.

Delinquent children   Many children who get involved in delinquent or criminal activities will not be achieving a reasonable standard of social or behavioural development. They might well benefit from services provided by the local authority and other agencies.

Children separated from one or both of their parents   The separation of children from one or both parents is known to affect emotional development. Similarly, regular and unpleasant disputes between parents can affect children's health or development. The sorts of children who might come within this category are children whose parents are divorced or separated, or who are in the process of doing so; children whose parents are in prison; children separated from their parents because of immigration difficulties, and refugee children.

Children whose parents or carers need a break   Many families experience stressful times which affect the health and development of the children concerned and, in some cases, can put them at risk of harm. Parents or carers in such situations are better able to cope and to care for their children if they are given a break from them, either on a one-off basis, or as a regular arrangement. Such a break could be provided by arranging a holiday for the child, day care, out-of-school care, babysitting or accommodation on either a short-term or respite basis.

In need – the gateway to services?

The fact that children have to be identified as being in need before local authorities owe a duty to them of promoting their welfare and their upbringing by their family, thus enabling the children to cross the threshold of entitlement to services, does indicate a policy shift away from a commitment to universal provision of services. Even if 'in need' is interpreted widely, there is a danger that professionals and consumers alike will see defining children in need as stigmatising. Such an outcome would be ironic, since a clear intention of amalgamating health and welfare legislation with child care legislation was to remove the stigma attached to receiving help from social services.

Establishing that a child is in need, although the gateway to the general duty in section 17, does not guarantee that the particular services needed in an individual case will be provided. The local authority must provide a range and level of services, on a general basis, appropriate to the needs of children in need within their area (s.17(1)). This obviously links with the duty to identify the extent of children in need in their area (para. 1, schedule 2). Local authorities have considerable discretion to decide on the range and level of services they are going to provide or facilitate others in providing. Their specific duties to provide certain services – for example, day care or family centres – are accordingly diluted by the addition of the phrases 'as appropriate' or 'as they consider appropriate'. Thus they do not have to provide the particular service or services that an individual child in need and/or their family requires. Children or families denied a service in these circumstances may well find it difficult to challenge that decision, providing the local authority can show that the overall level of service available is appropriate to the needs of children in need in the area (see Chapter 8 on complaints and judicial review).

Another problem is that, at a time of scarce resources, there will obviously be an element of targeting services – particularly those with limited availability, to the most needy children within the larger group of children identified as being in need. The alternative would simply be to provide services on a first come, first served basis. Anxiety over resources has led some individuals and authorities to be pessimistic about the provision of family support services, warning that it is lack of resources, rather than restrictive interpretations of the definition of 'in need', which is likely to limit most services exclusively to children involved in child protection procedures.

Information on the delivery of services under part III in the first year of the Act's implementation is contained in the government report on the Act (DOH & Welsh Office 1993). In addition, the government has published a very helpful book bringing together recent research findings on the provision of family support services, descriptions of individual projects, and suggestions for policy development in this area (Gibbons (ed.) 1992).

Strategies for good practice in the provision of family support services

For local authorities to provide only a small number of limited availability family support services because of concern over resources is contrary to the spirit of the Act and its emphasis on promoting children's upbringing by their families:

'The Act's emphasis on family support and partnership with parents requires local authorities to adopt a new approach to child care services. To give family support a high priority in resource allocation may require new thinking across departments on matters such as devolving budget management and accountability.' (DOH 1991(3), Vol. 2, para. 1.10)

A positive creative approach to the provision of services is required, and below are some suggestions for how this might be achieved (see also In Need Implementation Group 1991).

Changing attitudes

The question of attitudes is just as important as the question of resources. Family support work needs to be recognised as high-status, skilled work, on a par with child protection work or family-finding. Such a shift in perception would be assisted by the development of specialist family support teams or specialist 'in need' managers or workers. As well as helping to give family support work a higher status, the existence of specialist teams or workers would ensure that there is up-to-date information on all available services and resources in the area; that a corporate approach to the provision of services is maintained; that agencies work together in accordance with section 27 of the Act; that there is flexible provision to as many children as possible, and that gaps in resourcing are identified so that future strategies can look at ways of closing the gaps.

Information

Fulfilling the duty to publish information about services and to make such information widely available (para. 1, schedule 2) is an essential element of working in partnership with consumers. They are empowered by having equal access with professionals to clear information about all the options for family support services. Having this information available should also ensure that when people come into social services offices the staff they speak to are well-informed and able to hand over information as well as giving it verbally.

Retaining universal provision

Local authorities should make full use of their power to provide services to children *not* in need – day care and out-of-school care (s.18), family centres (para. 9, schedule 2) and accommodation (s.20) – and their duty to help facilitate the provision of services by others (s.17(5)), to ensure that some element of universal provision of services for children continues. Corporate working with recreation, leisure and education departments is another essential part of such provision.

It is important that when a family approaches social services for information, advice or help, information is given, and there is a range of universal services available which people can simply self-select, without being involved in any process of assessment. A family should not have to go through the hoop of assessment to establish whether or not their child is 'in need' before they are given any information.

Maintaining universal provision of some services is an effective way of ensuring that no stigma is attached to receiving these services.

In Newcastle upon Tyne midwives and social workers came together to set up a project which provides not only antenatal and postnatal support to young mothers on a large estate, but other forms of family support as well.

In Milton Keynes a family centre operates an open-door policy. There are no referrals, no files are kept, and the community is involved in running the centre, together with the social services and education departments. The centre provides part-time nursery education, school holiday play-schemes, a drop-in centre, adult education, a baby clinic and a lunch club, among other things. Staff and other users can provide help and support in sorting out practical and personal problems, and a community worker supports and encourages users in taking up local issues.

Ensuring that services are provided which cater for the needs of black and minority ethnic families and children

Some authorities may consider that, in developing anti-discriminatory policies under the Race Relations Act, they have ensured equality of service for all members of their community. However, equality of service will benefit everyone only if everyone's needs are identical, if they arise from the same set of circumstances, and if everyone receives the same level or type of resources. In some circumstances black children and their families will want the same services that are provided to a large section of the community, but they may, however, have additional needs which have to be met if they are to benefit fully from those services. An important underlying aim in developing an anti-racist approach to services should be to ensure equity of *outcome*, rather than equity of provision, for all children. This is why an anti-racist approach is required to begin to ensure that black children and their families are treated fairly within a system in which their particular needs can be undermined or overlooked so easily, with the result that they continue to remain oppressed.

Some agencies and individuals may argue that anti-racist work is not relevant in their area because the population is predominantly white. Even where there is only a small or isolated black population, those family members may well, at some point, want or need to use the services provided by local authorities. Services should be provided to them according to their expressed needs, not according to numerical proportions. Involving the black and ethnic minority communities and voluntary organisations in discussions about the interpretation of 'in need' in the area, and in the range and level of services to be provided, is an essential starting point for setting up services that respond to the needs of children and families from these communities.

It is particularly important that anti-racist practice is developed in relation to the delivery of family support services, to ensure that the underlying principle of promoting children's upbringing by their families benefits all children and their families.

Imaginative use of resources

While resources are limited, a positive approach needs to be taken in looking at ways in which they can be used to best effect.

In the hard-pressed area of North Tyneside the local authority has developed a scheme whereby the number of free places available in local authority day nurseries has been increased by inviting fee-paying individuals to use the same facilities and local businesses to sponsor places for employees. The scheme has continued to develop, and ensures greater choice in day care provision for all parents (*Social Work Today*, 20 February 1992).

In another deprived area, social workers, together with health visitors and the local nursery school, involved the community in setting up and then taking over the running of a community toy library.

In Oxfordshire, before the implementation of the Act, respite care (now accommodation) was provided to families needing a break from their children. Part of the fostering allowance was used to buy clothes and toys for the children concerned, rather than all going to the foster carers.

Some local authorities are making greater use of unqualified staff, including residential workers, to spend time giving support and assistance to families in their own homes, as part of an agreed plan for family support. In many areas authorities make use of voluntary sector schemes such as Home-start or NEWPIN (see **Useful Organisations**, page 219) to provide support to families. Such schemes use volunteers, many of whom are parents who have themselves received support from the scheme in the past. Families receiving support value the fact that the volunteers have had similar experiences to them, and the schemes are able to provide volunteers of the same ethnic, cultural, religious and class background as the families they are supporting.

There is likely to be a level of unmet need in most areas. If a child is in need, or their family is denied a service because it does not exist, or because it is oversubscribed, details of this should be kept, and regularly passed on to managers, elected members, MPs, and the relevant government departments in order to inform future planning of services and decisions from both local and central government on future resourcing.

Encouraging self-assessment

For limited-availability or specialised services local authorities need to devise means of assessing whether or not children come within the definition of 'in need', and then whether a particular service should be made available to them or a member of their family. Clearly a full-scale assessment based on the model contained in the Department of Health 'Orange Book' (DOH 1988) would be inappropriate in all but a tiny minority of cases where the issue is the type or package of family support services which should be provided. A model that encourages self-assessment by families assists in promoting partnership with consumers, and helps practitioners to concentrate on identifying what services are needed, rather than concentrating on identifying deficiencies in the family concerned.

Different types of self-assessment are being developed in different areas. Mainly they involve simple forms and questionnaires for families to complete which connect to the definition of 'in need' and the local situation in terms of the provision of services. Important elements of any self-assessment model include:

- explaining clearly to consumers the rationale of working in this way, so that they understand why they are being asked to take this on, and do not feel overburdened by it;
- supporting staff so that they recognise that they are not being de-skilled. They are facilitating self-assessment, not abdicating responsibility. They are using their skills to empower consumers;
- encouraging families to get help from people outside social services in making their assessments;
- ensuring that families are given all the information available about the range and level of services in the area;
- having as an aim that worker and client will reach a shared assessment of the need or problem and what would alleviate it or solve it.

The advantages of developing such a process are that it helps to reduce the likelihood of stigma being attached to the identification of a child 'in need'; it encourages families to have more confidence in the services then provided to them; it makes it easier to avoid mistakes or to rectify them quickly, particularly those that arise through untested assumptions.

With any assessment process – whatever model is used – it is very important for workers to be aware of the difficulties in achieving objectivity. Everyone carries with them a personal baggage of beliefs and experiences which influence and affect the way they assess a particular family's situation. Encouraging greater self-assessment is an aid to objectivity, and to preventing assumptions being made, for example, about what is 'normal' family life. In addition, self-assessment encourages workers to acknowledge the knowledge and expertise that families have about themselves, which is particularly important for black families and families from other minority ethnic groups.

All assessments must take account of race, culture and class, and the effects of poverty and racism. In all forms of assessment much more needs to be done to ensure that the assessment takes account of – and values – the different forms of family life and child rearing that are present in multicultural Britain. Standardised assessment procedures are often Eurocentric in outlook, leading to a 'deficit' view of minority ethnic cultures. For example, suggested questions about whether a mother shows pleasure at being with her child, encourages physical closeness with the child, or praises the child appropriately, all require great care. Information obtained needs to be assessed within the context of the family and its culture. This is not to say that 'respect' for cultures should lead to a 'blinkered' and uncritical acceptance of all practices. Cultures are complex, and practitioners should aim to avoid static and over-simplified notions about minority ethnic group cultures. They should also be willing to seek advice and support, rather than assume that they do, or should, have this knowledge already:

> 'Necessary experience and expertise should be provided for in staffing of services and through relationships with other professions and services and with the community.' Where there are few members of staff from black or other minority ethnic groups, or where services are provided only rarely to black families or those from other minority ethnic groups, local authorities need to ensure that they have identified sources of advice and help, 'so that the necessary experience, expertise and resources are available when needed' (DOH 1991(3), Vol. 2, para. 2.9; see also Macdonald 1991).

Providing services

Once the child has been identified as 'in need', and the specific need or needs of the child and family have been clarified, the local authority should then plan what services should be provided. In some cases this will simply mean matching the need to an existing service, but in other cases a more complex package will have to be worked out. It is important, where relevant services are not provided by the local authority itself, that attention is given to whether or not the service is provided locally by another statutory agency or voluntary organisation, or whether it is available in another local authority area (ss.17 and 27).

Partnership

> 'Partnership with parents and consultation with children on the basis of careful joint planning and agreement is the guiding principle for the provision of services within the family home and where children are provided with accommodation under voluntary arrangements. Such arrangements are intended to assist the parent and enhance, not undermine, the parent's authority and control.' (DOH 1991(3), Vol. 2, para. 2.1)

Reference was made in Chapter 1 to the key principle underlying the Act of partnership between families and the local authority. The duties and powers set out in the Act and schedule 2, and the accompanying guidance, all provide the framework for developing partnership practice. Consulting the community, consumers of services, and voluntary organisations about the level of need in the area, and the range and level of services to be provided; publishing and circulating information about services; encouraging self-assessment – these are all examples of working in partnership. In working with individual children and their families, the crucial aspects of working in partnership are providing information – once again – and involving families in planning and decision making.

Guidance recommends that a plan should be made which should 'identify how long the service may be required, what the objective should be and what else others are expected to do' (DOH 1991(3), Vol. 2, para. 2.10). It goes on to recommend that the plan should form the basis of a written agreement made with the parent or carer, and that this plan should be reviewed. There is no legal requirement to make and review written plans in relation to services provided to non-'looked-after' children, but in cases where there is a complex package of services, or where social services' involvement may be long-term, it is clearly good practice that requirements in respect of planning and review should apply (DOH 1991(3), Vol. 2, para. 2.10). Even for short-term arrangements, or for universally provided services such as childminding or playgroups, a written agreement setting out the terms of the arrangements is always helpful to consumers and service providers alike. (See Chapter 8 for more information on planning, reviews and written agreements.)

Types of service

The Act goes into some detail about the sorts of services that might be provided. This is not intended to be an exhaustive list. Local authorities are able to provide other services if they wish, and they may need to do so, depending on the identification of needs within the area.

The sorts of services that local authorities should consider providing are these:

- advice, guidance and counselling (para. 8, schedule 2)
- occupational, social, cultural or recreational facilities (para. 8, schedule 2)
- home help, including laundry facilities (para. 8, schedule 2)
- facilities for, or assisting with, travelling to and from home to take advantage of a particular service (para. 8, schedule 2)
- assistance to enable the child or family to have a holiday (para. 8, schedule 2)
- day care for under-fives (s.18)
- out-of-school provision for school-age children (s.18)
- assistance in cash or kind (s.17(6))
- family centres (day or residential) (para. 9, schedule 2)
- accommodation (short- or long-term) (s.20)
- assisting an adult who has ill-treated, or may ill-treat, a child living at the same premises to move out (para. 5, schedule 2).

The possibility of giving assistance in kind – or in cash in exceptional circumstances – is continued and extended from previous legislation. The 'exceptional circumstances' criterion for the giving of cash remains, but it is important to remember that this assistance is no longer linked either to preventing children coming into accommodation or care or to ensuring that they leave accommodation or care. It now forms part of the wider duty to promote the welfare of children and promote their upbringing by their family. Remember also that case law has established that the provision of assistance in kind includes the provision of housing, though not necessarily permanent housing (*AG (ex rel. Tilley)* v. *London Borough of Wandsworth* [1981] 1 All ER 1162, and *R.* v. *London Borough of Tower Hamlets ex p. Monaf and Others* [1987] 19 HLR QBD and [1988] 20 HLR 529 CA). It is to be hoped that local authorities will not develop restrictive policies in relation to giving assistance in cash or kind, as it is essential that each case is decided on its merits. Policies which restrict the exercise of discretion in individual cases may lay local authorities open to applications for judicial review.

Financial and practical support under section 17(6) can be provided for children who are returning to live with their families or friends after being in either accommodation or care.

If a local authority provides cash help, or assistance in kind, it can require that the money, or the value of the assistance, be repaid in whole or in part. Before giving assistance in cash or kind, or imposing a requirement to repay, the local authority has to have regard to the means of the child and each of the child's parents. In other words, it must carry out a means test. Note that for the purposes of this legislation the term 'parent' includes a non-married father, whether or not he has acquired parental responsibility. People are not liable to make repayments while they are in receipt of income support or family credit (s.17(7)–(9)).

Provision of accommodation

A new concept

The provision of accommodation replaces, but is very different from, voluntary reception into care under previous legislation. Although a considerable number of children prior to the implementation of the Act used to come into care on a voluntary basis, voluntary arrangements were not viewed positively. The duty to prevent children coming into care voluntarily or compulsorily often led social workers to refuse to receive children into voluntary care. In addition, there was concern about children drifting in voluntary care, and a general belief that compulsory powers led to better planning for children. Research refuted this view: 'Although the need for greater control is usually justified on the basis of better planning and stability, these studies show that it does not necessarily achieve this' (DHSS 1985(2), p.8). What the research showed instead was that compulsory intervention frequently led to children staying longer in care and having fewer links with family and friends, and that parents felt more isolated and disregarded than parents of children in voluntary care.

The Act was introduced with the clear intention that local authorities should make more use of voluntary arrangements: 'Services to families in need of help should be arranged in a voluntary partnership with the parents' (DHSS 1987(1), para. 5). It places no duty on local authorities to prevent children from coming into accommodation. Rather: 'The accommodation of a child by a local authority is now to be viewed as a service providing positive support to a child and his family' (DOH 1991(3), Vol. 2, para. 2.13). There remains, however, the duty to prevent compulsory proceedings being taken (para. 7, schedule 2).

Duties and powers

Local authorities have a *duty* in some circumstances to provide accommodation and a *power* to do so in others. They have a *duty* to provide accommodation for children in need in their area who require accommodation as a result of:

'(a)   There being no person who has parental responsibility for him;
(b)   his being lost or having been abandoned; or
(c)   the person who has been caring for him being prevented (whether or not permanently, and for whatever reason) from providing him with suitable accommodation or care.' (s.20(1))

In addition, local authorities have a *duty* to provide accommodation for 16- and 17-year-olds who are in need and who are within their area, if the local authority considers that their welfare would be seriously prejudiced if they were not provided with accommodation by the local authority (s.20(3)).

Local authorities have a *power* to provide accommodation to any child within their area if they consider that doing so would safeguard or promote the child's welfare. They also have a *power* to provide accommodation for 16–20-year-olds in community homes that take young people of that age, again if that would safeguard or promote the child's welfare (s.20(4) and (5)).

The circumstances giving rise to a *duty* to provide accommodation for younger children are quite widely drawn and, together with the local authority's *power* to provide accommodation, enable local authorities to meet a wide range of situations. These could range from giving parents a break away from children in need (through disability or other reasons) to making longer-term arrangements in circumstances of serious family breakdown.

The guidance emphasises this point:

'The Act makes no distinction between requirements applying to the provision of a series of pre-planned short-term placements and longer-term provision of accommodation. This is because in practice differences in the provision of a service are not easily sustained.' (DOH 1991(3), Vol. 2, para. 2.26)

Thus accommodation could be used for a short-term arrangement: if a lone parent needed to go into hospital; on a regular but periodic basis as part of a family support service to give families a break; or on a long-term basis when it is recognised that the child or children cannot live at home. The way the legislation is phrased, and the wording of the accompanying guidance, make it clear that provision of accommodation should always be considered by the local authority, even where the threshold conditions for a care or supervision order are established:

'In a case where a child is suffering or is likely to suffer significant harm (as defined in Section 31(9) and (10) of the Act) the local authority has to decide whether the provision of accommodation by agreement with parents is sufficient to safeguard the welfare of the child or whether application for a care or supervision order is appropriate. In the majority of cases local authorities will be able to agree on an arrangement that will best provide for the needs of the child and safeguard and promote his welfare. Work with parents to achieve an initial agreement to the accommodation of the child by the local authority will usually ensure that the ongoing plan for the child can be operated in partnership with his parents.' (DOH, 1991(3), Vol. 2, para. 2.30)

The arrangement is a purely voluntary one, and the Act provides the framework for this by making it clear that accommodation cannot be provided in circumstances where anyone who has parental responsibility for the child objects to the provision of accommodation, providing they are willing and able to provide accommodation for the child or arrange for accommodation to be provided. Similarly, anyone with parental responsibility can remove children at any time from the provision of accommodation without there being any statutory requirement for them to give notice to the local authority (s.20(7) and (8)). However, if there is a residence order in force in relation to the child, only the person or people in whose favour the residence order has been made can object to a child being provided with accommodation and have the right to remove the child.

It follows from this that when the local authority is considering providing accommodation for a child it must be clear who has parental responsibility for the child, and whether or not a residence order is in force. Suppose, for example, that a married couple were separated or divorced, no residence order had been made in relation to the child, and the mother with whom the child was living requested accommodation. If her partner could provide accommodation for the child or could arrange for accommodation to be provided, and was objecting to the provision of local authority accommodation, the local authority would not be able to offer that service. Those working with families will thus need to be able to advise people about private law remedies if the provision of accommodation is a service that they might require. If, in the above circumstances, the mother had a residence order in her favour, then it would be up to her to decide whether to accept the provision of accommodation. Similarly, if someone else, such as a grandparent, had a residence order then, although the parents would have parental responsibility, it would be the grandparent's decision whether or not to accept the provision of accommodation. Where a residence order is in force and accommodation is provided for the child, it would, of course, be open to anyone with an interest in the child to apply to the court to have the residence order varied or revoked.

The important issues to establish are: who has parental responsibility, and who, if anyone, has a residence order. Non-married fathers who have not acquired parental responsibility cannot object to the provision of accommodation or remove the child from accommodation. They are, however, parents, and so must be consulted by the local authority and involved in planning and decision making (s.22).

Sixteen- or 17-year-olds can decide for themselves whether or not to go into accommodation and when to leave. So someone with parental responsibility for them cannot overrule their wishes on these matters (s.20(11)).

Before providing accommodation for a child the local authority is required to ascertain and take into consideration the child's wishes in relation to the provision of accommodation, having regard to the age and understanding of the child. This provision emphasises the importance of taking into account what the child wants, as the local authority is already required to consult with the child and with the child's parents and people with parental responsibility for the child (ss.20(6) and 22(4) and (5)). If a child under 16 holds a very different view to their parents about whether accommodation should be provided, or whether they should leave accommodation, this will clearly be a matter on which the local authority will need to negotiate – and possibly mediate – with the family. Ultimately, the local authority could not prevent a child under 16 from being removed from accommodation unless the threshold conditions exist for applying for a care order. In such circumstances the child, or relatives or friends, might need to be advised about their rights to apply for section 8 orders (see pages 12–17).

The regulations relating to placement and planning require a local authority to make plans in relation to each looked-after child, and to enter into written agreements with parents, or 16- and 17-year-olds themselves, when accommodation is provided (reg. 3, The Arrangements for Placement of Children (General) Regulations 1991). This will set the framework for the placement, and should help to avoid children drifting, or their placements being disrupted suddenly by parents, local authorities or carers (see pages 157–60). The guidance on this issue states: 'Agreements between parents and the responsible authority should reflect the fact that parents retain their parental responsibility . . . Their continuing involvement with the child and exercise of their responsibilities should be the basis of the agreed arrangements' (DOH 1991(3), Vol. 3, para. 2.14), and:

'An agreement should include arrangements for the child leaving accommodation, such as a period of notice to allow time for preparation of the child for this event and to ensure that the child's wishes and feelings are taken into account. Where a child is provided with accommodation by voluntary agreement for a substantial period and has become attached to the carer, this will be important if the child and the carer are to have a sense of stability and security. An agreement should also include a statement of the steps each party should take if another party decided to change the agreement. For example, if the local authority was unable to provide a service it had agreed to provide or proposed to move the child to another carer, the agreement might state that the parent would withdraw the child from accommodation. Or if the parent decided to take action which was harmful to the child the agreement might state that the local authority would consider applying for an emergency protection order.' (DOH 1991(3), Vol. 3, para. 2.66)

Children who are provided with accommodation are children 'looked after' by the local authority (s.22(1) and (2)). Thus all the part III duties towards looked-after children apply. The detail of these, and the planning for such children, are considered in Chapter 8.

The legislation encourages the use of respite accommodation arrangements for all children in need. Prior to the Act, respite care schemes tended to be provided for the families of children with disabilities, with very few similar schemes for children 'in need' for other reasons. This sort of arrangement is such an important way of providing family support in many different situations that it should become a regular part of the service offered. A recent study of the imaginative use of respite accommodation for a wide range of children in one county authority noted that all those involved in the study thought that the provision of respite accommodation could be an advantageous means of preventing long-term family breakdown (Aldgate et al. 1989). Regulations relating to planning, review and fostering placements specifically provide for this sort of placement (reg. 11, Review of Children's Cases Regulations 1991; reg. 9, The Foster Placement (Children) Regulations 1991; reg. 13, Arrangements for Placement of Children (General) Regulations 1991). Local authorities may need to recruit different types of foster carers to provide this service. They will also need to liaise with voluntary organisations who provide such a service already.

This Act places specific duties on local authorities in relation to the provision of accommodation for 16- and 17-year-olds in need. This reflects, in part, the principle established in the Gillick case that as children become older they have more right to determine what should happen to them. It has considerable resource implications for local authorities, given the increasing numbers of homeless young people in cities and towns. Local authorities will need to work closely with the housing department and with housing associations and other agencies to fulfil their statutory duties, and they will be assisted in doing this by the requirements in section 27 about inter-agency co-operation and a corporate approach to the provision of services.

Charging and contributions

Charging generally

Local authorities can charge for any service provided under part III of the Act, other than advice, guidance and counselling. The charge must be a reasonable one; people must be means-tested before being charged, and those in receipt of income support or family credit are not liable to pay charges. Those liable for charging are the child's parents if the child is under 16; children themselves once they have reached 16, and, where a service is provided for a member of the child's family, that person (s.29(1)–(5)).

The Act refers to both parents being means-tested for the purposes of assessing a reasonable charge or determining whether assistance in cash or kind should be reclaimed. This means that non-married fathers without parental responsibility could be means-tested for these purposes.

It is important to remember that the Act gives local authorities a *power* to charge for services, rather than requiring them to do so. Guidance urges local authorities who intend charging to have clear charging policies that are understood by all staff (DOH 1991(3), Vol. 2, para. 2.38). It would be very helpful if local authorities would include details of their charging and means-testing policies in the general information they publish about services (see page 33). This would mean that those requesting a service would be clear about the possibility of facing charges. In developing policies, local authorities should ensure that the delivery of services is not delayed because of over-complicated means-testing or other bureaucratic hurdles in the finance department.

Parental contributions

Local authorities may require contributions when they are looking after a child (s.29(6)). Parents are liable to contribute until the child reaches 16. Those over 16 are liable themselves. A person is not liable to make contributions while in receipt of income support, family credit or disability working allowance (para. 21(3) and (4), schedule 2, and DOH Circular 12, September 1991).

The local authority has to consider whether or not to recover contributions in each case (para. 21(1), schedule 2), but it could decide not to do so in every case. It may recover contributions from a contributor only if it considers it reasonable to do so (para. 21(2), schedule 2). The contributions cannot be more than what foster carers would be paid per week for a similar child. A local authority can impose a standard contribution. In all cases the means of the contributor must be considered (para. 22(4) and (5), schedule 2).

The local authority has to serve a contribution notice on the liable person, setting out what they think the person should pay and the date on which the payments should start, which cannot be earlier than the date of the notice. If the liable person agrees to the amount they will have to put their agreement in writing, and they will then have to pay that amount from whenever specified in the notice, or as agreed. If they have agreed in writing to make the payments, and they do not do so, or fall into arrears, the local authority can go to court to recover the money. They cannot do this for any period after receiving a written notification from the liable person that they are withdrawing their agreement to pay. It is very important for people whose financial circumstances change, and find they can no longer keep up the payment, to write immediately to the local authority, withdrawing their agreement to pay (para. 22(1)–(2) and (7)–(9)).

If the local authority and liable person cannot reach agreement within one month of the notice being served, or the liable person has withdrawn their agreement to pay, the local authority can take the case to court. The court can make a contribution order, paying due regard to the means of the liable person (*Re C (A Minor: Contribution Notice)* (1993) *The Times*, 13 May). The contribution order could be backdated to the date of the contribution notice but, as this could mean people being faced with a large lump sum to pay off, the court should take this into account when deciding when the order should start (para. 23, schedule 2). Court orders can be enforced by the usual methods of enforcing a magistrates' court maintenance order. Appeals are dealt with by the High Court. Legal Aid is available for these proceedings (para. 2 of part 1 of schedule 2, Legal Aid Act 1988, as amended by para. 45, schedule 12, Children Act 1989).

Some of the problems identified with parental contributions in the past have included these:

- Money is dealt with by the finance department, and is often ignored by families' or children's social workers, yet often they could help to negotiate a lower charge or no charge, and they have an important role to play in explaining the process and helping people through it.
- The amount collected in contributions is often less than the costs of collecting them.
- For some families their financial hardship has been aggravated by the demand for contributions, to the detriment of the welfare of the child and of other children in the family.

If local authorities *do* continue to charge contributions, it will be particularly important for social workers to help and advise their clients and, if necessary, to advocate on their behalf.

4 Child protection procedures

Introduction

It is sometimes thought that the Children Act is a Child Protection Act. This is a misunderstanding for two main reasons.

First, most of the work carried out under the auspices of the Children Act will *not* be child protection work; it will either be general preventive and family support work with children and families in the community, or private family law cases.

Second, those parts of the Act which *do* concern child protection (ss.43–52) relate to only one small part of the work covered by local child protection procedures. Two-thirds of all children on child protection registers are not subject to any legal proceedings, and there are many more children not on the register who do receive services. Whilst it might be said that both these groups are covered by the local authority duty to investigate (s.47), the legislation pays only scant attention to the manner in which these investigations are to be conducted and none at all to how cases should be dealt with after the initial investigation is completed.

In practice the manner in which all professionals with child protection responsibilities are to respond to child protection concerns will be decided by their local Area Child Protection Committee (ACPC). The ways in which ACPCs decide membership, organise their deliberations, set standards, review cases, etc. is at their sole discretion, and is subject only to Government guidance, not regulation. Whilst ACPCs and their employees must act within the law, the law itself does not cover much of the child protection work that must be undertaken.

This chapter explains the tasks, the working methods and the powers of ACPCs. It discusses the relationship between ACPC procedures and the statutory framework. It considers the effects of registration and the mechanisms for challenge. It comments on how the Act's commitment to partnership with consumers can be realised in child protection work. Chapter 5 looks at emergency procedures covered by the Act.

Area Child Protection Committees

ACPCs started life as Area Review Committees, set up following the inquiry in 1974 into the death of Maria Colwell (Secretary of State for Social Services 1974). This was in response to the lack of co-ordination between agencies about the child protection service to be offered in an area. There are 116 ACPCs in England and Wales. One covers each local authority area.

ACPCs take their membership from the various agencies that provide child protection services in the area. They always include representatives from social services, the police, the education department (a teacher and/or an education social worker), the health authority, the family health services authority, and the probation service. Health representatives include GPs, hospital and community doctors, nursing staff, and health visitors. The National Society for the Prevention of Cruelty to Children (NSPCC) also has a representative if they have a child protection team or prcject in the area, as do the armed services if they have a local base. Some ACPCs include a local magistrate, even though their role in child protection is quite different from that of other members. No such appointment is recommended by the Government. Some ACPCs have recently provided for service users to become members, thereby providing a means of planning services in partnership.

In some large counties there is a County Child Protection Committee (equivalent to an ACPC) and a number of District Child Protection Committees beneath that. The frequency with which these committees meet varies from once or twice a year to once a month. Some ACPCs have sub-groups, or working groups, to deal with specific areas of work, such as training, or child protection for black children. Occasionally these groups include agency members who do not sit on the ACPC.

The Government issues guidance about how child protection work should be organised. This has been updated in line with the Children Act, and was published in 1991 as *Working Together under the Children Act 1989: A Guide to Arrangements for Inter-agency Co-operation for the Protection of Children from Abuse* (DOH 1991(2)).

Working Together recommends that ACPCs establish links with other related agencies, such as voluntary organisations who provide relevant services, and organisations who represent religious and cultural interests. ACPCs have generally failed to establish such links.

This may explain, in part, the experience many families and child care practitioners have of a remote, often unknown, usually unapproachable and seemingly unaccountable committee. *Working Together* recommends that agency members of ACPCs should be able to make decisions on behalf of the agency without first referring back to that agency. Whilst this certainly speeds up the decision making process, it can also result in inadequate discussion between agency members and the staff they are meant to be representing. It is rare to find that agency staff know who their representatives on the ACPC are, let alone that they are aware of, or consulted about, possible ACPC agenda items. This can make for a wide gap between procedures adopted by an ACPC and actual child protection practice.

ACPCs are normally chaired by a senior member of the social services department, but there is no uniform system governing how decisions are made. Voting seems to be rare. More commonly the chair makes decisions based on their personal assessment of the 'feel of the meeting'. This lack of clarity and formality can lead to unwarranted domination of some ACPCs by high-status and vocal members.

The major functions of an ACPC are:

'(a) to establish, maintain and review local inter-agency guidelines on procedures to be followed in individual cases;
(b) to monitor the implementation of local procedures;
(c) to identify significant issues arising from the handling of cases and reports from inquiries;
(d) to scrutinise arrangements to provide treatment, expert advice and inter-agency liaison and make recommendations to the responsible agencies;
(e) to scrutinise progress on work to prevent child abuse and to make recommendations to the responsible agencies;
(f) to scrutinise work related to inter-agency training and make recommendations to the responsible agencies;
(g) to conduct reviews required under Part 8 of this Guide (reviews of individual cases);
(h) to publish an annual report about local child protection matters.'
(DOH 1991(2), para. 2.12)

ACPCs can decide exactly how child protection concerns are to be dealt with in their area. Their right to do this is unregulated, and so the community is totally reliant on both their goodwill and their good sense. If the ACPC decided that where an allegation of child sexual abuse was made all children of the household should be medically examined, there would be virtually no possibility of a legal challenge. Similarly, the lack of attention in most child protection procedures to equality issues – such as race, culture and disability – are almost unchallengeable in law. There is the possibility of using judicial review – although there are limitations with this process (see pages 173–4) – or taking a case under the Race Relations Act or the Sex Discrimination Act. This resulting lack of accountability contributes significantly to the lack of contact that exists between the ACPC and the recipients of the services they provide.

However, *Working Together* gives ACPCs more detailed guidance than ever before about the exercise of child protection functions. In addition, the Government has made it clear that, whilst regulations do not exist and *Working Together* does not have the full force of statute, it should 'be complied with unless local circumstances indicate exceptional reasons which justify a variation' (DOH 1991(2), p.iii).

Local authority duty to investigate

Child protection procedures set out the framework for work under section 47 (the local authority duty to investigate). This needs to be distinguished from other sorts of investigation under the Act. So, invoking the child protection procedures should not be the automatic response to a court direction under section 37(2) requiring a local authority to investigate whether or not it would be appropriate to apply for a care or supervision order (see page 98). Local authorities will need to decide how to conduct these investigations but it would be wrong just to treat a section 37 referral as if it were a section 47 referral (see below).

Similar considerations apply to investigations of the child's circumstances under paras. 17 and 19, schedule 3. These relate to children subject to education supervision orders (ESOs) where, in the case of a court discharging an ESO, it may direct the local authority to investigate the child's circumstances. They apply also in cases where the local authority has been notified by a local education authority (LEA) of a child's persistent failure to comply with a direction included in an ESO.

In none of the above situations can it be said that, by virtue simply of the court's direction or the LEA's notification, the local authority has reasonable cause to suspect that the child is suffering, or is likely to suffer, significant harm. The court may suspect this, but section 47(1)(b) requires that the local authority has reasonable cause to suspect it. The LEA is not required to make any judgement; it is under a duty to notify the local authority if a court direction is resisted persistently. But it does not necessarily follow that, for instance, a child who persistently refuses to comply with an ESO direction to attend a particular school is suffering, or is likely to suffer, significant harm. An automatic link between school non-attendance and the need for care caused problems under CYPA 1969 proceedings, and was, therefore, excluded from the threshold criteria for care and supervision proceedings under the Children Act 1989. Although a case decided shortly after the implementation of the Act established a link between persistent failure to attend school and the new threshold conditions for a care order, this link should not be assumed to exist in every case of truancy (*Re O (A Minor)* [1992] 2 FLR 7).

Local authorities will need to adopt a preliminary – as opposed to a child protection – policy and procedure to start investigations of the situations described above. The investigation might result in no services being offered, it might lead to services being made available under part III, or it might lead to a section 47 investigation.

Section 47 investigation

Section 47 replaces and extends section 2 of CYPA 1969, which imposed a duty on the local authority to investigate situations where it seemed that there were grounds for care proceedings. An investigation under section 47 must be carried out if it is thought that a child is suffering, or is likely to suffer, significant harm. Previously, if an investigation concluded that care proceedings were not needed, no further duties applied but, under the 1989 Act, if a local authority concludes that care proceedings are not needed, it must also decide what, if any, other services are required, and it must consider whether a subsequent review is needed.

Section 47(1) provides that:

'Where a local authority –

(a) are informed that a child who lives, or is found, in their area –
   (i)   is the subject of an emergency protection order; or
   (ii) is in police protection; or
(b) have reasonable cause to suspect that a child who lives, or is found, in their area is suffering, or is likely to suffer, significant harm, the authority shall make, or cause to be made, such enquiries as they consider necessary to enable them to decide whether they should take any action to safeguard or promote the child's welfare.'

If the local authority choose to 'cause' others to make the necessary enquiries, these other people could be workers from either statutory or voluntary agencies.

Local authority decisions following investigation

Even if the local authority has not conducted the investigation itself, it retains the responsibility to consider the results of investigations and to decide what action should then to be taken to safeguard or promote the child's welfare (ss.47(3)(a) and 47(8)). In addition, if the local authority's decision is not to apply for a child assessment order, an emergency protection order or a care or supervision order it has to decide whether or not other services are to be provided, whether it would be appropriate to review the case later and, if so, on what date (s.47(7)). The same considerations apply to all subsequent reviews. It is important to distinguish between section 47(7) reviews and other reviews, such as child protection registration reviews and section 26 reviews of a child who is looked after by the local authority.

Relationship with emergency protection orders and police protection

If a child is subject to an EPO the local authority must decide:

- what action to take to safeguard or promote the child's welfare, and
- whether, if the child is not in accommodation provided by or on behalf of the local authority, it is in the child's best interests to remain in that accommodation while the EPO is in force (s.47(3)(b)).

If the child is in police protection (s.46) the local authority must decide whether or not to ask the police to apply for an EPO on their behalf, or whether to apply themselves.

Access to the child

Where investigations are being carried out under section 47, the local authority is under a duty, where reasonably practicable, to obtain access to the child themselves, or by someone whom they authorise to do so. This could be a worker from another agency, such as a teacher, religious leader or a representative of the NSPCC. They do not have to obtain access if they are satisfied that they already have sufficient information about the child (s.47(4)). If, however, they do not have sufficient information, *and* they are denied access to the child, the local authority must apply for a child assessment order, an emergency protection order, or a supervision or care order, unless they are satisfied that the child's welfare does not require this (s.47(6), see Chapter 5).

Co-operation between agencies

Section 47, subsections (5) (9) (10) and (11) give statutory force to the guidance in *Working Together* about the ways in which different agencies with a child care remit should co-operate in child protection investigations and assessments. So, if the local authority believes that matters relating to a child's education should be investigated, they must consult the relevant local education authority (s.47(5)). It is not clear how opted-out and public schools are to be dealt with, nor whether the duties laid upon LEAs in s.47(9)–(11) include such schools. Other named agencies now have a statutory obligation to assist with investigations if called upon by the local authority to do so (s.47(9)). These agencies are any local authority (for instance where a child lived previously), any LEA, any local housing authority, any health authority or National Health Service Trust, and any 'person' (currently the NSPCC) authorised by the Secretary of State (s.47(11)).

It is striking that neither the police nor the probation service are included, although their assistance is often vital. This point was raised during the Children Bill's passage through parliament. The Government explained that these two agencies could be omitted because 'police refusal to co-operate on any matter would be indefensible', and because probation officers, being officers of the court, 'are already under a duty to assist in these matters' (*Hansard*, 6 June 1989, col. 342). It is regrettable that these already existing obligations were not reinforced in the Children Act. The current partial list would not have helped the probation service to understand its obligations to disclose its knowledge of the background of Jasmine Beckford's stepfather (Brent 1985).

There is also some doubt about whether the reference to the health authority places the same duty upon a general practitioner. It seems that this kind of cover would be necessary to secure the co-operation of GPs in cases similar to that of Giselle (Derbyshire et al. 1990), where the GP failed to provide relevant information about the foster mother's mental health problems.

Local authorities may have further difficulties in obtaining the assistance they require because s.47(10) gives other agencies a 'get-out clause' by stating that they do not need to provide assistance 'where doing so would be unreasonable in all the circumstances of this case'. Unfortunately, the guidance states only that the circumstances will vary from area to area and that agencies need to have good inter-agency liaison.

If, when conducting an investigation, it seems to the local authority that the child normally lives in another local authority, they must consult with that other local authority, who have then to undertake the investigation on behalf of the first local authority. This duty leaves responsibility clearly with the first local authority, and so removes the kind of confusion that existed between Lambeth and Southwark about who had responsibility for the investigation concerning Doreen Aston (Lambeth et al. 1989).

What child protection procedures cover

While section 47 refers to local authority enquiries and reviews, the law is silent on the nature of such enquiries and on the conclusions and non-court actions that should result from them. There are also no regulations covering the nature and process of investigations and reviews. An ACPC is, therefore, left with total discretion about how to conduct its child protection service. There are no effective sanctions on an ACPC which does not follow the Government guidance contained in *Working Together*. Inspections of child protection services carried out by the Social Services Inspectorate (SSI) demonstrate the difficulty that can arise. For instance, the SSI report on Rochdale's services (SSI 1990) found that the ACPC had no procedure which enabled parents or children to participate in child protection conferences, although this had been recommended some two years previously in the earlier edition of *Working Together*. The SSI made clear and strong recommendations that the procedures should be changed to reflect *Working Together*, but it was powerless to enforce that recommendation.

The current version of *Working Together* is much more forceful, in both its recommendations and its clear expectation that ACPCs will implement them unless there are exceptional reasons for not doing so. Yet despite, for instance, the very clear recommendation that parents should normally participate throughout each conference about their children, some ACPCs have yet to adopt this practice. It remains to be seen what action, if any, can be taken to force an ACPC to follow Government guidance. Judicial review (see pages 173–4) is one possible course of action.

ACPC child protection procedures vary in detail and layout. *Working Together* gives guidance (in Appendix 6) on the content and format of local procedural handbooks. It recommends the following order:

- legal context;
- explanation of the different agencies involved and their role;
- how to make referrals for a child protection investigation;
- the initial steps taken to assess whether abuse or neglect has occurred;
- explanation of how the investigation is conducted, including details of how parents will be involved from the outset;
- details of the function and management of child protection conferences, which needs to include information on the participation of parents and older children in order to reflect the detail in *Working Together* about these matters;
- explanation of the criteria for abuse and neglect;
- the requirements for registration;
- the purpose of the child protection register;
- guidance about review child protection conferences and post-registration work;
- guidance on how statutory and voluntary agencies should work together;

- advice on special circumstances, for example, children of families in the services, or organised abuse;
- detailed procedures to be followed in individual agencies.

Participation by parents and children

Hitherto child protection procedures have tended to mention parents' and children's participation in relation to child protection conferences only. Such partial discussion prevents proper consideration of their participation throughout each part of the child protection procedures. *Working Together* highlights the need to adapt this wider vision of participation when it says:

> 'However, it cannot be emphasised too strongly that involvement of children and adults in child protection conferences will not be effective unless they are fully involved from the outset in all stages of the child protection process, and unless from the time of the referral there is as much openness and honesty as possible between families and professionals.' (para. 6.11)

Participation in conferences is just one means of achieving partnership with families, as underlined in the guidance.

Partnership will not flourish unless parents, other adults and older children are encouraged to participate throughout all the child protection stages, and unless they are helped to feel that they can participate at each stage. The child protection conference is a pivotal part of the process. It cannot be missed out, but it should not be seen as the most important part, nor as a part in which participation can be dispensed with. This need to work in partnership and with full participation from the outset will be further underlined when government research on disposal of child protection referrals is published (Gibbons (forthcoming)). This research demonstrates that most child protection referrals are diverted to other more appropriate services, before the conference stage is reached.

Many ACPCs had difficulties in incorporating the recommendations in the first edition of *Working Together* regarding the participation of parents and older children. The reasons varied – lack of commitment, differences of view held by ACPC members, pressure of other work. An added problem was getting to grips with the practical implications of altering a policy or a procedural statement. So, it had become increasingly common to find that, whilst the child protection procedures allowed for parents to participate in conferences, hardly any parents *did* participate, and certainly not for the whole of the conference. Without a thorough overhaul it is most unlikely that any policy would be satisfactorily implemented. The current edition of *Working Together* takes this problem seriously.

It does so by addressing the requirement for participation more thoroughly than before, and by making the requirement itself much tighter. ACPCs now have to have exclusion criteria which will need to be shown to apply in any individual case in which a parent is to be excluded for even a short part of an initial or review child protection conference. These criteria must be spelt out clearly. Blanket policies allowing for a 'mandatory' exclusion period in all cases will be contrary to the recommendations contained in *Working Together*. Similarly, the requirements for children's participation have been clarified and strengthened. The expectation is that children will soon be able to participate in some way in child protection conferences about themselves.

These policies cannot, and will not, be implemented without good planning. Attention needs to be given to writing procedures for participation, for invitations, for exclusions, for chairing, for the format of meetings, for how participants' views will be presented to the conference, for how decisions and recommendations will be made, recorded and circulated, for how decisions can be challenged, and for how all this information will be published for workers, parents and children. Training needs will have to be assessed and resourced. In addition to the guidance in *Working Together* the Department of Health is planning to publish in 1994 a practical guide for social workers about partnership with families in child protection work. The University of East Anglia publish an excellent practical guide to this aspect of working in partnership (Thoburn 1992).

ACPCs still have much work to do to build on the positive and helpful Government guidance and research. They must overcome the powerful resistance of that minority of professionals who oppose the Government's guidance about participation by parents and children. They must develop means to inform parents and children about their local child protection procedures and about their role within them. An increasing number of ACPCs use the Family Rights Group/NSPCC guide for families, *Child Protection Procedures: what they mean for your family*, available in English, Welsh, Urdu, Gujerati and Bengali (FRG/NSPCC 1992). A copy of the guide is then given to every family of a child who is the subject of a section 47 investigation.

A few ACPCs supplement this guide with a short useful guide to their own local procedures. It need not be long – two sides of A4 is common, but it is an important way of encouraging parents to see that they have a valuable role to play and that the professionals welcome their expertise. ACPCs committed to ensuring that *all* parents have accessible information might consider making this information available in braille and on audio tapes. Some local areas are providing training sessions for parents who participate in child protection conferences. Others have produced videos for families to borrow which explain the role and functioning of such conferences.

ACPCs will want to set up systems to monitor the participation of parents, other carers and children, and to ensure that this monitoring includes more than child protection conferences. The SSI report on Rochdale, for instance, found that many children were medically examined without seeking their parents' permission, or without seeking permission from children with sufficient understanding. In addition 10 per cent of parents did not know that their child's name was on the register, 20 per cent had not been told of case plans, and 80 per cent had not been involved in the assessment. Seventy-nine per cent of the children on the child protection register had no long-term plans made for them which identified clear, measurable objectives for parents. No attention whatsoever appeared to have been given to children's participation (SSI 1990). Such problems would be far less likely to arise if local child protection procedures alerted professionals, at every stage, to tell parents and children what was happening and why, to ask for their views about this, and to consult them about how they wanted to see the investigation conducted and matters resolved.

Equal opportunities

ACPC procedures should give attention to equal opportunity issues. The importance of this is underlined when users are being encouraged to participate more in the work. Some ACPCs have given thought to, and guidance about, race and cultural issues, and rightly so, since it is vital to ensure that procedures acknowledge that all children and families, of whatever race, receive a service that is responsive to, and positive about, their particular cultural background, ways of life, wishes and expectations. There is some evidence that Afro-Caribbean children are over-represented on child protection registers whilst children of Asian origin are under-represented. No national research has been conducted to investigate why this is so, but it would not be unreasonable to deduce that a service delivered predominantly by white professionals is unlikely to be appropriate for all who come into contact with it.

Equally, more thought needs to be given to gender issues. British society still holds mothers largely responsible for the care and upbringing of their children. Most of the work done in pursuit of good child protection is done with mothers, yet many of the most influential professionals involved in the child protection process are men. ACPCs could usefully give more attention, in both procedures and training, to achieving a better balance between work and workers, and to making child protection work more sensitive to gender inequalities.

Whilst the Children Act brings children with disabilities to the forefront of work with children and families, there is no recognition of the particular difficulties that might be experienced by parents with disabilities. Workers would benefit greatly by clear ACPC guidance on how their participation can be maximised.

Requirements for registration

Working Together clarifies that before a child's name can be entered on the child protection register the requirements for registration must be satisfied and the category of abuse identified. One of the following requirements must be satisfied:

' (i)   There must be one or more identifiable incidents which can be described as having adversely affected the child. They may be acts of commission or omission. They can be either physical, sexual, emotional or neglectful. It is important to identify a specific occasion or occasions when the incident has occurred. Professional judgement is that further incidents are likely;

or

(ii)   Significant harm is expected on the basis of professional judgement of findings of the investigation in this individual case or on research evidence.

The conference will need to establish so far as they can a cause of the harm or likelihood of harm. This cause could also be applied to siblings or other children living in the same household so as to justify registration of them. Such children should be categorised according to the area of concern.' (para. 6.39)

The categories of abuse have been reduced to four: neglect, physical injury, sexual abuse and emotional abuse. The category of 'grave concern' no longer exists in Government guidance, and should have been removed from all ACPC procedures. This removal resulted from research findings that its use varied widely from area to area; that it was used more to contain professional anxiety, and that these registrations were usually too vague to allow for a relevant and effective child protection plan to be negotiated. By using the 'requirements for registration', children who have not yet been abused or neglected can be registered – but now only under the category of the abuse or neglect whose likelihood can be identified and substantiated.

The intended effect of placing a child's name on the child protection register should be that co-ordinated protective and preventive services are provided to the child and to their family. Unfortunately, that has not always been the case, as many ACPCs have been unclear about the purpose of registration. Some have seen it as a list of children who had been abused or neglected, or were in grave danger of abuse or neglect, while others regarded it as a list of children in need of multi-disciplinary child protection services. The Government guidance sees the purpose of registration as identifying those children who have been abused or neglected, and who will continue to be at risk of abuse or neglect unless a multi-disciplinary child protection plan is implemented.

Effects of registration

Working Together is helpful in separating the criteria or definitions of abuse or neglect from the 'requirements for registration' (para. 6.39). Children's names should not be registered if, for instance, they have been physically abused but there is no significant risk of this occurring again. If there *is* significant risk of this or another form of abuse or neglect occurring in future, the registration should signal the existence of a multi-disciplinary child protection plan, and it should provide the structure to nurture that plan. This is the positive side of registration.

There are negative aspects, too. Although many professionals insist that the child protection register is mainly a list of children, most parents experience it as public registration of their failure as parents. The stigma they feel continues long after registration finishes, and it is felt keenly even when they were not responsible for the abuse that occurred. This stigma is not just perceived – it is also a reality. In some employment circumstances the local authority is asked if the applicant is known to the social services department. The fact of having had one's child's name on a child protection register is likely to act as a disqualification from work involving children.

Some areas appear to use registration as a criterion for the allocation of scarce resources. This has led workers to recommend registration in order to gain parents access to day care facilities, for example. There is a real possibility that the child protection functions of a local authority will be used in some areas to determine whether children are in need (for more on this see Chapter 3). One of the unintended and unwelcome effects of this is that registration will become a key to resource provision rather than occurring because a multi-agency protection plan is required. An awareness of these long-term disadvantages might help to prevent such abuse of the child protection process.

Another detrimental effect of registration relates to the way information is passed between professionals. Child protection professionals generally work to an unwritten rule that information is passed only to those 'with a need to know', but there is no clear guidance about who might 'need to know', and why. *Working Together* does not go beyond saying that 'the degree of confidentiality will be governed by the need to protect the child' (para. 3.15).

If a child's name has come off the register, do the next school headteacher and form teacher 'need to know'? If a mother had one child's name on a child protection register, does the GP have to inform social services when she becomes pregnant again? No doubt the answer is 'it depends'. But on what does it depend, and do parents and children know what rules of confidentiality are being operated? All too often a family and child's experience of confidentiality is that information about them is passed around, speculated on and recorded without either their agreement or their knowledge.

Confidentiality applies to a number of areas: between professionals, about sources and between family members. Professional workers need to make clear to all their clients, at the outset, those matters that may be discussed in confidence and those that cannot be guaranteed confidentiality. Professional workers could guarantee to clients that they will not pass on information about or from them without at least informing them of their intention to do so, and giving reasons for that decision. In many cases this would have the added advantage of enabling the clients to pass on that information themselves, thus leaving them with greater dignity.

The requirements of some agencies – voluntary as well as statutory – to start child protection investigations in all situations concerning possible child abuse or neglect has resulted, unintentionally, in a lack of a confidential counselling service. Some areas have sought to provide children with some control by, for instance, buying into the Childline service and advertising it widely. This gives children choice about how much control they will retain over their discussions. Similar alternative services could, and should, be provided for parents and other carers.

Child protection plans

If the primary purpose of registration is to list those children who are in need of a multi-agency child protection plan, one would expect to be able to locate this plan easily on agency files. One would also expect parents (or other primary carers) and older children to be aware of the plan and to have it in recorded form. What is needed is a clear structure for making decisions and recommendations, for holding meetings of the core group involved in a case, and for negotiating, agreeing and recording child protection plans.

If parents and other family members are to play their full part in ensuring better protection for their children in the future they will have to be involved in all these matters. Family members and professionals alike will have to:

- understand and accept that child protection conferences make both decisions and recommendations, and that there is a distinction between the two;
- appreciate that parents need to participate in the core group meeting which should make the child protection plan, incorporating the conference recommendations if those are agreed by the core group;
- ensure that child protection plans are negotiated in the first instance, and become stipulations only if agreement cannot be reached. The results of these negotiations should be put into a written (or otherwise recorded) agreement. Alternatives to a written agreement include an agreement on video tape, audio cassette, in braille or on computer disc. It should be made clear whether the record is of a freely-made agreement, or records the fact that the signatories agree to the stipulations by one or more of the agencies. Every participant will need to have a copy of this recorded agreement;
- the recorded agreement should always be made in the family's language.

These sorts of agreements are required under the Children Act for foster placements and placements of children in care with parents or those with parental responsibility (see pages 157–8). In line with these requirements *Working Together* recommends that a recorded agreement should be drawn up also when making a child protection plan. It says:

'It is essential that parents, and children where appropriate, should be fully involved in the discussions about what should constitute a plan. Agreement should be striven for between the professionals, the family and the child. Making a formal agreement is in itself a useful way to record plans. Authorities may find it helpful to consider the Family Rights Group model agreement.' (para. 6.8)

This model agreement form is published jointly by the Family Rights Group and the National Foster Care Association (FRG/NFCA 1991).

Challenging child protection procedures, decisions and recommendations

Whilst the Children Act provides a statutory framework to respond to users' concerns and complaints about the local authority services they receive, nothing comparable has yet been provided for child protection matters. If a parent or child is concerned about the behaviour or decisions of an individual agency, or of members of the agency, they can use that agency's complaints and representations procedure. If, however, their concern relates to the way in which the ACPC procedures were carried out, or to the decisions of the child protection conference, this is a multi-agency matter which cannot be resolved by one agency alone. The ACPC, therefore, holds responsibility for providing a fair means of review of these areas of concern. *Working Together* states: 'ACPC procedures should cover the handling of complaints about a conference as such. ACPCs could establish a special "appeals procedure", or look to the procedure of the local authority as the lead agency' (para. 6.21). The adoption of this latter recommendation would mean that one single agency would make decisions on behalf of, and binding upon, all agencies involved in a particular case. It seems unlikely that this would be satisfactory for any of the parties involved. The former recommendation involves the ACPC running its own appeals procedure, as has been established by a few ACPCs. This would be a welcome development throughout England and Wales.

5 Emergencies and assessments

Introduction

Chapter 4 dealt with child protection procedures and investigations under section 47 of the Children Act where there is suspicion or an allegation that a child is suffering, or is likely to suffer, significant harm. This chapter sets out the court orders that can assist with investigation and assessment when there is a need to protect children in an emergency. It also considers police powers and the provision of refuges for runaway children.

Local authorities have a duty to prevent all children in their area suffering ill-treatment or neglect, by ensuring that services are provided for them (para. 4, schedule 2). Child protection procedures link with this duty by helping to bring children who need, or may need, protection to the attention of the relevant agencies so that an appropriate package of services can be provided for the child and family. As noted in Chapter 4, the vast majority of children subject to child protection procedures remain living with their families, so the emphasis is, rightly, on professionals working in partnership with those families. There will, however, always be cases where compulsory powers are needed in order to protect children or to ensure that a proper investigation is carried out into their circumstances. Here too, as we shall see, partnership work can and should be achieved.

Emergency protection orders

During the late 1970s and early 1980s there was considerable and mounting criticism of the place of safety order, the order used for protecting children in an emergency. Criticism was levelled at the duration of the order; the lack of right of challenge for children or carers; the wide grounds – not necessarily related to an emergency – on which the order could be made, and the fact that the order was being used increasingly – and in some areas routinely – as a way of starting care proceedings. There was also confusion about the legal status of a child under a place of safety order, and this led to problems over consent to medical examinations and disputes about contact between children and their families. The Children Act responds to all of these criticisms.

It must be emphasised that an emergency protection order 'remains an extremely serious step' (DOH 1991(3), Vol. 1, para. 4.30). The unplanned and sudden removal of children from familiar surroundings is extremely traumatic for the child and such action should be taken only where it is absolutely necessary to protect the child from immediate and real danger.

Grounds

There are two distinct grounds for making an emergency protection order. The first is this:

> 'Where any person (the applicant) applies to the court for an order to be made under this section with respect to a child, the court may make the order if, but only if, it is satisfied that:–
>
> (a) there is reasonable cause to believe that the child is likely to suffer significant harm if –
>
> >   (i)   he is not removed to accommodation provided by or on behalf of the applicant; or
> >   (ii) he does not remain in the place in which he is then being accommodated' (s.44(1)(a)).

Before a court can be satisfied that the order should be made on this ground there must be clear evidence of the need to remove or detain the child immediately. In particular, the court will want to know whether the removal of the child can be arranged with the agreement of parents or carers instead. The court will bear in mind that local authorities have a duty to prevent children becoming subject to court proceedings (para. 7, schedule 2) and are able to offer accommodation as a service to children and families (s.20). The court may also want to know whether the applicant has considered, and discussed with the parents or carers, the possibility of an alleged abuser moving out of the home so that the child can remain there; the local authority can assist here by providing either accommo- dation or cash help (para. 5, schedule 2). There is no power under the Children Act for the court to *order* people who have been violent towards children to leave the home, but it is open to a parent or carer to apply for an injunction in private law family proceedings, or ancillary to proceedings under the Act, ordering their partner to leave the home because of violence towards them or the children (see page 14). The court may want to know whether these possibilities, too, have been considered. Note that it is the *court* that must be satisfied that the grounds exist. This first ground looks to the future, and evidence of past or present significant harm is relevant only in so far as it is evidence of the likelihood of the child suffering significant harm in the immediate future (DOH 1991(3), Vol. 1, paras. 4.41–4.43).

The second ground for an emergency protection order is this:

'Where any person (the applicant) applies to the court for an order to be made under this section with respect to a child, the court may make the order if, but only if, it is satisfied that:–

(b)   in the case of an application made by a local authority –

  (i)   enquiries are being made with respect to the child under Section 47(1)(b); and
  (ii) those enquiries are being frustrated by access to the child being unreasonably refused to a person authorised to seek access and that the applicant has reasonable cause to believe that access to the child is required as a matter of urgency; or

(c)   in the case of an application made by an authorised person –

  (i)   the applicant has reasonable cause to suspect that a child is suffering, or is likely to suffer, significant harm;
  (ii)   the applicant is making enquiries with respect to the child's welfare; and
  (iii) those enquiries are being frustrated by access to the child being unreasonably refused to a person authorised to seek access and the applicant has reasonable cause to believe that access to the child is required as a matter or urgency.'

(s.44(1)(b) and (c))

The 'authorised person' referred to in this section is the NSPCC. So, while any person can apply on the first ground, only a local authority or the NSPCC can apply on this second ground, which has become known as the 'frustrated access' ground. It must be shown that an investigation is under way, arising from suspicion that the child is suffering or is likely to suffer significant harm (s.47, and see Chapter 4), and that, in the course of those investigations, 'a person authorised to seek access' has not been allowed to see the child. Note that when the local authority is carrying out an investigation under section 47 they must arrange for the child to be seen (unless they already have enough information about the child), *and*, if they are not allowed to see the child, they must apply for an emergency protection order, a child assessment order or a care or supervision order, unless they are satisfied that the child's welfare can be satisfactorily safeguarded without them doing this (s.47(4) and (6)). The person authorised to seek access to the child could be a social worker, or it could be somebody else involved in the investigation, such as the health visitor. The issue is gaining access to the child, and not, for example, being able to take the child for a medical examination. If the person is allowed to see the child, though not in private, it might be difficult to argue that access to the child has been denied.

The denial of access must be unreasonable. Persons seeking access to a child must carry proper identification (s.44(3)) and, if they do not, it will not necessarily be unreasonable for them not to be allowed in to see the child. Depending on the circumstances, it might not be unreasonable to refuse to allow a person inside in the middle of the night to see a child who is fast asleep, or it might not be unreasonable to refuse to let someone in to see a child if the parent promises that the child will be taken immediately, or as soon as possible, to a local doctor or health clinic. However, this might not be a reasonable refusal of access if similar arrangements had not been followed through previously. Finally, there must be some evidence to support the applicant's belief that access to the child is required as a matter of urgency (DOH 1991(3), Vol. 1, paras. 4.39–4.40).

This 'frustrated access' ground for an emergency protection order needs to be distinguished from the grounds for a child assessment order (see page 90). Both orders are based on the suspicion of harm or likely harm but, with the 'frustrated access' ground, the issue is denial of access to the child together with evidence of the need to see the child urgently. This is an emergency order. The child assessment order is *not* an emergency order: the issue there is the need to have an assessment of the child which will not be carried out unless an order is made.

In addition to the grounds set out above, the court must also take into consideration the guiding principles that the welfare of the child is their paramount concern, and that the order must be better for the child than making no order. But the court is not required to go through the detail of the welfare checklist when dealing with these applications. And, since applications for emergency protection orders are not family proceedings, the court does not have the option of making any of the other orders under the Act (ss.1 and 8(3) and (4)).

Making the application

Anyone can apply for an emergency protection order on the first ground, although, in reality, applications are usually made by social workers from the local authority or the NSPCC. Applications on the 'frustrated access' ground can be made only by the local authority or the NSPCC. Applications must be made to the family proceedings court, unless they arise as a result of an investigation ordered by the High Court or county court under section 37, or if other *public* law proceedings concerning the same child are continuing in a higher court, in which case the application should be made to that court (article 3, The Children (Allocation of Proceedings) Order 1991).

Applications can be made to either a full court or a single magistrate. Since they are designed to deal with emergencies, applications will usually be made *ex parte* – this means without giving notice to the child's parents or carers. Prior authorisation to do this must be obtained from the court or the court clerk (rule 4(4), FPC 1991). If the application is made at a time when the courts are sitting, the application should be made to the court (DOH 1991(3), Vol. 1, para. 4.46). At other times, for example at night or on public holidays, applications can be made to single magistrates in their own homes (rule 2(5), FPC 1991).

If the applicant does not wish to seek leave to make an *ex parte* application for an emergency protection order, they must give the child's parents or carers at least one day's notice (rule 4(1)(b) and schedule 2, FPC 1991). This means ensuring that they receive the completed application form and the notice of the hearing. Since emergency protection orders should be applied for only in serious cases of emergency, where there is an immediate threat to the child's safety, it will often be inappropriate to give advance notice to parents or carers. Where consideration is being given to notifying parents or carers in advance, it should be borne in mind that they may well find it difficult to obtain legal representation at such short notice, and that they may be better off waiting until they are able to challenge any order made, after 72 hours (see page 81).

If the application is to be made without notice the applicant does not have to fill in the application form first, providing they undertake to do this immediately afterwards. The application form is detailed, requiring information about the child, where they live, who they live with, who their parents are, the marital status of their parents, and details about any brothers and sisters. Applicants must identify themselves by name and give their address and phone number and details of their solicitor. The specific grounds for the application must be indicated, together with a short statement explaining why the applicant believes that the grounds exist. The applicant must give details of any orders for directions that they are seeking, for example about contact or medical examinations (form 34, schedule 1, FPC 1991). The Government is planning to introduce amended court forms in June 1994.

If the application is to be made on notice the people who should be given notice are the child, the child's parents, anyone with parental responsibility, and anyone caring for the child at the time the application is made. Of this group, the child and anyone with parental responsibility will automatically be parties to the proceedings (rules 4 and 7, and schedule 2, FPC 1991). The other people given notice of the application will be able to apply to the court to become parties (rule 7). Children, their parents and anyone with parental responsibility are entitled to emergency Legal Aid, which will be granted without either a merits or means test (see page 107). At the hearing of the application for the order, whether on notice and whether in a court or in the magistrate's home, the applicant will need to give evidence – on oath or affirmed – in order to satisfy the court or magistrate that the grounds exist. If the application was on notice, the other parties will be able to cross-examine the applicant and call their own evidence. A note should be kept of any evidence given (rule 20, FPC 1991).

If an emergency protection order is made, a copy of the order, stating how long it will last and giving details of any directions that have been given (see pages 84–6), must be served within 48 hours on the parties to the proceedings and on anyone who has the actual care of the child. If the applicant is not the local authority, a copy of the order must also be served on them (rule 21(8), FPC 1991; rule 21(7), FP 1991). Where the application was made without notice the application form should be served with the order on the parties (rule 4(4)(ii)); it may be helpful, too, to serve a copy of the evidence that was given at the hearing. In any event, the form and the order should ensure that the parents or carers are clear about the grounds for the application, the length of the order made, and the details of any directions given. Both the form and the order tell parents or carers about the Law Society's Children Panel, and advise them to find a solicitor immediately. The order also explains the effect of the order, and informs parents or carers of their rights to apply to vary any directions made and for the discharge of the order (see pages 81 and 84). Whoever serves the application and the order should also give parents or carers this information verbally. The courts have made no provision for translating applications and orders into different languages. Where English is the family's second language it would be helpful if translated documents could be provided, or if an interpreter could be present when the documents are served.

There is provision for a guardian *ad litem* to be appointed when an emergency protection order is to be applied for (s.41(4)(g)). Where the application is without notice there will be little for the guardian *ad litem* to do, other than help the court check the evidence of the grounds and consider alternatives. An advantage of appointing a guardian *ad litem* at this stage is that they will be able to make an immediate start on their duties of investigating the case.

The court or magistrate is allowed to take into account hearsay evidence, providing it is relevant to the application. This means that relevant records, reports or opinions can form part of the evidence, even if the person who made them is not present (s.45(7)).

Length of the order

An emergency protection order can be granted initially to last for up to eight days, with special provisions for an extension if the eighth day is a Sunday or public holiday (s.45(1) and (2)). The court can extend an emergency protection order for up to seven days, but only if it has reasonable cause to believe the child is likely to suffer significant harm if the order is not extended. The court will want to be satisfied that there are good reasons for delaying the start of care and supervision proceedings if the local authority think it likely that such proceedings will be started. The applicant for an extension must give at least one day's notice to the parents and the child of their application for an extension, and parents and children are entitled to argue against the extension. They may argue that there is no need for the order to continue because there is insufficient evidence of the likelihood of the child suffering significant harm, or they may propose alternative arrangements for the child which they consider will be adequate to ensure the child's safety. Only one extension can be granted (s.45(4)–(6)).

Applications to discharge

It is not possible for parents or children to appeal against the making of an emergency protection order, nor for an applicant to appeal against the refusal to grant one (s.45(10); *Essex CC* v. *F* [1993] 1 FLR 847). However, children, parents, people with parental responsibility, and anyone with whom the child was living before the order was made are entitled to apply to the court for the emergency protection order to be discharged (s.45(8)). No application can be made until 72 hours after the order has been made. Thereafter, an application can be made at any time until the order comes to an end. Judicial review (see Chapter 8) is a possible means of challenging the order within the 72-hour period.

No application can be made to discharge the order if the person otherwise entitled to make the application was given at least one day's notice of the emergency protection order *and* was present in court when the application was heard and the order made (s.45(11)). This is because it is presumed they would have had the chance then to challenge the application. Even where people are given notice of the application for an emergency protection order it might be more sensible for them not to go to court, but instead to wait 72 hours before applying to discharge the order. Although this is a very stressful time for families, and their feeling of desperation is very great – particularly if they feel the order is unjustified – a delay of three days should ensure that they are clearer about the case against them, and have had more opportunity to produce their own evidence or alternative proposals, and instruct a solicitor properly.

Similarly, no application to discharge an emergency protection order can be made if the court has already extended the original order. Again, this is because those entitled to apply for discharge would have been given notice of the application for an extension, and would have had the opportunity to be present at the hearing and argue against it (s.45(11)).

A person applying to discharge an emergency protection order must give at least one day's notice of this application to everyone involved in the case, including the people currently caring for the child, who may be foster carers or relatives (rule 4 and schedule 2). There is a standard application form for this, as there is for all applications under the Act. Basic details must be given about the applicant, the child, the existing order, and the reasons for the application.

The applicants will be arguing that there was no basis for the order to be made in the first place, that the need for protection no longer exists, or that alternative arrangements can be made which will ensure the child's protection. Particularly relevant to these applications will be issues about the provision of part III services to the family; the power of the local authority to assist an alleged abuser to move out of the home (para. 5, schedule 2); the local authority's duty to try to prevent court proceedings (para. 7, schedule 2), and the provisions about not removing children, or returning them if they would be safe at home (see page 85). Providing there is still clear evidence of the child being likely to suffer significant harm without the protection of the order, the fact that the local authority or NSPCC has been unable to complete its assessment or investigations would not be a reason for discharging the order.

Possible problems in exercising the order

An emergency protection order operates as a direction, to anyone who is able to do so, to produce the child at the applicant's request. Anyone who refuses such a request, without reasonable excuse, is guilty of an offence (s.49(1)). So is anyone who tries to prevent a child from being removed under an emergency protection order (s.44(15)). The fact that someone may be guilty of an offence if they interfere with the order being put into effect is stated clearly on the back of the order.

In some circumstances the person applying for an emergency protection order may not know where the child is, but may know that someone else has that information. In that case the emergency protection order can include a requirement that a named person, if asked to do so, shall reveal any information they have about the child's whereabouts. The person cannot refuse to give this information on the basis that it might incriminate themself or their spouse, but the information they give cannot be used against either themself or their spouse in any criminal proceedings (s.48(1) and (2)). Where an emergency protection order has been granted but the child has been taken away, or is being kept away, from the applicant, the applicant can apply for a recovery order (s.50). The court also has the power under this order to order a named person to give information about the child's whereabouts, and the making of a recovery order operates as a direction to any person who is able to do so to produce the child to any authorised person.

An emergency protection order does not automatically enable the applicant to enter premises in order to search for the child, but a specific direction can be given authorising this. Applicants should always consider whether they might need such a provision; guidance recommends that it should be asked for as a matter of course (DOH 1991(3), Vol. 1, para. 4.52). Where the order does contain such a provision it will be written on the order, and it is an offence for anyone to obstruct the applicant entering and searching for the child in such circumstances (s.48(3) and (7)).

If an applicant has been unable to remove a child under an emergency protection order because they have been denied entry to premises where the child is, or denied access to the child, or they think this is likely to happen, they can apply for a warrant authorising the police to accompany them and help them by using reasonable force, if necessary. A warrant can also direct that a GP, nurse or health visitor accompanies the police officer and applicant when carrying out the order. The likelihood of needing this extra help should always be considered (s.48(9)–(13)). In addition to the above, the police have the power to enter premises without a warrant if there is a threat to life and limb (s.17(1)(e), PACE 1984).

Effect of an emergency protection order

Parental responsibility　If an emergency protection order is made, the applicant acquires parental responsibility for the child. The only exception to this is if the police apply for and obtain an order after taking a child into police protection (see page 87). In such circumstances they are deemed to be applying on behalf of the local authority, and parental responsibility is given to that authority (ss.44(4)(c) and 46(7)). Once an order is made, parental responsibility is shared between anyone who had it before the order was made and the applicant.

If the applicant for the emergency protection order is not the local authority, there is provision for the authority to be treated as if it had been granted the order. The local authority must be of the opinion that it would be in the child's best interests for the order to be transferred to them, and, in forming their opinion, they must take into account:

- the wishes and feelings of the child;

- the child's physical, emotional and educational needs;
- the likely effect on the child of any change in his or her circumstances;
- the child's age, sex and family background;
- the circumstances which gave rise to the application;
- any directions made by the court or other court orders;
- the relationship (if any) between the child and the applicant;
- any plans the applicant has for the child.

If the local authority wishes to take over the order it must give written notice of this to the court, the applicant and anyone who had notice of the original application. It will be assumed that the transfer took place on the date given on the notice. Local authorities will not be able to use this procedure if the child concerned is in a refuge recognised with a certificate under the Act (The Emergency Protection Order (Transfer of Responsibilities) Regulations 1991, see page 89).

Directions for examination or assessment   The parental responsibility gained through an emergency protection order is limited. The applicant can only take such action in meeting their parental responsibility as is 'reasonably required to safeguard and promote the welfare of the child' (s.44(5)). This limitation, coupled with the requirement on applicants to state whether they are seeking any directions in relation to medical or psychiatric examinations or other assessments, and with the power of the court to make such directions (s.44(6) and (8)), indicates that applicants granted an emergency protection order are not entitled to consent to medical or psychiatric examinations or other assessments, although they would be able to authorise urgently needed medical treatment.

When requesting directions, the applicant should be as specific as possible, both at the hearing and on the application form, as to what directions are being sought. They should specify, for example, who is to carry out the examination and assessment, for what purpose, and where and when. The court could direct that no examination or assessment takes place (s.44(8)). If it does decide on an examination or assessment, the order will explain this. Any party to the proceedings, and anyone named in the direction, can apply to vary or discharge the direction (s.44(9)(b); rule 2(4), FPC 1991). One day's notice must be given. Directions for examination or assessment will usually be made when the order is made but, if not, they can be applied for and made at any time while the order is in force (s.44(9)(a)).

Public inquiries into child protection investigations and procedures, particularly the Cleveland Inquiry, identified the distress and trauma caused to children by having to undergo several examinations or assessments (DHSS 1987(2)). The use of directions should help to limit this excess and to ensure, as far as possible, that the examination or assessment is carried out by an agreed person and in an agreed manner. The order advises parents that, if directions were made at a hearing of which they were not given notice, they can ask the court for a doctor of their choice to be present at any examination directed, or they can apply for a variation of the directions – for example, that the examination be carried out by a different person.

Even if directions have been given for an examination or assessment, a child of sufficient understanding is able to refuse to give their consent to such examination or assessment (s.44(7)). If a guardian *ad litem* has been appointed, one of their tasks will be to advise the court on whether or not the child has sufficient understanding, and whether or not the child will give consent. If no guardian *ad litem* has been appointed, another professional who knows the child may be called to give evidence to the court about the child's level of understanding and likely attitude to examination or assessment. It is important for all those working with children to advise them of their rights. If a direction is made, it is ultimately the responsibility of the person carrying out the examination or assessment – doctor, nurse, psychiatrist, or social worker – to decide whether the child has consented. Particular care needs to be taken with children who have English as their second language, or who have a sensory disability that makes communication difficult, or children who have learning difficulties. Interpreters and alternative communication methods may need to be used to help establish the child's views (DOH 1991(3), Vol. 1, paras. 3.50–3.51). A case decided after the implementation of the Children Act has thrown doubt on children's rights to refuse directions for assessment and examination. The judge distinguished between the stage of assessment and examination and that of treatment, saying that the High Court could order a child to undergo treatment if that was in the interests of her welfare, even if that was not what she wanted (*Re W (A Minor)* [1993] 1 FLR 1). Another case indicated that the High Court could invoke its inherent jurisdiction to override a child's wishes and give consent on their behalf to assessment and treatment (*South Glamorgan CC* v. *W and B* [1993] 1 FLR 574). In a case concerning parental refusal to agree to a blood transfusion, the judge commented that proceedings under the Act for a specific issues order, interim care order or emergency protection order were inappropriate, and applications should be made to the High Court to exercise its inherent jurisdiction (*Re O (A Minor)* (1993) *The Times*, 19 March).

Removal and return   An emergency protection order authorises the applicant to remove the child from home or to prevent the child being removed from, for example, hospital or local authority accommodation. However, the Act also states specifically that the power to remove or detain should be exercised only in order to safeguard the welfare of the child (s.44(4)(b) and (5)(a)). Clearly, if an emergency protection order is granted on the basis of the first ground – the urgent need to remove or detain the child because otherwise they would suffer significant harm – the power to remove or detain *would* be necessary to safeguard the child's welfare. If, however, an order is made on the 'frustrated access' ground, it may be that when the child is presented, in compliance with the order, it is apparent there is no immediate danger of the child suffering significant harm. In that case the child should *not* be removed. Social workers exercising an order made on this second ground will need to consider the issue carefully, and may find it helpful to have a GP, nurse or health visitor on hand to advise them.

If the child is removed or detained but subsequently, while the order is still in force, it appears to the applicant that it is safe to return the child, the child must be returned. Children can be returned to their parents, to someone else with parental responsibility, or to anyone else the applicant considers 'appropriate'. For this last category the applicant must first obtain the court's agreement. Such 'appropriate' people could be relatives or friends. The emergency protection order will still be in force, and if circumstances change and the child is once again in danger, the applicant may – and indeed should – remove the child again (s.44(10)–(12)).

It is clearly traumatic for children to be removed suddenly from home and taken to a strange place, even if they have been suffering abuse or neglect. It is therefore crucial that, if there are relatives and friends who can look after and protect the child, or if the abusing parent or carer leaves the home, the duty to return the child should be complied with.

Contact   When an emergency protection order is in force, the applicant must allow the child to have reasonable contact with parents, non-parents with parental responsibilty, any person with whom the child was living before the order was made, any person with an existing contact order, and anyone acting on behalf of any of these people (s.44(13)).

The court is able to give directions about contact. So, if an applicant wishes to prevent someone seeing a child, or wishes the court to specify how and when contact should take place, this request should be set out on the application form and dealt with when the order is made. Details of any such directions will be set out in the order, and the parties to the proceedings, or anyone named in the directions, have a right to apply – on one day's notice – for the directions to be varied or discharged. If directions are not applied for initially, they can be applied for at a later date (s.44(6), (8), and (9); rule 2(4), FPC 1991). (For further details about contact see Chapter 7.)

Police protection

The police no longer have the power, as they did under previous legislation, to bring care and supervision proceedings, but they retain the power to remove or detain children in an emergency. Police officers can exercise this power only if they have reasonable cause to believe that the child would be likely to suffer significant harm if not removed immediately, or if kept where they are. A child removed or detained in these circumstances is a child in police protection (s.46(1) and (2)).

The police do not acquire parental responsibility for a child in police protection, but they are entitled to do whatever is necessary to safeguard the welfare of the child (s.46(9)). They could not, therefore, arrange and give consent for a medical or other examination or assessment, but they could arrange for a child to receive urgently needed medical attention.

The police cannot keep a child in police protection for longer than 72 hours (s.46(6)). They can apply for an emergency protection order during that time. If an order is made in these circumstances the maximum period of eight days will run from the first day on which the child went into police protection (s.45(3)). Any such application is made on behalf of the local authority in whose area the child is ordinarily resident and, if the emergency protection order is granted, parental responsibility is acquired by that particular authority. The police *do* have the power to make such an application without the knowledge of the local authority (s.46(8)), but this should never occur, because the police are duty-bound to inform the local authority where the child was found of what has happened and why, and what steps the police are proposing to take next. If the child normally lives in another local authority area, that local authority must also be notified and told where the child is (s.46(3)(a) and (b)). It is, of course, important for the local police and social services department to set up a clear system of communication for dealing with such emergencies. It would not make sense for the police to apply for an emergency protection order if this was opposed by the local authority, as the police cannot apply for an extension of the order, nor can they start care proceedings.

A child who is taken into police protection should be placed in local authority accommodation or a refuge (see page 88) immediately, or taken there as soon as possible after being removed (s.46(3)(f)). It can be traumatic and distressing for children to be kept for any period of time in a police station; local inter-agency arrangements should ensure that speedy transfers are possible and that disputes about placement are avoided. For example, the police might not be happy with the local authority's proposal to place a child in police protection with a relative or friend, and they could hold on to the child until the local authority made another proposal. Once the local authority takes over responsibility, if an order is made, the issue of where the child is to be placed rests solely with that agency.

Each police area must have an officer designated by the Chief Police Officer to deal with child protection cases. This officer has to start making investigations as soon as a child is removed into police protection (s.46(3)(e)). If, after completing the investigation, the designated officer finds that the child is not likely to suffer significant harm if released, the child must be released even if 72 hours have not elapsed. Otherwise the child will be kept for the full 72 hours, and beyond that only if an emergency protection order is made (s.46(5)). The local authority which has been notified of what is happening is also under a duty to begin an investigation into the case (s.47).

Besides notifying the relevant local authority, the officer who removed the child into police protection should also tell the child what is happening, and should try to find out the child's wishes and feelings. In addition, the officer should contact the child's parents, anyone else with parental responsibility, and anyone caring for the child at the time of removal, to let them know what has happened and why, and what is likely to happen next (s.46(3)(c) and (d) and (4)). A child in police protection must be allowed contact with their parents, with people with parental responsibility, with people caring for them when removed, and with anyone with a contact order. The police can decide what level of contact, if any, would be reasonable and in the child's best interests (s.46(10)).

These requirements to contact the relevant local authorities and the child's family should ensure that the police can establish quickly whether anyone close to the child might be able to care for them in the short term.

Refuges for runaway children

For some years before the Act, voluntary organisations, primarily The Children's Society, had been addressing the problems of children who ran away either from home or care, and had set up refuges for them. However, by providing this sort of safe haven organisations laid themselves open to prosecution: for child abduction (s.2, Child Abduction Act 1984) and for assisting a person in being absent from detention (s.32(3), CYPA 1969). They were also at risk of falling foul of the new legislation, for abducting a child in care (s.49).

Now children's homes or foster carers can apply to the Secretary of State for a certificate authorising them to provide a refuge for runaway children, and this certificate exempts those running the home, or the foster carers, from prosecution. Any foster carers who apply must already be approved in accordance with the Children (Foster Placement) Regulations 1991, and the relevant home must comply with the Children's Home Regulations 1991. The local police and social services department have a chance to comment before the certificate is issued, and the Social Services Inspectorate has to prepare a report on the proposed refuge and then carry out regular inspections (s.51).

Children can be taken into, and remain in, a refuge if it appears that they are at risk of harm (reg. 3(2), The Refuges (Children's Homes and Foster Placements) Regulations 1991). Within 24 hours of the child first coming into the refuge the person running it must contact the police officer designated by the area Chief of Police to deal with refuges. The officer must be told that the child has been taken into the refuge, and must be given a contact telephone number. If possible, the officer should also be given the child's name and last known address. If this isn't found out until later, it should at that stage be passed on to the police. As soon as possible, attempts must be made by those in the refuge to find out the identity of the person 'responsible' for the child. This will usually be the child's parent or carer, or a person with parental responsibility, but it could, in addition, be a local authority if the child is under a care order or an emergency protection order (reg. 3(3)–(5)). This information must be passed on to the police within 24 hours of being discovered.

As soon as the police have details of the parents, carers, and any relevant local authority, they must contact them and tell them that the child is in the refuge, and who provides the refuge. The police must pass on the contact telephone number but *must not* give the address of the refuge (reg. 3(6) and (7)).

The prime purpose of the refuge is to enable children to return home, or to set in motion other arrangements that will enable them to leave the refuge safely. They should not remain there for longer than either 14 consecutive days or 21 days in a three-month period (reg. 3(9)). If children do stay longer, those providing the refuge will still be exempt from prosecution but may end up having their certificate withdrawn.

If the people running the refuge consider that a child would suffer significant harm by leaving, they could ask the local police to take the child into police protection (s.46), or they could apply for an emergency protection order themselves (s.44(1)). This is the case even if the child is in care, because police protection or an emergency protection order overrides the existence of a care order. The police can put a child in police protection into a refuge (s.46(3) (f) (ii)). If the refuge obtains an emergency protection order, the local authority cannot use the Emergency Protection Order (Transfer of Responsibilities) Regulations (see page 84) to remove the child from the refuge while the order is in force.

Child assessment orders

The child assessment order in the Act is rather different from the original proposal for such a provision made in the inquiry report into the death of Kimberley Carlile (Greenwich 1987). The original proposal was for an order requiring a parent or carer to take a child for a medical or developmental examination or assessment. Initially, the Children Bill did not contain any such provision. There was sustained lobbying for it, but disagreement among the lobbyists – particularly between the NSPCC and the Association of Directors of Social Services – about what exactly was required. Finally, the provisions relating to an emergency protection order were amended to include the 'frustrated access' ground, and a new provision for a child assessment order was included.

There are important distinctions between these two orders:

- An emergency protection order is for emergency situations. A child assessment order is not.
- An emergency protection order is based on evidence of significant harm or, if the 'frustrated access' ground is used, there must be suspicion of significant harm coupled with unreasonable denial of access to the child, and some evidence indicating that access is required as a matter of urgency. A child assessment order, like the 'frustrated access' ground, is based on suspicion of harm, but the issue here is not access to the child, but obtaining a satisfactory assessment of the child to find out whether he or she is suffering, or is likely to suffer, significant harm.
- Anyone can apply for an emergency protection order on the first ground, but only the local authority or the NSPCC can apply for an emergency protection order on the 'frustrated access' ground, or for a child assessment order (ss.44(1) and 43(1)).

The grounds for a child assessment order are these:

'(a) the applicant has reasonable cause to suspect that the child is suffering, or is likely to suffer, significant harm;
(b) an assessment of the state of the child's health or development, or of the way in which he has been treated, is required to enable the applicant to determine whether or not the child is suffering, or is likely to suffer, significant harm; and
(c) it is unlikely that such an assessment will be made, or be satisfactory, in the absence of an order under this section.' (s.43(1))

In addition to being satisfied that these grounds exist, the court must also take into account the welfare principle and the principle that making the order would be better for the child than no order (s.1(1) and (5)).

Suspicion of significant harm

The applicant will need to bring evidence supporting their reasonable suspicion of existing or likely harm. Guidance suggests this might be evidence of failure to thrive, or of possible neglect, or of possible sexual abuse – cases where 'the harm to the child is long term and cumulative rather than sudden and severe' (DOH 1991(3), Vol. 1, para. 4.9). Given that the application is based on the suspicion of existing or likely significant harm, it will have been preceded, where the local authority is the applicant, with an investigation under section 47, and the court will want to hear details of that investigation.

No satisfactory assessment without an order

There must be evidence that the necessary assessment cannot be carried out in co-operation with the child's family: 'There should have been a substantial effort to persuade those caring for the child of the need for an assessment and to persuade them to agree to suitable arrangements voluntarily' (DOH 1991(3), Vol. 1, para. 4.23).

Parents or carers may have simply refused to co-operate, or may have refused to accept that there is a problem or, having agreed initially to co-operate, may have failed later to keep appointments made for them or take the child to the doctor or clinic as promised. In this last case it will be important to find out from the family why this has happened, as there may be good reasons for it. It should not be assumed that the examination or assessment suggested by professionals is the only acceptable one. People may be reluctant to use the normal child health services, or they may wish their own alternative health practitioner or therapist to be involved in an assessment. Practitioners should be particularly sensitive to issues of gender, race and culture when proposing an assessment, as the family may well prefer the child to be seen by someone of the same gender or ethnic background as the child. The family may want their GP or an independent professional to either carry out the assessment or be involved.

Where parents are reluctant to co-operate they should be told of the possibility of a child assessment order being applied for. It will be hard to do this without it immediately being seen as a threat, but, nevertheless, attempts to negotiate should continue, and families should be referred to independent sources of advice. Guidance suggests that parents or carers should be given written information explaining the order, its effects, the powers and duties gained by local authorities, and its impact on the rights and responsibilities of parents (DOH 1991(3), Vol. 1, para. 4.27).

Assessment necessary to establish existence or possibility of significant harm

Guidance recommends that assessments 'should always have a multi-disciplinary dimension', involving all the professionals working with the family (DOH 1991(3), Vol. 1, para. 4.25). Applicants for child assessment orders must be able to explain in detail to the court what the assessment will involve, where it will take place, and who will do it. This information must be on the application form and, if an order is made, it will appear on the order itself.

The application

Guidance recommends that, before an application is agreed on, a child protection conference should be called to consider the matter (DOH 1991(3), Vol. 1, para. 4.23). The need for a section 47 investigation, this requirement to call a child protection conference, and the fact that an application for an order can be made only after giving notice to the relevant people, all emphasise that child assessment orders are *not* emergency applications.

Applications for child assessment orders must be made to magistrates in the family proceedings court. The only exceptions are where the application arises out of an investigation ordered by the High Court or county court under section 37, or where public law proceedings concerning the same child are continuing in a higher court, in which case the application is made to that court (article 3, Allocation of Proceedings Order 1991). Arrangements for the allocation and transfer of proceedings (see page 19) apply to these proceedings. The applicant must give at least seven days' notice of the application (rule 4 and schedule 2, FPC 1991), and must complete a standard form, setting out the details of the applicant, the child, the child's family, the grounds for the order, and the details of the assessment sought. Notice of the application must be given to the child, the child's parents (including a non-married father without parental responsibility), anyone else with parental responsibility, anyone who is caring for the child, and anyone in contact with the child as a result of a contact order either under section 8 or section 34 (s.43(11)).

Automatic parties to the proceedings are the applicant, the child, and anyone else with parental responsibility. The other people given notice of the proceedings can apply to be parties. Children, their parents, and anyone with parental responsibility will be automatically entitled to Legal Aid without a means or merit test. Other people will be able to apply for Legal Aid. A guardian *ad litem* will normally be appointed for the child (s.41 and rule 7, FPC 1991).

It is likely that, before the final hearing, there will be a hearing for directions to establish who might be joined as parties and to set a timetable for the filing of evidence and reports. As with all other proceedings under the Act, witness statements and reports and documents will be disclosed and circulated in advance of the hearing, in accordance with directions given, and the guardian *ad litem*'s report must be available seven days before the hearing unless the court specifies otherwise (rules 11(7), 14 and 17, FPC 1991).

Effect of the order

If the court is satisfied that the grounds exist, it may make the order, but only if that is in accordance with the welfare of the child and would be better than making no order. Since these are not family proceedings (s.8(3) and (4)) it is not open to the court to make any other order available under the Act (s.10(1)). There is one exception: if, after hearing the evidence, the court is satisfied that there are grounds for making an emergency protection order rather than a child assessment order, it should make an emergency protection order instead (s.43(3) and (4)). This possibility is something that should be included in the written information given to parents or carers (see page 91).

The court can order an assessment lasting for up to seven days. The order will specify when the assessment is to start, which may not necessarily be as soon as the order is granted (s.43(5)). The timing of the assessment should have been sorted out by the applicants before the hearing. One reason for the assessment being limited to seven days is that it is a lesser order than an emergency protection order, based only on *suspicion* of harm, and so it would be illogical for it to last longer than an emergency protection order. The other reason is to cause the least possible disruption to the child. It is probable that in many cases only an initial assessment will be achieved in that time, but that should be sufficient to produce some evidence of whether or not the child is suffering, or is likely to suffer, significant harm. To some extent this order can be seen as an order to 'fish for evidence'.

Once the process has started it will be important to sustain efforts to work in partnership with the child and family, and to obtain their co-operation in the assessment. They should already be fully informed about the concerns of professionals, and the assessment process that has been planned. Once the order has been obtained and the process of assessment started, it could be that the parents will then agree to co-operate with a continuing assessment beyond the seven days, or to receive services offered, or to agree to the child going into section 20 accommodation for a period of time.

If the parents remain unwilling to co-operate or to acknowledge a problem, and if there is evidence of existing or likely significant harm to the child, the local authority or NSPCC could start care or supervision proceedings and apply for an interim care order or interim supervision order, with directions as to examination or assessment (s.38(6)). Note that a supervision order can impose conditions on the parent or carer, if they consent, as well as the child (para. 3, schedule 3; see also Chapter 6).

Where two parents with parental responsibility are involved, but disagree as to whether or not to co-operate, court proceedings may be necessary to help resolve the dispute. Under a child assessment order the applicant does not acquire parental responsibility and is, therefore, authorised simply to carry out the assessment ordered by the court. Children of sufficient understanding can refuse to submit to the assessment, even if the court has made an order (s.43(8), but note the case of *South Glamorgan CC* v. *W and B*, see page 85). The court will seek guidance from the guardian *ad litem* about the child's level of understanding and attitude to the application. If a child is clearly refusing consent it is very unlikely that the court would make an order. If the order is made, it is still important that whoever is carrying out the assessment should establish for themselves whether or not the child consents. A child assessment order authorises an assessment of the child, not the whole family. The adults in the family would need to give their consent to be involved in any assessment.

Unlike an emergency protection order, a child assessment order does not give a blanket power to remove a child, but the applicant can ask for directions to be made that the child should be removed from home. The court must be satisfied that the removal is necessary for the purposes of the assessment, and the child can be removed only for the period or periods of time specified in the order (s.43(9)). Guidance stresses that:

> 'This is intended to be a reserve provision, and if used the number of overnight stays should be kept as low as possible . . . It is important that the child assessment order is not regarded as a variant of the emergency protection order with its removal power. The purposes of the two orders are quite different.' (DOH 1991(3), Vol. 1, para. 4.15)

Removal from home should be ordered only in exceptional circumstances, not just for the convenience of those carrying out the assessment. There must be a clear link with the assessment, such as where the child has eating or sleeping problems which need a period of continuous observation.

If the court does give directions authorising removal, it must also make directions about contact between the child and their family (s.43(10)). The court should bear in mind the presumption in favour of reasonable contact in relation to emergency protection orders and care orders under the Act.

Particular consideration should be given to arranging for the parents or carers to stay with the child. The court must, of course, have regard to the welfare of the child and to the child's wishes, expressed through the child's solicitor and the guardian *ad litem*, when making these directions (DOH 1991(3), Vol. 1, para. 4.16).

Any party to child assessment order proceedings can apply to have the order varied or discharged (s.43(12)). Two days' notice of such an application must be given to all the parties and all those who received notice of the original application (rule 4(1)(b)). Any of the parties can also appeal against the making of the order or the refusal to make the order (s.94). The Notice of Appeal must be filed within 14 days, and appeals from the family proceedings court go to the High Court, while appeals from care centres or the High Court go to the Court of Appeal (rule 4.22, FP 1991).

Although this order is a lesser order than an emergency protection order, an interim care order or interim supervision order, it is still a substantial intervention in the life of the child and could lead to even further intervention. It should never be applied for or made lightly, or used as a matter of routine, but only where there is serious concern.

6 Proceedings for care and supervision orders

Introduction

This chapter gives details of the court procedures involved in applying for a care or supervision order, and considers practice issues that arise during the course of proceedings. Although the chapter is concerned specifically with care and supervision orders, the procedures described apply to all proceedings under the Children Act, both private and public.

The changes to care and supervision proceedings introduced by the Act are a response to sustained criticism over a long period about the complexities, anomalies and injustices of previous legislation. Children could come into care by many different routes, with varying criteria for entry; the legal position of children differed depending on which route had brought them into care; local authorities could assume parental rights by an administrative procedure; parents were not automatically parties to care proceedings; children, parents and other relatives were unable to challenge local authority decisions about contact with children in care, except in very limited circumstances; there was unequal access to the wardship jurisdiction of the High Court. Most of these anomalies and injustices have been tackled effectively by the new legislation.

Applications

Only the local authority or the NSPCC can make an application for a care or supervision order (s.31(11)), and this is now the only way in which a local authority can take control over a child. The local authority can no longer use the inherent jurisdiction of the High Court for such a purpose, nor can it apply for a residence or contact order under section 8 of the Children Act (ss.9(2) and 100). It has only limited powers to apply for a specific issue or prohibited steps order (see page 16).

It is not possible for a court dealing with private law family proceedings to make a care or supervision order simply because it thinks the conditions are met. However, in the course of hearing any family proceedings, and if it thinks that it might be necessary to make a care or supervision order in relation to the children involved, a court can adjourn the proceedings and direct the local authority to carry out an investigation of the child's circumstances (s.37(1)), which can include seeking psychiatric evidence relating to the child's carers (*Re H (A Minor)* (1993) Fam. Law 205, April).

On receiving such a direction the local authority must carry out its investigation within eight weeks, or the time directed by the court. The local authority has to consider whether to apply for a care or supervision order, or provide services to the child or the family, or take some other action. If the local authority decides not to start proceedings they must let the court know, in writing, why they have reached that decision, what services or assistance they are providing to the child or the family, and what other action, if any, they are taking or propose to take (s.37(2) and (3)). If a local authority refuses to take any action under part IV of the Children Act, the court has no power to force it to take action (*Nottingham CC v. P* [1993] 1 FLR 514 and [1993] 2 FLR 134; see also page 102).

The threshold conditions

There is now one single set of conditions that must be established before the court can consider making a care or supervision order. Besides considering whether these conditions are satisfied, the court must also consider whether making the order would be better for the child than making any other order or no order at all (s.1(5)). Additionally, it must have regard to the principle that the welfare of the child is the paramount consideration and, in doing so, it must consider the factors set out in the prescribed checklist (s.1(1) and (3)).

The threshold conditions are these:

'(a)   That the child concerned is suffering, or is likely to suffer, significant harm; and
(b)   That the harm or likelihood of harm, is attributable to –
   (i)   The care given to the child, or likely to be given to him were the order not made, not being what it would be reasonable to expect a parent to give to him; or
   (ii)   The child's being beyond parental control.' (s.31(2))

The definitions of 'harm' in the Act make it clear that the term is intended to cover physical and sexual abuse; the impairment of physical, intellectual, emotional, social or behavioural development, and the impairment of physical or mental health (s.31(9)). The Act states that, where the issue is harm to the child's health or development, then, in deciding whether that harm is significant, the health or development of the child concerned should be compared with that of a similar child (s.31(10)). This raises rather more questions than answers, as it is not clear how a similar child will be identified – will it be simply by age, or will issues such as poverty, class and ethnicity come into it? One case which decided that persistent truanting could bring a child within the threshold conditions also decided that, in this context, 'similar child' means a child of equivalent intellectual and social development who is going to school (*O* v. *Berkshire CC* [1992] 1 FLR 498).

Beyond this there is no definition of 'significant'. In the debate on the Children Bill the Lord Chancellor said: 'It speaks of significant harm – namely that which, being more than minimal, indicates that compulsory care or supervision may be justified' (*Hansard*, House of Lords, 19 January 1989, col. 343). It is important to note that the conditions to be established relate to present or future harm. This means that action can be taken where there is clear evidence to show that the child is likely to suffer significant harm but where no harm has yet occurred. Thus, it is possible to bring proceedings in relation to children who are in accommodation or are newly born.

One case has decided that 'likely to suffer significant harm' should not be equated with 'on the balance of probabilities': in looking to the future all the court can do is to assess the risk of harm occurring (*Newham LBC* v. *AG* [1993] 1 FLR 281). Another case made it clear that, in relation to the words 'is suffering' significant harm, the court is not confined to looking at the conditions obtaining at the date of the hearing. The fact that at that date the child had been removed from any possible harm was not decisive of the matter (*Re B* [1993] 1 FLR 815; *Northampton CC* v. *S and Others* [1993] 1 FLR 554).

In the case of *Re B* it was stated that care goes beyond physical care, and includes emotional care which a reasonable parent would give a child. In the case of a child who has been sexually abused, that includes listening to the child and monitoring its words and actions so that a professional assessment can be carried out. This reasoning, it should be noted, was being used in order to justify the making of an interim care order so that an assessment could be carried out.

The threshold conditions require evidence on two issues before they can be established. The first is establishing the existence – or likely occurrence – of significant harm, and the second is establishing that the harm derives from lack of reasonable parental care. Lack of care could mean either that the parent or parents caused the harm themselves or that they allowed it to happen. The parents' care is tested objectively, while the child concerned is considered subjectively. So the court has to consider what would be a reasonable standard of parental care for this particular child; it will not be asking itself what sort of care this *particular* parent could reasonably be expected to give to this particular child. The conditions could, therefore, be satisfied when parents are limited by disability or their inability to provide proper care, but remember that these are only the threshold conditions. The court must then go on to consider the welfare principle, and to determine whether or not the order would be better for the child (*Humberside CC v. B* [1993] 1 FLR 257).

Considerations before proceedings are taken

Whenever a local authority is considering making an application for a care or supervision order, whether as part of an investigation directed by a court dealing with family proceedings or as part of a child protection investigation or otherwise, they must consider what other options might be available. Local authorities have a duty to take steps to reduce the need to bring care and supervision proceedings (para. 7, schedule 2), and a general duty to promote the welfare of children in need by, where appropriate, promoting their upbringing by their family (s.17(1)). The local authority should consider whether the provision of services or assistance to the family might avoid the need to bring proceedings and, in particular, whether it would be appropriate to provide accommodation for the child:

> '. . . a care or supervision order will be sought only when there appears to be no better way of safeguarding and promoting the welfare of the child suffering, or likely to suffer, significant harm . . . This means that voluntary arrangements through the provision of services to the child and his family should always be fully explored.' (DOH 1991(3), Vol. 1, para. 3.2)

Local authorities will need to consider carefully what would be achieved by acquiring compulsory powers over the child. Research studies have shown that there is a widely-held belief that having compulsory powers leads to better planning for children, but there is no research evidence to support this belief. There is, however, considerable evidence of the damage caused to children and families by compulsory intervention (DHSS 1985(2), and see Chapter 3).

The local authority should discuss the options with the children concerned, their parents (including non-married fathers), anyone else with parental responsibility for the children, and any other relevant person.

Other relevant people may be other professionals who have been involved with the family, or relatives and friends of the family who might be able to offer support or help, including looking after the child or children in the short or long term.

Guidance recommends that local authorities hold a child protection conference before taking any action. This will enable the local authority to discuss the case thoroughly with other professionals before reaching a decision on what action to take, and this may be particularly helpful where others have had more contact with the family than the local authority. It is recommended that parents, children where old enough, and other family members should be fully involved in the decision-making process, and should be invited to attend any child protection conference so that they have the opportunity of discussing the options in detail and making their own suggestions as to how problems might be resolved and the children protected adequately (see Chapter 4). Guidance points out that:

> 'Involvement will mean more than just attendance; families should be able to participate in the decision-making process and they will need to be kept informed of decisions as they are made, the reasoning behind those decisions and their likely consequences.' (DOH 1991(3), Vol. 1, para. 3.10)

Guidance goes on to state:

> 'No decision to initiate proceedings should be taken without clear evidence that provision of services for the child and his family (which may include an accommodation placement voluntarily arranged under section 20) has failed or would be likely to fail to meet the child's needs adequately and that there is no suitable person prepared to apply to take over care of the child under a residence order.' (DOH 1991(3), Vol. 1, para. 3.10)

Applications by the NSPCC

The NSPCC have a duty to consult the local authority, providing it is reasonably practicable to do so, before they make an application for a care or supervision order (s.31(6)). If a care or supervision order is subsequently made, the local authority will be the ones who gain parental responsibility for the child and who will have the specific powers and duties in relation to the child, as set out in part III and schedule 2 of the Act. For this reason, guidance stresses that it is good practice for the NSPCC to keep the local authority informed of their concerns about any children, including those who are accommodated by the local authority. Where possible, the NSPCC and the local authority should agree a course of action (DOH 1991(3), Vol. 1, paras. 3.13–3.14).

Legal issues

Before applying for an order the applicant, whether it be the local authority or the NSPCC, will need to consider some specific legal issues. The guidance to local authorities makes it clear that they should seek legal advice on the following matters:

- Will there be sufficient evidence to satisfy the threshold conditions, and will all the circumstances of the case be such as to justify the making of an order, bearing in mind the welfare checklist and the principle of not making an order unless it can be shown to be better for the child?
- Will the applicant be seeking an interim care or supervision order, and if so, for how long? Applicants should also consider possible alternatives to this, such as a residence order made in favour of a relative, or a specific issue order requiring the parent or parents to take the child regularly to a clinic or a day nursery. Criticism by the High Court and Court of Appeal of one local authority which was seeking section 8 orders as an alternative to taking care proceedings should not be interpreted as detracting from this guidance. In that case the local authority were trying to use a prohibited steps order to exclude a father from the home. The court was right to query the *local authority's* use of a section 8 order for this purpose, as opposed to the mother making the application, and on the specific facts of this case, probably right to query why the local authority were not instituting care proceedings. The judge had found that the children were at serious risk of being sexually abused by their father and that their mother was unlikely to protect them adequately. He had ordered the local authority to carry out a section 37 investigation. He refused the local authority's application for a prohibited steps order because section 9(5) prevented the local authority from obtaining a contact order through the means of a prohibited steps order. This decision was upheld on appeal. The comments by the Court of Appeal that the local authority should always use part IV court proceedings to protect children have unfortunately led local authorities to take the view that section 8 orders should be avoided. There remain many cases where they will still be appropriate (*Nottinghamshire CC* v. *P* [1993] 1 FLR 514, and [1993] 2 FLR 134).
- Who are likely to be parties to the proceedings, and what applications are they likely to make?
- What procedural matters arise? These might include whether the case should be transferred to the county court or High Court, who will need to prepare witness statements, what sort of timetable there

should be, and whether or not a guardian should be appointed (DOH 1991(3), Vol. 1, para. 3.12).

In emergency cases, whether or not an emergency protection order has been made, time for such consultation and consideration will be limited. Nevertheless, it is extremely important that these issues are considered to some degree. Proceedings should never be commenced lightly, as they will always have a traumatic effect on children and their families.

Starting proceedings

The proceedings must be started in the magistrates' family proceedings court, unless they have been started as a result of a section 37 direction by a county court or High Court or there are continuing public law proceedings concerning the same child going on in another court, in which case they should start in that court (article 3, The Children (Allocation of Proceedings) Order 1991). It is possible for proceedings to be transferred then to another family proceedings court, or to a county court care centre or the High Court. (For details on transfer see Chapter 2.)

Applications

All proceedings must be started by filing an application on the standard form (rule 4(1) and form 19, schedule 1, FPC 1991). As with all application forms under the Act, the form is detailed. It requires information about the child's family, and background about the applicants, too. The applicants must also set out their reasons for believing that the threshold conditions exist; whether any interim order is being sought and, if so, the grounds for this; details of any directions being requested under the interim order; details of any direction being requested under a final supervision order, and details of the plan for the child, which must include the arrangements for contact and should also make reference to why the order would be better for the child. At the end of 1993 the forms were being reviewed and new forms are to be introduced in 1994.

Parties

Certain people will be parties automatically to care and supervision proceedings. These are the applicant, the child or children concerned, and the people with parental responsibility for them. Any other person can apply to be joined as a party to the proceedings (rule 7). So grandparents, non-married fathers who do not have parental responsibility, and other relatives or friends or foster carers who wish to make applications in relation to the child can apply to be parties. Non-married fathers without parental responsibility must be given notice that proceedings have been started (rule 4(3) and schedule 2, FPC 1991). Where a guardian *ad litem* is appointed for the child, the guardian has a specific duty to notify those people whose involvement in the proceedings would be likely to 'safeguard the interests of the child' of their right to apply to be parties, and the guardian should give the court details of these people (rule 11(6)). The court rules provide that, when a court receives an application for someone to be joined as a party to the proceedings, it has three options: it can deal with the application itself, invite representations from the other parties, or arrange a hearing to decide the matter (rules 7(2)–(4)). A case looking at how these applications should be dealt with decided that the test to apply was the same as that set out in section 10(9), which applies when anyone seeks leave to make a section 8 application (see pages 15–16). As well as considering these criteria, the court should also assess whether a substantive application would have a reasonable prospect of success (*G v. Kirklees MBC* [1993] 1 FLR 805).

Appointing a guardian *ad litem*

The court must, in all specified proceedings, appoint a guardian *ad litem* for the child, 'unless satisfied that it is not necessary to do so in order to safeguard his interests' (s.41(1)). Specified proceedings are all public law applications, including applications to place children in secure accommodation and applications for emergency protection orders (s.41(6) and rule 2(2)). A guardian can and should be appointed as soon as possible after the application is made. Guardians are appointed from a panel of guardians *ad litem* and reporting officers. They must not:

- be a member or officer of the NSPCC or the local authority bringing the application, unless they are employed solely as a member of the panel of guardians *ad litem*;
- have been directly involved in the care, accommodation or welfare of the child during the five years prior to the commencement of proceedings;
- be a probation officer, unless they work part-time and are acting as a guardian in their spare time (rule 10(7)).

The appointment of a guardian *ad litem* will continue for the period specified by the court, unless the court otherwise terminates the appointment. If the guardian's appointment is terminated, the court must give written reasons for this (rule 10(9) and (10)).

Guardians are under a duty to safeguard the interests of the child. They have to act in accordance with the principle that delay is prejudicial to children, and they have to consider all the factors on the welfare checklist when carrying out their duties. Court rules make it clearer than it was under previous legislation that guardians are officers of the court. They have to advise the court on matters such as timetabling, the appropriate court for hearing the proceedings, the child's wishes, the level of the child's understanding in relation to such matters as consent to medical treatment or attendance at court, the options available to the court and the suitability of each option, and who should be parties to the proceedings (rule 11(1) and (4)).

In addition, guardians are under a duty to appoint a solicitor for the child unless one has been appointed already. They will instruct that solicitor, unless the child wishes to instruct a solicitor themself and has sufficient understanding to do so. In such circumstances the guardian must continue to carry out all their other duties and, if the court agrees, can have legal representation in the conduct of those duties (rule 11(3)). In such circumstances, however, guardians *ad litem* are not entitled to Legal Aid (reg. 3, The Civil Legal Aid (General) (Amendment) (no. 2) Regulations 1991), so panels will need to be clear about the arrangements for paying for legal representation in such circumstances.

Guardians have to investigate the background to the case thoroughly. If, in the course of their investigations, they come across people who they think should be a party, they have a specific duty to inform them of their right to apply to become a party, and they must tell the court about them (rule 11(6)). The Act gives guardians a specific right of access to local authority and NSPCC records, and the right to copy relevant documents and produce them as evidence to the court (s.42). Guardians must attend all directions appointments and hearings unless excused by the court (rule 11(4)).

Guardians can be asked by the court to produce interim reports. Their final report must be filed with the court at least seven days before the hearing, and the justices' clerk must then serve the report on each party (rule 11(7)). So, guardians are there both to instruct the child's solicitor and also to be independent advisers to the court about a number of matters. Their most important role, however, is to make recommendations about what the court should decide. A case decided after the implementation of the Act made it clear that, while the guardian's evidence and recommendations were not binding on the court, it should give careful consideration to them, and should be very clear about its reasons for departing from them if it decided to do so (*S* v. *Oxfordshire CC* [1993] 1 FLR 452).

It has always been important for guardians *ad litem* to remain independent of the local authority or NSPCC so that they can take a critical look at past actions or future plans, and so that they are seen to be independent by children and families. This is why many people have called for an independent service to be set up to administer the panels and to recruit members. In a case brought by guardians *ad litem* against Cornwall County Council, the President of the Family Division, whilst not arguing for an independent service, did say:

> 'It is vital that the independence of the guardian *ad litem* in carrying out his or her duties on behalf of the child in any proceedings should be clearly recognised and understood . . . It is important that the court and the public should have confidence in the independence of the guardians. It is also important the guardians *ad litem* themselves should feel confident of their independent status.' (*R v. Cornwall CC, ex p. Cornwall and Isles of Scilly Guardians ad litem and Reporting Officers Panel* [1992] 1 WLR 427)

It is, therefore, regrettable that the court rules allow local authorities and the NSPCC to employ their own guardians, if they so wish (see rule 11(7)). It is difficult to see how someone employed by an authority – and perhaps employed by them previously in a different capacity in their social services department – will be able to keep sufficient detachment and be able, where necessary, to criticise actions taken or plans made by people who are, or have been, colleagues. It will be even harder for other parties in the proceedings to accept such guardians as independent.

All panels administering guardians *ad litem* must have a complaints procedure with an independent element (reg. 3, Guardians *ad Litem* and Reporting Officers (Panels) Regulations 1991). Children, family members and their lawyers should make use of this procedure if dissatisfied with the way a guardian *ad litem* has handled a case.

Solicitors for children

Solicitors for children in these proceedings should be appointed from the Law Society's Children Panel, as this will ensure that they have had some specialist training and are experienced in this area of work. Solicitors will be appointed by either the guardian *ad litem* or the court (s.41(3) and rule 11(2)). The court has a duty to appoint a solicitor if the child does not have one and:

- no guardian *ad litem* has been appointed, or
- the child has sufficient understanding and wishes to instruct a solicitor, or
- it would be in the child's best interests to be represented by a solicitor (s.41(4)).

When a solicitor has been appointed by the court and there is no guardian *ad litem*, the solicitor must follow the child's instructions. If there *is* a guardian, then the solicitor must follow the guardian's instructions, unless the child wishes to give instructions which conflict with those of the guardian. In that case the solicitor must take into account the views of the guardian and, if the solicitor considers that the child is able to give instructions, having regard to the child's understanding, the solicitor must conduct the case in accordance with the instructions given by the child. A case looking at whether a child had sufficient understanding to instruct a solicitor decided that a high level of emotional disturbance could remove the level of understanding necessary. If there was a dispute about this, the court should hear specific expert opinion on this issue (*Re H (A Minor)* [1993] 1 FLR 440). If there is no guardian, and the child is not able to give instructions, the solicitor must represent the child in furtherance of the child's best interests. It is to be hoped that this latter situation will rarely, if ever, arise.

The Law Society produces a list of all solicitors on their Children Panel, which is regularly updated, and available free. Parents, relatives and friends of children involved in care proceedings may find it helpful to choose a solicitor from this list, which should ensure that they are represented by someone with experience and knowledge of this specialist area of law.

Legal Aid

Certain people are automatically entitled to Legal Aid in care and supervision proceedings, which means they do not have to pass either a means or a merits test. They are: children, their parents (including non-married fathers without parental responsibility) and anyone else with parental responsibility (s.15, Legal Aid Act 1988, amended by article 2, Legal Aid Act 1988 (Children Act 1989) Order 1991). Anyone else who wishes to apply to be a party may apply for Legal Aid and will be means-tested only, not merits-tested. Grandparents who are seeking an interim residence order in their favour, and who are successful in obtaining it, will then become people with parental responsibility entitled to automatic, non-means-tested, Legal Aid.

Where a person is automatically entitled to Legal Aid, the solicitor can start work on the case immediately without waiting for approval from the Legal Aid Board. Providing the application for Legal Aid is received by the board within three working days, Legal Aid will be backdated to when the solicitor started doing the work (reg. 8, The Civil Legal Aid (General) (Amendment) (no. 2) Regulations 1991).

Directions appointments

On receiving an application for a care or supervision order, the court will set a date for a hearing. The applicant is responsible for serving the other parties to the proceedings with a copy of the application form, which will now have the date, time and place of this first hearing. The form is served by either giving it to the other parties personally or by posting it to them. People who are not parties but are entitled to notice, such as non-married fathers without parental responsibility, must be given a written notice that sets out the date, time and place of the first hearing and gives details of the application. The applicant must ensure that the parties are given three days' notice of the hearing (rule 4 and schedule 2, FPC 1991). Since it is extremely unlikely that anyone will be ready to go ahead with the full hearing within that time-limit, it is likely that the first hearing will become a directions appointment. At a directions appointment the court can do the following (rule 14(2)):

(a) Set a timetable for the filing and service of witness statements and documents. All evidence must be in the form of written witness statements, signed by the person making them. All witness statements, documents and reports must be disclosed to all the parties in advance of the hearing, in accordance with the timetable decided by the court. In an unreported case, the court warned that a local authority which served its evidence after the date specified and thereby caused an adjournment was liable to pay the costs thrown away (*R* v. *Nottingham CC*, 1992 July 14, Douglas Brown J).

(b) Deal with the appointment of a guardian *ad litem* for the child (if one has not been appointed already) and, possibly, deal also with the appointment of a solicitor for the child.

(c) Deal with any applications by people who wish to be joined as parties, or any issues about who should be joined.

(d) Deal with the question of expert witnesses. This may involve deciding whether expert evidence is needed and, if so, giving leave for the child to be medically or psychiatrically examined or otherwise assessed. Such examinations or assessments for the purpose of providing evidence for the proceedings cannot take place *without* the court's leave (rule 18(1), and see page 114).

(e) Set the date for any subsequent directions appointment or hearing.

(f) Deal with the question of the attendance of the child or children who are the subject of proceedings.

(g) Arrange for the case to be transferred or consolidated with other proceedings concerning the same family, if this has not been done already.

(h) Deal with any applications for interim orders.

(i) Deal with any other matters that the court considers appropriate.

During the course of proceedings the need may arise for further directions, or for existing directions to be varied or revoked. If so, further directions appointments can be arranged, either on the court's initiative or at the request of any of the parties to the proceedings. Normally everyone should be given two days' notice of a further directions appointment, although in an emergency the court can deal with an oral request without notice having been given to the other parties. If everyone is in agreement with the application for a new direction, or for a variation or revocation of an existing direction, and they have all signed the written request, the court, if it agrees, can simply make, vary or revoke the direction in accordance with the agreed application (rule 14(5)–(8)).

Directions appointments can be dealt with by a single justice or a justices' clerk (rule 2(5)). Single justices or justices' clerks are not entitled to deal with an initial application for an interim order so, if one was being applied for at the first directions appointment, that hearing would be dealt with by the full court.

Interim orders

The local authority or the NSPCC might wish to seek an interim care or supervision order, and other parties to the proceedings might wish to make applications for section 8 orders. The court has the power to adjourn proceedings at any time and – where they are dealing with an application for a care or supervision order or where family proceedings have been adjourned so that a local authority can carry out a section 37 investigation into whether or not an application needs to be made for a care or supervision order – the court is able to make an interim care or supervision order (s.38(1)). The court is also able to make interim section 8 orders in any family proceedings, including, of course, care and supervision proceedings (s.11(3)).

A residence order, even if made as an interim measure, gives the person in whose favour it is made parental responsibility for the child for as long as the order is in force. It may contain directions about how it is to be carried out, and conditions can be attached to it, such as about the child's education, or contact with parents and others, or ensuring the child attends a nursery or family centre. These matters could also be dealt with by other section 8 orders instead.

Single justices and justices' clerks can make interim care and supervision orders, and interim section 8 orders, but only when:

(a)   everyone has agreed in writing that the order be made,
(b)   a previous interim order has been made already in the same proceedings, and
(c)   the terms of the order being made are the same as in the previous order (rule 28).

If proceedings are commenced in, or are transferred to, the county court, district or circuit judges can deal with directions appointments. Circuit judges can deal with any applications for interim orders which are opposed, but district judges have only limited powers to deal with such matters. In the High Court, district judges can deal with any applications, opposed or unopposed (Family Proceedings (Allocation to Judiciary) Directions 1991, September 1991).

Grounds

The court can make an interim care or supervision order only if 'it is satisfied that there are reasonable grounds for believing the circumstances with respect to the child are as mentioned in Section 31(2)' – i.e., that the conditions for the making of a care or supervision order exist (s.38(2)).

Having established the specific conditions for an interim care or supervision order, the court must, of course, then consider the welfare principle, the welfare checklist, and whether the order will be better for the child than no order or any other order (s.1(1), (3) and (5)). If the court makes an interim care order, it must ask the local authority to explain their proposed arrangements for contact, and all the parties can comment on this. If necessary, contact orders can be made (s.34(11)).

If the court chooses to make an interim residence order in the course of care or supervision proceedings, then it must also make an interim supervision order, unless it is satisfied that the child's welfare will be safeguarded satisfactorily without the existence of such an order (s.38(3)). Before making any interim section 8 order the court must consider the welfare principle, the welfare checklist and the efficacy principle in section 1(5).

Given that there are now specific conditions that must be satisfied before the court can consider making an interim care or supervision order, the applicant clearly needs to present evidence to establish these conditions. This needs to address the significant harm suffered, or likely to be suffered, by the child and how this relates to a lack of reasonable parental care. In addition, in view of the welfare and non-intervention principles that apply to all court decisions, it also needs to provide clear details of why the order will be better for the child, and what the applicant intends to do as a result of the order. If directions relating to medical, psychiatric or other assessments are being sought, the applicant will need to give details of what the examination or assessment will involve and why it is necessary.

If the court is satisfied that the conditions for making an interim care or supervision order exist, that does not mean they will necessarily find the conditions established for a final care or supervision order. At this point they only have to be satisfied that there are reasonable grounds for believing the conditions exist, not that they do *in fact* exist.

After implementation of the Act, concern was expressed at the length of time interim hearings were taking. Perhaps to address this problem, the judge in one case set out some guidelines for family proceedings courts. These made it clear that justices were not required to make a final conclusion, but if they were going to make an interim order they should state their findings and reasons concisely and summarise the essential factual issues between the parties. They also suggested that only a minimal amount of evidence should be heard, restricted to the issues essential to the interim stage – there should not be a dress rehearsal of the final hearing. Finally, it was also suggested that justices should be wary of orders that would lead to a change in a child's residence (*Hampshire CC* v. *S* [1993] 1 FLR 559). On this last point it should not be forgotten that looked-after children – particularly those removed in an emergency – are likely to face changes in placement. Sometimes a move, into the extended family for example, can provide greater security.

Applications for interim care or supervision orders should never be rubber-stamped. Even at second or subsequent applications where there is no real change to the evidence available, the court will always have to consider whether or not making the order is better for the child, and whether some other order might be more appropriate:

'The consequences of interim care are potentially so serious for the child and those with parental responsibility for him that such a step should always be fully examined by the court. The parents and others concerned should never be encouraged to consent to an interim order just to avoid the trauma of a court hearing.' (DOH 1991(3), Vol. 1, para. 3.40)

Before the preliminary hearing all those involved will need to think carefully about the options available, which they might want to press for, and why. In particular, applicants will need to weigh up very carefully whether they actually need to apply for an interim care order. They will need to be clear why that would be better for the child than, for example, an interim supervision order, or that plus a residence order in favour of a relative or friend. All of those involved should bear in mind the possibility of using section 8 orders as an alternative to either an interim care or interim supervision order (see also page 102):

'Where a suitable relative or other person connected with the child is prepared to look after him and is likely to be able to meet his needs at least for a trial period, the residence order – supported where necessary by an interim supervision order – offers an attractive alternative to the interim care order. The local authority should always weigh carefully the pros and cons of such an arrangement . . . The authority should ensure that support services provided under Part III are made available to help the person caring for the child under a short-term residence order to meet the child's needs while the order is in force.' (DOH 1991(3), Vol. 1, para. 3.42)

Time-limits

The first interim care or supervision order in adjourned proceedings can be made for up to eight weeks. Second or subsequent orders can usually be made for up to four weeks only, but can be longer if that brings the total period of the interim orders to eight weeks. So, if a first interim order is made for three weeks, the second order could be for five weeks, or if the first order is for one week and the second for two weeks, then the third could be for five weeks (s.38(4) and (5)).

The same time-limits apply if an interim order has been made in family proceedings following a direction to the local authority to carry out a section 37 investigation.

There is no limit on the number of interim applications that can be made, but the courts will be guided by the principle that delay is prejudicial to children (s.1(2)) and by the timetable set at the directions appointment. Everyone involved in the case should make every effort to ensure that proceedings are not unnecessarily lengthy, and guardians *ad litem* have a specific duty to advise the court on the timing of proceedings (rule 11(4)):

'. . . a balance will have to be struck between allowing sufficient time for enquiries, reports and statements, and risking allowing the child to continue in interim care or supervision for so long that the balance of advantage is distorted in favour of continued intervention.' (DOH 1991(3), Vol. 1, para. 3.46)

Many courts have adopted policies of aiming to complete cases within 12 weeks. This timescale was suggested as an average timescale in a pilot project on timetabling carried out before the implementation of the Act. This project was evaluated by the Department of Health, who published a report on the project (DOH 1992). The timetable of 12 weeks was proposed as a target, and as such it is helpful, but it should not be adhered to too rigidly.

Effects of interim orders

Interim care and supervision orders are similar in effect to full orders, except that the court sets the time-limit for them and is able to give directions about medical or psychiatric examinations or other assessments of children.

Under previous legislation it was not possible to make an interim *supervision* order. This option should now be seen as a very real possibility, particularly as the order can require not only the child but also the person with parental responsibility for the child, or if different, the person with whom the child is living, to attend at a particular place in order to take part in particular activities. The Act clarifies that the supervisor must be allowed access to the child (schedule 3, paras. 2, 3 and 8). The sort of close monitoring that is now possible under a supervision order, combined, if necessary, with directions for an examination or assessment, may be sufficient in many cases to protect children while proceedings are pending. The making of an interim supervision order rather than an interim care order will also have the important effect of enabling children to stay in known surroundings within their family, rather than having to cope with the trauma of separation while the case proceeds.

If an interim *care* order is made, all the duties and responsibilities of local authorities in relation to children in care will apply. So, for example, the local authority must review the case after four weeks (s.26, and the Review of Children's Cases Regulations 1991); must comply with its duty to consult with children, their parents, people with parental responsibility and other relevant people, and must take into consideration the child's religious persuasion, racial origin and cultural and linguistic background in making any decision about the child (s.22). The duties in relation to planning, contact and, where appropriate, restoring children to their families also apply (The Arrangement for Placement of Children (General) Regulations 1991; para. 15, schedule 2, and s.34; s.23(6)). This should have the effect of ensuring that the local authority continues to work with the child and family, even while proceedings are continuing. This is welcome, given that research has shown that work with the family virtually ceased in the past while proceedings were continuing, in some cases for many months.

Directions for medical or psychiatric examinations or other assessments

Examinations or assessments of children should, where children are of insufficient understanding to give consent themselves, be carried out with the agreement of their parents or carers. Where this is not forthcoming, the Act gives the court a number of specific powers to order that an examination or assessment should take place: a specific issue order (s.8, see Chapter 2), a child assessment order (s.43, see Chapter 5), directions attached to an emergency protection order (s.44, see Chapter 5) or directions attached to an interim care or supervision order (s.38(6)–(9)).

Note however the comments made in *Re O (A Minor)* (1993) *The Times*, 19 March (see page 85).

It is quite possible that, by the time the preliminary hearing in care or supervision proceedings takes place, there will already have been an examination or assessment of the child. However, if no such examination or assessment has taken place and it is thought necessary to have one, or if it is thought necessary to have a further examination or assessment, there must be some discussion about this and, possibly, some negotiation with children and their families.

Once court proceedings have started no one can arrange for a child to be medically or psychiatrically examined or otherwise assessed for the purposes of obtaining evidence for the court proceedings without the leave of the court (rule 18). So, even if everyone is in agreement at the start of proceedings that an assessment or examination should be carried out, the court's authorisation must still be obtained. Although there is no specific reference in the Act or rules about children being able to refuse consent to this type of agreed examination or assessment, the general principles of the Gillick case should ensure that children of sufficient understanding would be able to refuse consent, subject to the court decisions which have cast doubt on this principle (see chapter 5, page 85).

In those cases where an interim order is being applied for, or where there is no parental agreement to an examination or assessment, then the court should be asked to use its power to attach directions as to the examination or assessment of the child to an interim care or supervision order. It should be noted that a local authority with an interim care order on a child is bound to comply with any direction made, even where the directions have resource implications for the local authority (*Re O (Minors)* (1993) *The Times*, 19 March; *Berkshire CC v. C and Others* [1993] 1 FLR 569).

Guidance points out that care proceedings should not be used simply to obtain an examination or assessment (DOH 1991(3), Vol. 1, para. 3.43). This provision for court directions is there in order to prevent children being subjected to a series of examinations or assessments purely for the purpose of collecting evidence for court proceedings. The clear intention is that the court should be able to control the examination and assessment of children under interim orders; these matters should not be left to the discretion of either the local authority or the supervisor.

Children have a specific right, if of sufficient understanding, to refuse to submit to a medical or psychiatric examination or other assessment directed under an interim order (s.38(6), but see *Re W (A Minor)* [1993] 1 FLR 1 and other cases, page 85). One of the duties of the guardian *ad litem* is to advise the court on whether the child is of sufficient understanding to refuse to submit to such examination or assessment (rule 11(4)) but at the initial hearing the guardian may not have been appointed, or may not have been in the appointment long enough to have discussed these issues with the child. The applicant should be in a position to give some information on the child's attitude. Ultimately, it is the responsibility of the person carrying out the examination or assessment to decide whether or not the child has sufficient understanding to refuse consent. Nevertheless, all those working with the child – the social worker, guardian *ad litem*, and solicitor – have responsibility to make sure the child is aware of their rights, and that the child's views are made known. Specialist help will be needed where English is the child's second language or where, because of a child's sensory or physical disability, communication methods other than speech or writing are required.

Discussion with parents and people with parental responsibility is important, first, to inform them of what the applicant would like to arrange under directions, and second, to see whether or not agreement can be reached as to the examination or assessment to be carried out. Guidance states that: 'The aim should be to secure the agreement of all concerned to a single programme of examination or assessment, which could if necessary be observed by, or conducted jointly with, a medical practitioner nominated by the parents' (DOH 1991(3), Vol. 1, para. 3.49). Guardians *ad litem* and legal representatives of children and other parties will need to be prepared for discussion and negotiation on the issue and to make their own suggestions and representations to the court, both about the nature of any examination or assessment and about who should carry it out. Families and/or the child concerned may well wish the assessment or examination to be carried out by someone of the same gender as the child, or someone of the same ethnic or cultural background, or someone who understands the child's and family's culture. Guidance underlines the importance of these issues when deciding who should carry out assessments (DOH 1991(3), Vol. 1, para. 3.48).

In particular, it will be helpful if agreement can be reached as to the person who is to carry out the examination or assessment, or alternatively to agree that, for example, a medical examination be carried out jointly by two medical practitioners, one nominated by the applicant and one by the parents. If agreement can be reached, it may not be necessary for the court to make any interim orders. If, however, agreement cannot be reached, it is obviously helpful that the court can decide the matter by making an interim order with directions attached.

Directions for examination or assessment attached to interim orders can be made when the order is made, or at any time while the order is in force. Any party can apply to vary such directions, and they must give three days' notice of their application (s.38(8) and rule 4(1)(b)). Parties also have the right to appeal against any directions made (*Re O (Minors)* (1993) *The Times*, 19 March.

What if the applicant does not wish to apply for an interim care or supervision order, or is unable to satisfy the conditions for one, but wants some assessment or monitoring of the child and the parents might not agree to that, or might withdraw their agreement later? At that stage it would be possible for the applicant to seek leave to apply for a specific issue order. The application might be for the court to direct the parents to take the child to a health clinic or family centre or medical practitioner, either once or on a regular basis. No specific conditions would need to be established for such an order, but the court would be guided by the welfare principle and checklist and by the principle of non-intervention. In addition, the local authority would have to obtain the leave of the court to make the application. The issue of leave could be sorted out in the course of the preliminary hearing. It should be noted that, even if the applicant were not seeking any order in relation to the child, it would be open to other parties, for example the child acting through the guardian *ad litem* or solicitor, or the parents or other relatives, to apply for, or seek leave to make an application for, a section 8 order such as a specific issue or prohibited steps order. Such orders could be coupled with an interim residence order (see above), or made alone.

Final hearing

Disclosure

Before the final hearing takes place, and in accordance with the timetable set by the court, the parties must have disclosed to each other their signed witness statements and any documents they wish to rely on. The guardian *ad litem*'s report to the court has to be available seven days before the hearing. No one may rely on evidence or documents which have not been disclosed in advance, or change their disclosed evidence, without the leave of the court (rule 17). A private law case under the Act stated that in dealing with an application for a section 8 order the court could, in exceptional circumstances, receive and act on evidence adduced by one party which had not been disclosed to another (*Re B (A Minor)* (1992) *The Times*, 31 July).

Witness statements, documents and reports relating to the proceedings cannot be disclosed without leave to anyone other than the parties, their legal representatives, the guardian *ad litem*, any welfare officer appointed in private law cases, or the Legal Aid Board (rule 23). Thus, leave will need to be obtained to disclose any such document to, for example, an expert witness. Before the case is heard the magistrates or judge will read all the written evidence, documents and reports (rule 21(1), FPC 1991).

Prior disclosure gives all parties the opportunity to consider the different options being proposed. It should also help them identify those areas where there is agreement and those where conflict remains.

Attendance at court

The hearing will be held in private (rule 16(7)), in the presence of all the parties and their legal representatives. Children may attend court hearings of public law cases, but they are not obliged to attend unless the court specifically orders them to do so (s.95(1) and (2)). If they do attend, the court has the power to exclude them from the whole or part of the hearing if that would be in their interests, providing those children have a guardian *ad litem* and/or solicitor to represent them. Children of sufficient under-standing and their guardian and solicitor may all make representations about this (rule 16(2)). One judge in the High Court has indicated concern about children attending hearings and has said that guardians *ad litem* should expect to be asked to justify why the child is attending (*Re G (A Minor)* (1992) *The Times*, 19 November).

Evidence

All evidence is based on the written evidence disclosed in advance. As these are civil proceedings concerning children, there is a relaxation of the hearsay rule (s.96(3)–(5)). This means that witnesses can refer to something that they have been told rather than being limited to what is within their direct knowledge. It is important that any hearsay evidence is clearly identified as such, that it is directly relevant to the proceedings, and that there is a real need for producing it in this form (*Edwards* v. *Edwards* [1986] FLR 187; *Re H, Re K* [1989] 2 FLR 313).

Evidence at the hearing is given orally, and witnesses, experts and the guardian *ad litem* may all be cross-examined. The evidence is recorded, by either a handwritten note or a tape recording. All those who have prepared witness statements should be called, so that the other parties can cross-examine them. Witness statements cannot be received as evidence if the relevant witness does not attend court, unless all the parties agree that this should happen.

Children can now give evidence in civil proceedings, even if they do not understand the nature of the oath. The court can hear evidence from a child if it considers that the child concerned understands that they must tell the truth and the child has 'sufficient understanding' to justify their evidence being heard. This change brings civil proceedings into line with criminal proceedings (s.96(1) and (2)).

Other parties, or anyone else present in court, can be asked by the court to leave the room while a child gives evidence, or at any other point in the proceedings, if the court considers this would be in the child's interest, and the person concerned is represented by a solicitor (rule 16(2)).

The Act specifically provides that, in care, supervision or child protection proceedings, no one can refuse to give evidence on the basis that doing so would incriminate themselves or their spouse in an offence. If they do make an incriminating statement or admission it will not be admissible in evidence in criminal proceedings against them or their spouse. This should ensure that care and supervision proceedings are never delayed pending criminal proceedings against any adult involved (s.98).

Clearly, evidence needs to relate to whether the threshold conditions are satisfied. In addition, all parties should address the issues listed in the welfare checklist, and should be able to tell the court why they consider that one particular order, or no order at all, would be better for the child than the order proposed.

The local authority should always present a detailed care plan to the court, explaining what it intends to do under the order sought, to enable the court to decide whether the order will be better for the child. Case law has indicated that a local authority should follow the format for a plan set out in paragraph 2.62 of Volume 3 of *Guidance and Regulations* (DOH 1991(3), and see pages 154–5) (*Manchester City Council* v. *F* [1993] 1 FLR 419).

Options for the court

There are a wide variety of options open to the court. It can:

- Make no order at all. The court may decide that the threshold conditions for a care or supervision order have not been established, and that the welfare of the child does not require any other order being made instead. If the threshold conditions have been established, the court may decide that the provision of services by a local authority under part III of the Act, perhaps including the provision of accommodation, would be sufficient to prevent the child suffering, or further suffering, significant harm (ss.1(5) and 31).
- Make a care order (s.31). Before making a care order the court must consider what arrangements the local authority has made for contact between the child and their family. If necessary, the court can also make a contact order (s.34, see Chapter 7).
- Make a supervision order (s.31).
- Make a residence order, combined perhaps with another section 8 order, or make any section 8 order alone – about contact, a specific issue or a prohibited steps order. Case law has established that a

court should not make a care order where an application for a residence order is pending and needs delay for an assessment before it can be considered (*Hounslow LBC* v. *A* [1993] 1 FLR 702).

* Make a family assistance order (s.16).

The court must make its decision 'as soon as is practicable'. In one case the judge suggested that, as the drafting of findings and reasons can take time even when the decision has been made, it might be better if they were presented the following day (*Hampshire CC* v. *S* [1993] 1 FLR 559).

Another case emphasised that, while the period of the adjournment should be kept to a minimum, the preparation of findings and reasons should not be conducted under time pressure (*Devon CC* v. *S and Others* [1992] 2 FLR 244).

This last case also established that, where justices were dealing with a case where everyone was in agreement as to what should happen, it was inappropriate for them to insist on lengthy oral evidence at either the interim or final hearing stage. If they intended to make an order substantially different to the one agreed on by the parties, they must give an indication of this and allow the parties to make submissions.

When giving its decision the court must give reasons, indicating any findings of fact and specifying why it considers that its decision will be better for the child. Cases have made it clear that magistrates must give reasons for preferring one course of action against another, having set out the facts and the issues in dispute. If reasons are not given this makes the order void (*Re B (Minors)* (1992) *The Times*, 16 July; *W* v. *Hertfordshire CC* [1993] 1 FLR 118; *S* v. *Oxfordshire CC* [1993] 1 FLR 452). One early case gave magistrates detailed and helpful guidance on exactly how to construct their judgements (*Oxfordshire CC* v. *R* [1992] 1 FLR 648). A copy of any order made, including a refusal to make an order, should be sent or given to all the parties by the justices' clerk (rule 21(4)–(8)).

Effect and duration of orders

Care order

If a care order is made, the local authority acquires parental responsibility for the child (s.33(3)). They now share it with parents or guardians. The local authority has the power to determine the extent to which parents or guardians can meet their parental responsibility, but they can do that only if this is necessary in order to safeguard the child's welfare (s.33(4)). There will thus need to be negotiation in every case about how far parental responsibility is to be limited. (For more discussion on this issue see Chapter 8.)

The Act sets some specific limits on the parental responsibility gained by local authorities through a care order. So, local authorities cannot:

- Make the child be brought up in a religion different to the one they would have been brought up in if the care order were not made (s.33(6)). Although the wording of this duty does not necessarily encourage local authorities to ensure that children continue to be brought up in the religion that they were being brought up in before the order was made, it should be read together with the duty in section 22 to take into consideration the child's religious persuasion when making any decisions about the child.
- Consent or refuse consent to an application to free a child for adoption, or to an adoption order (s.33(6)).
- Appoint a guardian for the child (s.33(6)).
- Change the child's surname, or allow anyone else to change it unless they obtain the written consent of everyone with parental responsibility, or obtain the leave of the court (s.33(7)). In exceptional circumstances an application to change the surname can be made *ex parte* (*Re J (A Minor)* [1993] 1 FLR 699).
- Remove the child from the United Kingdom for a period of longer than a month, unless they obtain the written consent of everyone with parental responsibility, or obtain the leave of the court (s.33(7)).

In relation to these last two points, local authorities should ensure foster carers are aware of the legal position and that they liaise with the local authority, particularly over things such as holidays, as an application to the court may need to be made. Local authorities may not arrange for children to live outside the United Kingdom permanently unless they seek the approval of the court. The child concerned, and everyone with parental responsibility, must give their consent, or have their consent dispensed with on specific grounds (para. 19, schedule 2).

Children under a care order are children who are 'looked after' by a local authority, so all the duties and powers of the local authority contained in part III and schedule 2 of the Act will apply to these children. (For more detail about these powers and duties see Chapters 8 and 9.) The making of a care order discharges any existing section 8 order, and any supervision order, school attendance order or wardship in relation to the child (s.91(2)–(5)). A care order lasts until the child is 18, unless it is discharged before then (s.91(12)).

Once a final care order has been made, the local authority has absolute discretion to decide how it will exercise its powers under the order, and the courts cannot make directions which are binding on the authority, except that the courts can make orders in relation to contact. Case law has established that it is contrary to this principle for a court to make a series of interim orders so that it can review the process of the reunification of child and family (*Kent CC* v. *C* [1993] 1 FLR 308). If the court thinks the local authority is about to embark on a course of action it considers would not be in the interests of the child's welfare, it should think very carefully before making a care order. Very detailed contact orders are one way of setting a framework for reunification (see pages 124–5 and Chapter 7).

Supervision order

Supervision orders are likely to be more effective than they were under previous legislation. The supervisor has a duty to advise, assist and befriend the child; to take such steps as are reasonably necessary to give effect to the order, and, where the order is not wholly complied with or the supervisor considers it may no longer be necessary, to consider whether or not to apply for the variation or discharge of the order (s.36).

In addition, supervision orders now enable requirements to be imposed, not only on the child who is the subject of the order, but also on a 'responsible person', which the Act defines as any person with parental responsibility for the child and any other person with whom the child is living. The requirements that can be placed on the child are that the child lives at a particular place for a specified period of time, or that the child attends at a particular place once or on a regular basis, or that the child participates in specified activities, or that the child does a combination of all of these things (para. 2, schedule 3).

If requirements are to be imposed on the responsible person, they must consent to that. The requirements can be that they take reasonable steps to ensure that the child complies with any of the above directions; that the child complies with any requirements about psychiatric or medical examination or treatment, and that the responsible person attends at a particular place for specified activities (para. 3, schedule 3). This would allow for directions such as that the parents and child attend a family centre on a regular basis, or go to some other place that can help with parenting skills or any other particular difficulties. Case law has established that conditions attached to a supervision order could require a mother and child to live at a family rehabilitation centre (*Croydon LBC* v. *A* (no. 3) [1993] Fam. Law 70, February).

A supervision order can require the responsible person to keep the supervisor informed of the child's address and to allow the supervisor reasonable contact with the child. Children can be required to allow the supervisor to visit them at the place where they are living (para. 8, schedule 3).

The court can include specific requirements in the order relating to psychiatric and medical examinations and treatment of children. Where the child has sufficient understanding to make an informed decision about this, the court can only include such requirements if the child consents (paras. 4 and 5, schedule 3).

Supervision orders can initially be made for a period of up to one year only. A supervisor can apply to the court for the order to be extended, but the total period for which the order is in force can only be three years (para. 6, schedule 3). In any event, a supervision order will automatically come to an end when a child reaches 18 (s.91(3)).

If either the child or the responsible person fails to comply with directions given under the supervision order, the supervisor has a number of legal remedies, but it will be important first of all to find out why the child and/or family are not co-operating, and to see whether the directions need to be changed so that co-operation can be achieved. The supervisor should also tell the child and parents carefully what the effects of non-co-operation might be. Guidance recommends:

> 'The local authority should at all times respond to non co-operation in a positive and constructive way designed to regain that co-operation. Failure to work closely with those concerned with the child's welfare, in particular with the parents, may lead to a breakdown in the local authority's relationship with the parents, and consequent deleterious effects on the welfare of the child.' (DOH 1991(3), Vol. 1, para. 3.95)

If agreement cannot be reached, the supervisor can apply to the court to vary or discharge the order, or could apply for a care order (s.36). The threshold conditions for a care order would have to be established before the court could make a care order in those circumstances. If denied access to the child, the supervisor could apply to the court for a warrant which would authorise a police officer to assist them in carrying out their powers (s.102). Alternatively, in circumstances where there were grounds for it, the supervisor might need to apply for an emergency protection order.

Discharge and variation of interim and full care or supervision orders

The child, any person with parental responsibility for the child, and the local authority (where there is a care order) or supervisor (where there is a supervision order) are entitled to apply to the court for the discharge of the order or, in the case of supervision orders, the discharge or variation of the order (s.39(1) and (2)). On an application to discharge a care order the court may, providing one of the parties has applied for this, substitute a supervision order for the care order without there necessarily being evidence to establish the threshold conditions. However, where the application seeks to replace a supervision order with a care order, the threshold conditions *must* first be established, and the court must then consider whether making a care order would be better for the child than any other order or making no order at all (s.39(4) and (5)).

If, under a supervision order, requirements have been imposed on a responsible person who does not have parental responsibility for the child and is therefore not entitled to apply to discharge the supervision order, that person can nevertheless apply to the court for a variation or discharge of the requirements imposed on them under the order (s.39(3)).

There are no specific conditions to establish before care or supervision orders are discharged, but the welfare principle will apply, together with the checklist, and the court will be required to consider whether no order or any other order would be better for the child. The option of a section 8 order is again available to the court in place of a care order.

Non-married fathers who have not acquired parental responsibility, other relatives of children, and friends and foster carers are not able to apply to discharge care orders. However, if an application to discharge a care order was in progress, they could apply to be joined as parties to the proceedings and, in those proceedings, they could apply for a residence order. Alternatively, even if no proceedings were pending, they could apply, or seek leave to apply, for a residence order. A residence order is the only section 8 order that can be made in relation to a child in care, and the making of a residence order in such circumstances discharges the care order (ss.9(1) and 91(1)).

Under previous legislation, when relatives or friends wished to offer a home to a child who was in care but the local authority was not prepared to place the child with them, those relatives or friends had no legal remedy unless the local authority agreed to the matter being resolved through wardship proceedings. The important change introduced by the Act is that relatives and friends are now able to seek leave to apply for a residence order when a child is in care.

The Short Report was quite specific in recommending that, in future, the court should not be able to control the exercise of a local authority's discretion in relation to children it was looking after (House of Commons 1984). The Government's consultation document continued this recommendation, but specified that the courts should have the final say in two crucial areas: contact between children in care and their families, and the final decision about where a child should live (DHSS 1985 (1)). This is why the courts are now able to hear, not only applications to discharge care orders, but also applications for residence orders in relation to children in care. Some relatives or friends who make applications for residence orders in these circumstances will be entitled to make the application, while others will have to seek leave of the court.

When dealing with an application for leave, the court is required to consider the parents' wishes and feelings and the local authority's plans for the child. A case decided shortly after implementation concerned a foster carer seeking leave to apply for a residence order in relation to foster children who had been removed from her. Neither the children nor their mother supported the application. The Court of Appeal rejected the argument that leave should never be granted if this was contrary to the local authority's plans, but did say that, as the local authority is under a duty to safeguard and promote the welfare of children in care, then any departure from their plans 'might well disrupt the child's life to such an extent that he would be harmed by it' (*Re A and W (Minors)* [1992] 2 FLR 154). It is to be hoped that courts will not automatically assume that the local authority's plan is best for the child, and that these criteria will not become an impossible hurdle for relatives and friends, but that the courts will be willing to grant leave so that the substantive issue about where the child's future lies can be dealt with by the court.

The question of whether or not a care order should be discharged is a matter that *must* be considered by a local authority when it carries out reviews of the cases of children in care (reg. 5 and schedule 2, Review of Children's Cases Regulations 1991). It will be important for those working with the child to give this issue proper consideration and to advise children of their right to make an application to discharge the care order themselves.

When children have been living away from home for some time, they will need to be prepared carefully for their return home if that return is to be successful. In particular, regular contact with their family will be essential, and overnight and longer stays at home, or where it is intended they will live, are highly desirable. Where a local authority is working to return children to parents, relatives or friends, the duties in part III and schedule 2 should ensure that this careful process is carried out.

There will, however, be circumstances – where parents apply for the discharge of a care order, or other relatives or friends apply for a residence order – when the local authority is opposed to the child returning home or living with relatives or friends, and where the effect of making the order will be a sudden change in circumstances for the child. The court is unable to make a specific order for a phased return home, but could, in such circumstances, use its powers to make contact orders together with its powers to adjourn proceedings to establish, in effect, a phased return.

Thus the contact order could specify an increasing amount of contact leading to overnight or longer stays within a specified time-limit, at which point the case would come back for a final decision on whether or not the order should be discharged or a residence order made.

Alternatively, where the relationship between parents or relatives and foster carers is good, and where the foster carers are in agreement with the child returning to parents or relatives, it will be possible for the court to make a residence order in favour of the foster carers for a limited period of time, and a contact order under section 8, thus facilitating increasing amounts of contact between the child and family.

It may be that the local authority changes its position in the course of the hearing, perhaps as a result of evidence given, or perhaps as the result of the involvement of a guardian *ad litem*. In that case it might be possible to agree that a phased return home will occur after the care order has been discharged, with parents and the local authority agreeing that the child should be accommodated initially by the local authority and that return home will then be implemented gradually. On an application for discharge of the care order, the court also has the option of replacing the care order with a supervision order.

If an application to discharge a care order or a supervision order is unsuccessful, no further application for discharge can be made for six months, unless the court specifically grants leave (s.91(15)). If an application for a residence order in relation to a child in care is unsuccessful, there is no time-limit on when a further application can be made, but the court does have the power to specify that a particular person cannot make any further application without the leave of the court (s.91(14)). This latter power should be used sparingly (*F* v. *Kent CC* (1992) *The Times*, 6 August).

Appeals

All parties to the proceedings have a right of appeal (s.94(1)). Appeals from the magistrates' court will be heard by the High Court. Appeals from the county court and the High Court go to the Court of Appeal. Appeals will not be re-hearings, but will be based on the court's reasons for its decision, the evidence given and recorded, and the reports filed. The decision of the lower court will be overturned only if it is obviously wrong in law (*Croydon LBC* v. *A* (no. 3) [1993] Fam. Law 70, February; *G* v. *G* [1985] 1 WLR 647). A Notice of Appeal must be filed with the court and served on all the parties to the proceedings within 14 days of the decision being appealed against. In the case of appeals against the making of an interim order, the Notice of

Appeal has to be filed and served within seven days (rule 4.22(2) and (3), FP 1991). Case law has indicated that it will be difficult to obtain leave to appeal out of time (*Re M (Interim Care Order)* [1993] 2 FLR 406).

All courts now have the power to make orders pending the hearing of an appeal. Where a court refuses to make a care order on a child who is the subject of an interim care order, the court may make a care order pending the appeal. If a court refuses to make either a care order or a supervision order on a child subject to an interim supervision order, the court may make a supervision order pending the appeal (s.40(1) and (2)). If a care or supervision order is made in either of these circumstances, the court has the power to give specific directions 'as the court sees fit'. This could mean very detailed directions to control the exercise of a local authority's discretion under the order. Similarly, if the court grants an application to discharge a care or supervision order, it can order that the care or supervision order continues until the hearing of the appeal, or that it continues subject to any directions that the court may make. It is only in these circumstances that the court can give detailed directions to a local authority when it makes a care or supervision order (s.40). Where a court refuses to make an order pending appeal, the High Court cannot make an order under s.40(1), but can make an interim care order under s.38 (*Croydon LBC v. A. (no. 2)* [1992] 2 FLR 348).

Before making or continuing an order pending appeal the court must, of course, consider whether or not the order would be better for the child. It will also need to bear in mind the principle that delay is prejudicial to children. A clear case will need to be demonstrated for an order being made or continued.

Note that a family proceedings court does not have the power to stay a care order pending an appeal – in other words to make the order and then say it will not have any effect. If an appeal is being considered and a stay is required, then an application should be made immediately to the High Court which has an inherent power to grant a stay (*O v. Berkshire CC* [1992] 1 FCR 489).

7   Contact

Introduction

This chapter looks at the background to the current legislation, sets out the legal provisions in relation to contact, suggests how practice can be developed to promote successful contact, and looks at how disputes can be resolved or otherwise dealt with. The final section deals with the appointment and role of independent visitors.

During the 1980s a growing body of research in both the UK and the USA was showing that, when children are separated from their families and are being looked after by local authorities or other agencies, their well-being is enhanced if they maintain links with their families and friends. Maintaining links is an essential ingredient in ensuring that children can leave accommodation or care and return to families and friends, as a majority (80 per cent) of children do. It is also important for children who may never return home, because they function better psychologically, socially and educationally, and develop a better sense of identity, if they are able to maintain links (Millham et al. 1986; Thoburn 1988; Maluccio & Sinanoglu 1981, and Fanshel & Shinn 1978). Regrettably, research over the same period showed that little was being done by social workers to help children maintain these links, even in circumstances where contact was not being actively discouraged:

> 'Only two sets of parents said their social workers had actually *helped* them over visiting.' (Packman et al. 1986)

> 'We were frequently dismayed and sometimes angered by the way in which social workers so often failed to provide the necessary support and encouragement to maintain visiting.' (Rowe et al. 1984)

Millham et al. (1986) found that looked-after children faced two barriers to maintaining contact with family and friends: specific restrictions placed by social workers on contact with a particular person, which affected one-third of the 450 children in their study; and non-specific restrictions arising from the practical problems of travel, cost and commitment to other children at home, or unwelcoming placement attitudes, which affected two-thirds of the children. This research painted a graphic and depressing picture of a sizeable group of children remaining in long-term care or accommodation, without a stable placement, who by the end of a two-year period had lost all contact with their families, although there were no social work reasons for this.

In the early 1980s the Government responded to growing concern over the issue of contact, and the evidence that was beginning to emerge from research studies, by introducing new legislative provisions in relation to contact – a Code of Practice on Access, and amendments to the Child Care Act 1980, which gave parents – no one else – a limited right to challenge a local authority's decision to terminate access (s.12(a)–(g), Child Care Act 1980). At the time the Government indicated that further legislative change, shifting decision making about contact from local authorities to the courts, would be necessary if practice in relation to the promotion of contact did not improve. A study of the new legislation and Code of Practice (Millham et al. 1989) showed that they had been of limited effect in changing practice.

The crucial importance of contact is now recognised and acknowledged in both legislation and guidance:

> 'For the majority of children there will be no doubt that their interest will be best served by efforts to sustain or create links with their natural families . . . Contacts, however occasional, may continue to have a value for the child even where there is no question of returning to his family. These contacts can keep alive for a child a sense of his origins and may keep open options for family relationships in later life.' (DOH 1991(3), Vol. 3, para. 6.9)

A number of the principles set out in *Principles and Practice* (DOH 1989(1)) stress the importance of contact:

> 'Every effort should be made to preserve the child's home and family links.' (principle no. 5)

> 'Family links should be actively maintained through visits and other forms of contact. Both parents are important even if one of them is no longer in the family home and fathers should not be overlooked or marginalised.' (principle no. 14)

> 'Wider families matter as well as parents – especially siblings and grandparents.' (principle no. 15)

> 'Continuity of relationships is important, and attachment should be respected, sustained and developed.' (principle no. 16)

Legal provisions

Contact is not specifically defined in the Act, although the definition of a contact order (s.8) makes it clear that it covers visits, stays and other forms of contact. Guidance indicates that these include letters, telephone calls, and such things as the exchange of photographs (DOH 1991(3), Vol. 3, para. 6.9).

Guidance on contact, replacing the Code of Practice on Access under previous legislation, is contained in Chapter 6 of Volume 3 and Chapter 4 of Volume 4 of *Guidance and Regulations* (DOH 1991(3)). The relevant regulations are the Contact with Children Regulations 1991.

The Act sets out the following duties in relation to contact:

- Local authorities have a duty to promote contact between all children they are looking after and their parents, relatives and friends, unless this would not be practicable or consistent with the child's welfare (para. 15(1), schedule 2). Voluntary organisations and the people running registered children's homes are placed under a similar duty in relation to children they are looking after (reg. 6, Arrangements for Placement with Children Regulations 1991).
- Local authorities are under a duty to promote contact between children in need living away from home and their families and friends, where these children are not looked after by the local authority (para. 10, schedule 2). These could be children living in nursing or mental nursing homes or fostered privately. This duty links with the duty on local authorities, when notified of children living in local education authority or health authority or private health establishments for longer than three months, to consider what services they should make available to the child and family (ss.85 and 86), and the duty on local authorities to satisfy themselves that the welfare of children who are fostered privately has been adequately safeguarded and promoted (s.67 and reg. 2(j), Children (Private Arrangements for Fostering) Regulations 1991).
- Local authorities have a duty to allow children in care reasonable contact with their parents, with guardians (if they have any), and with anyone who had the care of the child under either a residence order or a High Court order that was in force immediately before the care order was made (s.34; *Re P (Minors)* [1993] 2 FLR 156).
- When a child is under an emergency protection order, the applicant for the order has a duty to allow the child reasonable contact with parents, non-parents with parental responsibility, anyone with whom the child was living immediately before the order was made,

and anyone with a contact order in favour of the child (s.44(13)). The court may, at the time of making the order or subsequently, direct that a particular person should not have contact with the children. Alternatively it may specify how often they should see the child, and it could, for example, direct that contact be supervised (s.44(6)(a)).

- When a child is removed into police protection (see Chapter 5) the police have a duty to allow the child contact with parents, non-parents with parental responsibility, anyone with whom the child was living immediately before being removed, and anyone with a contact order in relation to the child. The police have the right to decide what level of contact would be reasonable and in the child's interests, and they could decide not to allow contact (s.46(10)).

- If the court makes a child assessment order and authorises the removal of the child from home for any period under that order, the court must also make directions about the arrangements for contact between the child and their parents, relatives and friends (s.43(10)).

- Local authorities have a duty to keep parents, and non-parents with parental responsibility, informed of their child's address. The only exception to this is if the child is in care and disclosing the address would prejudice the child's welfare (para. 15(2) and (4), schedule 2).

These duties to promote and allow contact link with the duties to promote the upbringing of children in need by their families (s.17), the duties to enable children to live with their parents, relatives or friends (s.23(6)), and the duty to place children near their home and together with their brothers and sisters (s.23(7)).

Promoting contact for looked-after children

Planning and reviews

The failure of social workers to make proper plans in relation to contact was noted by research studies (Fruin & Vernon 1985; Millham et al. 1986). The arrangements for contact between children and their parents, relatives and friends is now one of the essential issues discussed and decided on when plans are made in accordance with the Arrangements for Placement of Children (General) Regulations 1991.

It is important that the local authority recognises that it is *its* duty to ensure that proper arrangements for contact are made, in consultation with – and in most cases by agreement with – children, their families, their foster carers or residential staff. It should never be the case, as unfortunately it was in the past, that families are left to make their own arrangements with the foster carers or the residential staff.

Forms of contact other than visits – such as phone calls, letters, exchanging photos – should always be considered in addition to, or in place of, visits.

Whatever arrangements for contact are made, they should be carefully monitored and reviewed. This must happen as part of the general reviewing process in accordance with the Review of Children's Cases Regulations 1991, but may need to happen more frequently, particularly where problems arise or when restrictions have been placed on contact. Millham et al. found: 'Restrictions on contact do not receive continual scrutiny by social workers and constraints on unwelcome family members are frequently allowed to linger long after the original reasons for discouraging visits have evaporated' (1989, p. 3). A decision that contact should be supervised is, for example, one that should be regularly and frequently reviewed. 'Contact should be monitored to check whether the arrangements are working as intended and to identify any problems which have arisen and any changes which are needed: whether, for example, the arrangements are unnecessarily restrictive' (DOH 1991 (3), Vol. 3, para. 6.38).

Importance of participation in planning and discussion

A prime duty of agencies is a duty to consult with children, their parents, non-parents with parental responsibility, and other relevant people before making any decision about a child (s.22). This consultation process will need to be gone through in relation to all decisions about contact arrangements with children. It is important that the discussions about contact take into account the overall plan for the child, and that arrangements for contact are not seen in isolation.

When children are consulted it is particularly important that they are given information about all the possible options. On the whole, children will usually want to see their parents, brothers and sisters and other relatives and friends as well. Social workers should be proactive in raising the issue of contact. The fact that a child does not, of their own accord, ask to see someone should never be taken as an indication that they do not want to see that person. There are many reasons why they may not raise the issue themselves, an obvious example being that they may not know that they are allowed to make such a request.

Sometimes a child is ambivalent about having contact with a particular person, or always shows reluctance to go on a visit, or is quite clear that they do not want contact. Sometimes reluctance to go on a visit may arise from the way the arrangements have been set up, for example so they conflict with an activity or TV programme a child enjoys. A change in the arrangements, or more flexibility, may be all that is required. Ambivalence, or a clearly expressed wish for no contact, may arise from something the child is worried about or needs more explanation about. A discussion with a trusted adult, either a professional or family member or friend, may help the child to express their concerns and take a different view. Every effort should be made to help the child take a long-term view.

If the problem cannot be resolved, forms of contact other than visits, such as letters and phone calls, should be discussed with everyone concerned. Even if there is no contact, the issue should continue to be reviewed so that children have the opportunity to change their minds at a future date if they wish to do so.

If social workers consider that the child has valid reasons for not wanting contact with a person the local authority has a duty to allow contact with – parents, and those with parental responsibility before a care order was made – then they should seek legal advice about whether it should be the local authority or the child who makes the application to the court to stop contact (s.34(4), and see page 143).

Importance of written information

Providing written information to children and families is crucially important. It ensures that they have something they can regularly refer to, can mull over at home or with a friend, or take to an adviser. It is also an essential method of helping to avoid mistakes or to prevent misunderstandings from arising.

The Act and *Guidance and Regulations* emphasise the importance of written information by requiring it to be available. Guidance recommends that children and families be given an information pack when a child starts to be looked after, which should cover general information about the law and about what being looked after means, including brief details of the local authority's duties and the procedures for reviews and for making complaints (DOH 1991(3), Vol. 3, paras. 10.16 and 6.34). It is suggested that children's homes should produce their own leaflets about the facilities for visiting and details of the available public transport (DOH 1991(3), Vol. 3, para. 6.34).

The specific arrangements for contact in an individual case will be part of the written plan for the child, and the details will also be in the written agreement (reg. 4 and schedules 1–4 Arrangements for Placement of Children (General) Regulations 1991, and see pages 154–5). A copy of the plan or agreement, or those parts of it which are relevant to them, must be given to parents, others with parental responsibility, and anyone who is having contact with the child, as well as to foster carers or staff in a children's home (reg. 5 and DOH 1991(3), Vol. 3, paras. 2.68–2.72 and 6.33–6.35). Thus all those involved in the contact arrangements should have that information in writing, and be clear about what the arrangements are. Where a section 34 contact order in relation to a child in care is varied by agreement, all those people must be given details of the variation in writing (see page 145).

Problems for families

A major problem for some families when their children go into accommodation or care, particularly the latter, is that they do not know how important it is for contact and good channels of communication to be set up immediately. This knowledge is learnt, as many social workers will appreciate when they consider how they first came to understand the importance of contact for looked-after children. Even those families who want to see as much of their children as possible are unlikely to fully comprehend the strong links between contact and their chances of having their child returned to them. Families need help and support, at the earliest possible stage, in understanding how important contact is.

A further problem is the guilt felt by parents and other family members when a child is removed into care, and often when the child goes into accommodation. This sense of guilt and of failure can make contact a difficult and painful experience. Again support and encouragement to maintain contact is important. Problems of feeling a sense of guilt or failure are exacerbated when children are removed on an emergency or compulsory basis, and research has shown that, before the implementation of the Act, children removed from home in this way had fewer links with their families and friends and remained longer in care than children admitted on a voluntary or planned basis (Millham et al. 1986; Packman et al. 1986).

Children are often upset by visits. They show their upset in different ways – difficult behaviour towards their families during a visit; tears and clinging to them at the end of the visit; or difficult behaviour before or after a visit which affects their foster or residential carers. Often families find this upset, particularly tears at the end of the visit, so painful that there is a danger they will decide it would be better not to visit. In the same way foster and residential carers often wonder whether contact is worth the upset it can cause before and after a visit. Research has explored the difficulties faced by children separated from their families (Bowlby 1952; Rutter 1972) and has shown that it is better for children to keep in contact and be upset than not to have contact. Although this research was mainly based on children in hospital it is relevant to the majority of looked-after children.

Children, families and carers need careful social work support to cope with this upset, together with information about the different reasons for children being distressed, so that they can continue to visit or support the visits. It is particularly important that this work is done in the first few weeks of the child becoming looked after. Unfortunately, as Millham et al. (1986) point out, all too often 'we find balm and comfort applied to the wounds of separation when they should be kept open and salted' (p.232). Researchers also found that social workers' visits to children, their families and their carers declined over time. Families, however, continued to need encouragement to maintain contact and to feel that they could contribute. Without encouragement and support from social workers, in many cases contact begins to deteriorate and then to stop altogether (Millham et al. 1986 and 1989; Rowe et al. 1984).

Foster carers and residential staff

The majority of looked-after children are now placed with foster carers, and many families will visit children in their foster homes. Many families find this a difficult experience for a number of reasons.

Families often find it hard to cope with the thought – and sometimes the experience – of someone else doing their job better than they can at that time. However welcoming the foster carers, families can still feel undermined. If there is a difference, as there still often is, between the economic circumstances and class background of the family and the foster carers, this can be felt very deeply by the family. They can feel ashamed about what they have to offer their children by comparison, and may well have salt rubbed into their wounds by the children themselves, who understandably enjoy and make specific reference to the greater material benefits they experience in the foster home. Families can be deeply hurt by comments made by children in such circumstances.

The development of attachment between children and their foster carers can also cause anguish to families, and a fear that they will eventually be excluded from their child's affection. This anxiety was often exacerbated in the past when families found that their child was using the foster family's surname. This should never happen in short-term placements, and should never happen without the parents' consent or the approval of the court in long-term placements (s.33(7)).

Families are very quick to pick up on negative or unwelcoming attitudes towards them from foster carers or residential staff. This can quickly become an unspecific and informal barrier to contact, causing visits to be a stressful time for all concerned, and possibly leading to a reduction in visiting.

All of these are matters which families should be given the opportunity to discuss. Careful monitoring of the arrangement should ensure that these sorts of problems are noticed speedily, and the arrangements varied if necessary, including changing a placement, to ensure that the family are able to continue to feel important to the child and involved in that child's life.

When making the arrangements for contact, account must be taken of the foster carer's own family arrangements, and the possible problems arising from them going away for weekends or holidays should be anticipated and dealt with. The arrangements should not, however, simply be fitted around what the foster carers can manage.

For foster carers, managing contact – particularly if visits occur in their own home – is often one of the most difficult parts of their jobs. The assessment process for foster carers now requires that those carrying out the assessment must take into consideration the prospective carer's ability to work with families and to deal with contact from the children's family and friends (DOH 1991(3), Vol. 3, para. 3.26). When a child is placed with them, the written placement agreement will include details about the arrangements for contact (see page 184), and hopefully this will have been negotiated at a meeting attended by both foster carers and the families. This should mean that foster carers are clear from the time that they are approved that working with families will be as important an aspect of their role as providing care for children.

As important as recruiting foster carers with a positive attitude to contact and to families as well as to children is ensuring that they receive proper training so that they are able to understand the importance of contact: so that they can learn about the feelings children and families may experience, the problems they may encounter, how to deal with these, and what they can do to make contact an enjoyable and meaningful experience for all concerned.

Continuing and regular contact and consultation with their own linked social worker is also crucial in helping foster carers continue their good work, as is reasonable payment for their work. Foster carers should really receive a proper wage, but until this is accepted they should at least receive an enhanced allowance for helping local authorities in their duty to promote contact.

Residential staff also need training on the importance of contact, possible problems that may arise and how to overcome them. Regulations now require children's homes to provide welcoming and private facilities in which visits can take place (reg. 7(3), Children's Homes Regulations 1991, and DOH 1991(3), Vol. 4, para. 1.65). Regulations also make it clear that stopping any form of contact between a child and their family or friends must never be used as a way of punishing the child (reg. 8(2)(c) and (3)(d)).

Choice of placement

The plan for the child – which must include the arrangements for contact – should, where possible, be made before the child is placed (reg. 3, Arrangements for Placement of Children (General) Regulations 1991). This means that the contact arrangements should inform the decision about what placement would be best for the child. Guidance points out that a placement 'with a family of the same race, religion and culture in a neighbourhood in reach of family, school or day nursery, church, friends and leisure activities' is the one most likely to ensure continuity for the child (DOH 1991(3), Vol. 3, para. 4.4). It is also the one most likely to enable the child's family and friends to feel comfortable when visiting, and to enable the child to maintain good links with family, friends and community.

For many children the reality is that placements cannot be planned so carefully. Despite this, local authorities should always bear in mind their duties to place children near their homes and to place brothers and sisters together (s.23(7)). The monitoring and review of the arrangements for contact should always take into account the possibility that a particular placement may need to be changed because it is interfering with the maintenance of good contact. This could arise, for example, because of distance, because of a number of siblings being placed in separate foster homes, or because the carers, whether foster carers or residential workers, have a negative attitude towards contact or towards the family, which is undermining the arrangements.

Practical help with visits

Problems arising from distance, lack of public transport, cost of travel and commitments to other children are all some of the non-specific barriers to contact that cause links between looked-after children and their families to wither (Millham et al. 1986 and 1989, and Rowe et al. 1984). It is thus very important for local authorities to make use of their powers to provide practical help with visits (para. 16, schedule 2). Such help can be given if the visit could not take place without 'undue financial hardship' and the circumstances warrant making the payment. The payments are not just to cover travel expenses, but can also be given to pay for food, for childminding, for overnight accommodation, or a treat for the looked-after child. Payments can be made to any parent, relative or friend to help them visit the child; or to the child to enable them to visit parents, relatives or friends in their own homes. When children make overnight stays at home, which because of their timing do not allow their parents to claim child benefit or income support for the child for that period, use should be made of this power to provide them with financial assistance so that contact does not end up taking much-needed resources from the rest of the family.

All children and families should be given written information about this power to provide financial help with the information they get when the child starts to be looked after.

As well as providing financial help, other practical support may be needed. Parents should have met the foster or residential carers before or at the time of the placement, and have visited the placement then (DOH 1991(3), Vol. 3, para. 4.17), but in an emergency this may not have been possible to arrange. If the parent has never been to the placement before, the social worker should firstly make every effort to arrange a meeting with the foster carers before the visit and secondly, should go with them on the first visit. If parents have not been able to meet the foster carers beforehand, time should be set aside, separately from the time allowed for the visit, for the adults to meet and exchange information on the first visit. Even if the family has been to the foster carer's home before, the social worker should check whether they would like to be accompanied on the first visit (DOH 1991(3), Vol. 3, para. 6.20). Families should have clear instructions in writing about how to get to the foster or residential home, including available public transport.

Preparations for the visit should include advice to parents and other relatives about what is likely to happen, and suggestions about what they might do during the visit. Sometimes advice may be needed about what to say or what not to say to the children, in particular how to respond to the question 'When can I come home?'

It has not been unknown for social workers to fail to provide families with this type of support to overcome the non-specific barriers to contact, in order to test the family's motivation. This should never happen. Families should be told if their motivation is being tested, and given every support in maintaining contact before social workers make a judgement on whether they are motivated to maintain links.

When, where and for how long?

The location, duration and frequency of visits will be the subject of the consultation process, and set out in the written arrangements.

It should never be automatically assumed that visits will take place in the foster home or children's home. Wherever possible, children should be able to visit and stay at their own home or at the homes of relatives and friends. This enables contact to be a much more natural experience (DOH 1991(3), Vol. 3, para. 6.18).

Visiting looked-after children can, particularly for parents, be a very artificial experience. Few parents spend an hour or two simply sitting with their children with perhaps a few games or books, unless waiting for an appointment at the hospital, doctor, or dentist. As much as possible, visits should enable parents and others to engage in normal everyday activities with their children. Outings can be enjoyable to everyone, but people should not be expected to go out on every visit. 'If possible, parents should be encouraged to participate in some way in the child's daily life, by preparing tea, for example, or shopping for clothes or putting a young child to bed' (DOH 1991(3), Vol. 3, para. 6.18).

If visits can neither take place at the child's home, the home of relatives or the foster carers, an alternative venue should be found, and only as a last resort should social services offices be used. Offices are frequently lacking in privacy, bring in an element of formality, and are likely to make families and friends feel ill at ease. 'Whatever the venue the aim should be to ensure that privacy and a welcoming and congenial setting are available' (DOH 1991(3), Vol. 3, para. 6.18).

For most children the aim will be that they should return home, so visits – particularly for babies and young children – should be as frequent as possible. In arranging the timings for visits, thought should be given to people's working hours and the length of their journey to and from the visits.

If visits have to be supervised, everyone should be clear about why this is happening, and some indication should be given about how long it will go on for. If the supervision is part of an assessment of a person's relationship with a child or their ability to parent, then it should be carried out by a qualified worker, the persons involved should be clear about what is happening, and the workers should discuss their observations with them. This type of supervision is unlikely to need to continue for any great length of time. Supervision might, alternatively, be to ensure that some behaviour does not occur – such as snatching or injuring the child, or that something is not said. Again the person involved needs to be clear what the concerns are. A much wider group of people can perform this supervisory task, even relatives or family friends, as well as foster carers, unqualified workers or volunteers.

Issues of race, culture, language and religion

In making the arrangements for contact these matters must be taken into consideration (s.22(5)). Clearly the principle of enabling children to experience continuity of background in their placement is crucial here (see comments on placement above, and Chapter 9 on placement). All the difficulties that families face in maintaining contact when their children are living in another family are immediately doubled if the child and family are black and the carers white; if English is the second language of the child and family, but the carers speak only English; or if the child and family practise one religion and the carers another, or none at all. For some children and families all of these problems may exist.

If carers cannot be found who share the same ethnic background, language or religion as the child, then the promotion of contact will be essential, not only for enabling the child to maintain links with their family but also to enable them to maintain and develop a sense of identity and pride in their background.

Attention should be paid to the important role played, not only by relatives but by family friends, such as godparents, in the lives of some black families. Workers should make sure that they have full information about the network of relatives and friends important to the child. In some cultures it is important that children initiate contact with adults, rather than the other way round, and that children go to visit the adults rather than be visited. In making the arrangements for contact, cultural expectations and norms must be respected. Knowledge can be gained through consultation and discussion with black and minority ethnic colleagues and others who have direct knowledge of the particular culture.

When English is a family's second language they should always be offered the use of an interpreter at meetings, and written information should be translated for them.

Wider family and friends

By requiring agencies to promote children's contact, not only with their parents but also with their other relatives and friends, the Act recognises the importance to children of creating and/or sustaining their links with their wider family generally, with friends, and with their community. Too often, in the past, the benefit to children of such links has been overlooked, with the focus limited to parental contact only. As a result, if contact with parents was severely restricted or ended altogether, it often followed that contact with other family members was dealt with in the same way. Such limitations on contact, or failure to promote contact, limit the options for children who cannot return to live with their parents. Promoting contact with relatives and friends keeps open the option of children eventually going to live with them.

In looking at children in long-term placements Rowe et al. (1984) found: 'A continuing contact with grandparents appears to be almost wholly beneficial' (p.116). Brothers and sisters are also important, not least because they provide our longest-lasting relationships. Studies of admissions to care or accommodation show that most young children are admitted with brothers and sisters (Millham et al. 1986). Studies have also shown brothers and sisters like being together, but more often than not they are separated from each other (Whitaker et al. 1985; Rowe et al. 1984; Berridge 1985, and Berridge & Cleaver 1987). Social workers should ensure not only that contact with siblings at home is promoted, but that those who are being looked after, but are placed separately, are able to keep in regular contact with each other.

Disagreements, complaints and court procedures

When children are *in accommodation* the local authority does not acquire parental responsibility for those children. Nor does it have the power to limit the parents' exercise of their parental responsibility. The plan for the child while in accommodation, including the arrangements for contact, will have been sorted out by agreement between the local authority and the child's parents or carers. Given that accommodation can be used for both short- and long-term placements, and can be used in situations where the conditions for a care order could be established, it is quite possible that disagreements over the arrangements for contact may arise – they could be about the frequency, duration, nature or place of contact. In cases where a child has been abused, the local authority may feel that visits should be supervised. They might even take the view – particularly if this is what the child wants – that there should be no visits or other forms of contact at all. Attempts should be made to resolve disagreements at meetings, but if they cannot be resolved, parents or others with parental responsibility are entitled to use the complaints and representations procedures. Alternatively, an application could be made to the court (see pages 142–3).

When children are *in care*, parents still retain parental responsibility, but the local authority now acquires it, too, and it has the power to limit the parents' exercise of their parental responsibility (s.33). Local authorities have to allow parents and people with parental responsibility reasonable contact with the child in care (s.34). Within this framework the local authority should consult and negotiate with the parents, and attempts should be made to reach agreement on the arrangements for contact. If the parents do not think that what the local authority is proposing is reasonable, this is something to try and sort out first in a meeting. If that fails to resolve the problem, parents can use the complaints and representations procedure. They can also apply to the court. In one case where a parent and local authority could not agree on contact the case was taken to court and, in making a defined contact order, the judge stated that the previous practice of contact at the discretion of the local authority should not be the regular practice, as section 34 provides that reasonable contact should be the norm, not contact at the local authority's discretion which is not the same. 'Reasonable' contact implied agreement with the parents and, if no agreement was possible, contact which was objectively reasonable (*Re P (Minors)* [1993] 2 FLR 156). Note that a local authority cannot stop parents or people with parental responsibility having contact with a child in care except by applying to the court for a court order, unless there is a sudden emergency (s.34).

Relatives and friends who wish to have contact with children in accommodation or care may or may not be 'other relevant people' that the local authority must consult, involve in planning and invite to reviews. Whatever their position, if they wish to have contact with a child they should approach the local authority, and their proposal should then be discussed with the children concerned and their parents. If relatives and friends are dissatisfied with the arrangements for contact that are made for them, or if the local authority refuses to allow them contact with the child, they could try to resolve this by requesting a meeting with the social workers and their seniors, by using the representations and complaints procedure, or by seeking leave to go to court. The representations and complaints procedure can be used by anyone whom the local authority considers 'has a sufficient interest in the child's welfare' (s.26(3)(e)). Guidance stresses that local authorities should have a flexible approach on this so as not to overlook relevant people (DOH 1991(3), Vol. 3, para. 10.7). In relation to contact, it states specifically: 'responsible authorities should ensure that the representations procedure recognises the need to accept complaints from people, other than parents, who have contact with children who are being looked after' (para. 6.36, Vol. 3).

What if relatives and friends who are seeking contact with a child do not get on with the child's parents, or don't get on well, with the result that the parents may be opposed to their having contact with the children? There may be a history of conflict in the family, or relationships may have become strained over the issues that led to the child being accommodated or in care. A local authority may believe that it is in a child's interest to promote contact with relatives and friends but be concerned that this would conflict with the parents' wishes. Attempts should be made to negotiate with all concerned and to suggest alternatives, such as contact by letter or telephone rather than visits. If agreement cannot be reached, this, too, is a matter for the complaints and representations procedure or for an application to court.

Court proceedings

Care should always be taken that family members and friends are not diverted and delayed from going to court by being advised to make a complaint first.

Children accommodated under section 20   Section 8 orders can be made in relation to children in accommodation and it is these proceedings that might be used to resolve disputes over contact which cannot be resolved by negotiation. An application may be made for a contact order or, possibly, a prohibited steps order. A section 8 contact order is a permissive order, requiring the person with whom the child is living to allow the child contact with the applicant. Government guidance suggests that where the aim is to stop contact, a prohibited steps order should be applied for (DOH 1991(3), Vol. 1, para. 2.30). However, case law has contradicted this, stating that no contact *could* be ordered under a contact order (*Nottinghamshire CC* v. *P* [1993] 1 FLR 514, and 2 FLR 134).

Parents, and anyone with a residence order in their favour, are *entitled* to make applications for a contact or prohibited steps order. Children have to *seek the leave* of the court before they can make either of these applications, and the court can grant the child leave to make the application only if it is satisfied that the child has sufficient understanding to do that (s.10(4) and (8)). Local authorities are not allowed to apply for a contact order (s.9(2)), but they may *seek leave* to apply for a prohibited steps order.

The Nottinghamshire case (see above) suggests that a local authority could not be granted leave to apply for a prohibited steps order if the aim of the order was to deal with the issue of contact because of the restriction in section 9(2). This would leave the burden of applying to stop contact on the child who was in accommodation.

Relatives, friends and foster carers will always have to *seek leave* to apply for a prohibited steps order. Relatives and friends are *entitled* to apply for a contact order if they have the consent of everyone with parental responsibility for the child or, where a residence order is in force, if they have the consent of the person with the residence order, or the child has been living with them for three years within the last five, and has stopped living with them not more than three months before they make their application. Otherwise they have to seek leave first (s.10(5)(b) and (c)).

The application for a contact order or prohibited steps order should be made on the standard application form and lodged with the family proceedings court, the county court or the High Court. If other proceedings are under way involving the same family, this application should be heard in the same court. Fourteen days' notice of the application must be given (rule 4, schedule 2 (as amended by SI 92/2067 and SI 92/2068)). The people, apart from the applicants, who will be parties automatically to the section 8 application will be those people who have parental responsibility for the child. The local authority which is providing accommodation, and the people currently caring for the child, must be given notice of the application (rule 4, schedule 2). As the dispute about contact is between the local authority and the applicant, an application should be made to have the local authority joined as a party. Foster carers can apply to be parties (rule 7).

Where the applicant needs to seek leave to apply, the court will deal with that issue first, either by granting the request without a hearing, or if there is some dispute over whether the application should be made or concerns that there might be, arranging for a hearing of this preliminary issue (rule 3; *G* v. *Kirklees MBC* [1993] 1 FLR 805).

Children will not be parties to section 8 proceedings automatically, as they would be for applications for a contact order if they were in care (see page 144). They may apply to be made parties, and they clearly *will* be parties if they have been granted leave to make the application themselves. In these circumstances they may instruct a solicitor if the court considers they have sufficient understanding to do so. Otherwise they have to act through an adult (rules 9.2 and 9.2A, FP 1991). A guardian *ad litem* from the panels of guardians and reporting officers will not be appointed, instead the court is likely to ask a welfare officer to prepare a report (s.7).

The hearings will follow the standard procedure, with an initial hearing for directions to sort out parties, the filing of evidence, and disclosure of all evidence and reports in advance of the hearing. If a contact order or prohibited steps order is made, this can subsequently be varied or discharged by the court on the application of any of the parties. While the court order is in force all the parties must abide by it. The order will last until the child is 16, unless it is discharged before then (s.91(10)).

It remains to be seen how far the courts will encourage or limit the use of section 8 orders when children are in accommodation. Where the application is to stop someone from having contact with a child in accommodation, the court may feel that such an application would be better made by one of the parents or by the child, rather than the local authority (see page 142), particularly if the decision is based on the child's expressed wishes.

If relatives or friends obtained a section 8 order in relation to a child in accommodation, that would, of course, override a parent's unwillingness to agree to their having contact with the child.

Children in care   The making of a care order automatically discharges any section 8 order that is in existence in relation to that child (s.91(2)), and the only section 8 order that can be made in relation to a child in care is a residence order (s.9(1)). So, issues of contact for a child in care cannot be dealt with under section 8. They are dealt with under section 34. The duty on local authorities to allow reasonable contact with children in care is owed only to parents or to those who had parental responsibility immediately before the care order was made. Thus, the duty is not owed to relatives such as grandparents but, of course, the duty to promote contact between children and their relatives and friends still applies.

Parents, people with parental responsibility for the child, the child and the local authority are all *entitled* to apply for a contact order under section 34. Anyone else must first seek the leave of the court before making the application (s.34(3)).

Under section 34 the court has the power to order that there should be no contact at all or, alternatively, to set out in detail what the arrangements for contact should be (s.34(2)–(4)). Some family proceedings courts initially took the view that they had no power to make an interim contact order under section 34. However, the fact that the section allows the court to impose any conditions that it thinks are appropriate should mean that orders can be made to last until the next or final hearing (s.34(7); *Re B (A Minor)* [1993] 1 FLR 421, *West Glamorgan CC* v. *P* (no. 1) [1992] 2 FLR 639). Where an interim care order has been made, contact should be maintained, save where there is exceptional or severe risk to the child. The court should not rule out the possibility of reunification at an interim stage (*A* v. *M and Walsall MBC* [1993] 2 FLR 244).

Applications under section 34 for contact to be defined by the courts or to stop contact should be made on the standard application form and lodged with the family proceedings court (article 3, Allocation of Proceedings Order). If existing public law proceedings are continuing in relation to the same child in another court, this application should be dealt with in that court. Any of the parties may request a transfer of the case to a higher court (articles 3 and 7, Allocation of Proceedings Order). The child, anyone with parental responsibility for them, or who had parental responsibility before the care order was made, the local authority and the person whose contact is the subject of the application will be parties automatically (rule 4 and schedule 2). Foster carers must be given notice of the proceedings, and can apply to be parties (rules 4 and 7, and schedule 2). Children will have a guardian *ad litem* appointed for them unless that is not necessary in order to safeguard their interests, and they will be represented by a solicitor (s.41). The parties to the proceedings are entitled to apply for Legal Aid. A minimum of three days' notice must be given to the parties before the hearing of the application (rules 4 and 7, and schedule 2). As with all proceedings under the Act, there is likely to be a hearing for directions first, and all the evidence and reports will be disclosed in advance.

A local authority cannot stop someone entitled to reasonable contact with the child from seeing the child unless it obtains a court order, except in emergency situations. Once a court order setting out the arrangements for contact has been made in relation to any person, a local authority cannot prevent that person from having contact with the child in accordance with the court order, nor can it change the arrangements for contact, except in the circumstances set out below.

Local authorities are able to suspend contact that would otherwise take place under a court order, or in accordance with their duty to allow certain people reasonable contact with the child, if the local authority is satisfied that the suspension is necessary in order to safeguard or promote the child's welfare and the issue has to be decided as a matter of urgency. Such suspensions can only last for up to seven days (s.34(6)). As soon as the local authority has decided to suspend contact in these circumstances it must write to:

- the child
- the child's parents
- the child's guardian (if there is one)
- anyone who had a residence order or care and control in wardship before the care order was made, and
- any other relevant person.

In the letter it must set out:

- the details of the decision
- the date on which it was made
- the reasons for it
- the length of the suspension, and
- the remedies available (reg. 2, Contact with Children Regulations 1991).

Local authorities should use this procedure in a genuine emergency. Attempts by local authorities to make repeated use of the procedure instead of applying to the court should be challenged by judicial review.

When a court order is in force setting out the arrangements for contact, these arrangements can usually be varied only by another court order. However, a variation in the arrangements can take place by agreement and without going to court if:

- the local authority and the person who has the order in their favour agree the variation;
- the child concerned also agrees to the variation, providing they have sufficient understanding to do so;

and

- written notification setting out the details of the changes and the date on which the agreement was made is sent to all those who have to receive notification of a suspension (see above) (reg. 3, Contact with Children Regulations 1991).

The Regulations also require the local authority to notify in writing all these people listed above of any variation or suspension of the contact arrangements made for any friend or relative of the child (reg. 4, Contact with Children Regulations 1991).

The decision to give courts the power to make orders in relation to contact between children in care and their families and friends is based on clear evidence of poor practice in relation to the promotion of, and decisions about, contact (see page 127). It is important that lawyers who represent children and families, and magistrates and judges, are familiar with the research evidence, and that the courts are prepared to use their powers to make sure that, where appropriate, children are able to keep in touch with relatives and friends. There has been a worrying tendency in some court judgements to suggest that contact should not be ordered if this is in conflict with the local authority's plans for the child. This type of decision assumes firstly, that local authorities are always right, and secondly, that contact should only rarely continue when children will not be returning home. Neither of these assumptions is supported by the research (*West Glamorgan CC* v. *P* (no. 2) [1993] 1 FLR 408, and *Re S (A Minor) (Access Application)* [1991] 1 FLR 161). However, a later case decided by Butler-Sloss LJ emphasises that under the Act parliament has given the court, and not the local authority, the power to make decisions about contact, and the principle of the court not interfering with the local authority's plans does not apply to applications for contact made under section 34 (*Re B (Minors)* [1993] 1 FLR 543). It has also been established that magistrates were wrong to make an order for no contact simply on the basis that they accepted the local authority's decision that the children could not return home (*Devon CC and Others* v. *S and Others* [1993] 1 FLR 842).

Independent visitors

Local authorities have a duty to appoint an independent visitor for any child they are looking after if there has been infrequent communication between the child and their parents or people with parental responsibility, or if the child has not been visited by such people within the last 12 months, and such an appointment would be in the child's best interest. Independent visitors can be appointed for *any* looked-after child, whether in accommodation or care and whether in a foster or residential placement (para. 17, schedule 2).

Local authorities have a duty, at every review, to consider whether an independent visitor should be appointed (reg. 5, and schedule 2(6)). This is a decision requiring consultation with the child, family and carers (s.22(4) and (5)) and requiring the local authority to take into consideration the child's religion, race, culture and language (s.22(5)). The requirement to consult with the child is backed up by a specific provision in the Act that an independent visitor should not be appointed if the child has sufficient understanding to make an informed decision and objects to the appointment (para. 17(5), schedule 2). Even if the criteria exist, it may not be appropriate to make an appointment if, for example, the child is in regular contact with other relatives or friends, or is well settled in a permanent placement and has sufficient contacts and friends.

Where a child is living with foster carers of a different ethnic or religious background, or is in a residential placement where there are no or few staff of the same background, and the child is not in contact with relatives or friends or – in the case of a child with mixed parentage – is in contact with only white relatives or friends, serious consideration should be given to appointing an independent visitor of the same religion or ethnic background. This regular contact with someone from the same background would help the child make and develop links with their community and give the child a positive adult role model who shares their religion, language or ethnic background.

Who can be an independent visitor?

In order to be 'independent' the person appointed cannot be an elected member of the local authority, or sit on any of its committees as an elected or co-opted member, or be an officer of the social services department, or be the spouse of any such person (reg. 2, Definition of Independent Visitors (Children) Regulations 1991). Guidance recommends that a partner of any such person should not be appointed either (DOH 1991(3), Vol. 3, para. 7.7).

Guidance also recommends that independent visitors should have an ability to relate to children and communicate with them, and should be committed to and interested in the welfare of children (DOH 1991(3), Vol. 3, paras. 7.14 and 7.22). A range of qualities will be needed to cater for different children: some children may prefer a younger person who could be like an older sibling, while others may prefer someone older (DOH 1991(3), Vol. 3, para. 7.15). For children likely to remain looked after for some time, the person appointed may need to be prepared to make a lengthy commitment (para. 7.19). Gender, class, and ethnic background should also be of central importance in choosing a visitor for a particular child.

'Imaginative and energetic' recruitment campaigns are recommended to recruit independent visitors (DOH 1991(3), Vol. 3, para. 7.18), with consultation with local community groups and voluntary organisations. It is suggested that the recruitment, assessment and support of visitors should be based on existing knowledge and skills in recruiting foster carers. Prospective independent visitors should be required to give details of any previous convictions or cautions, and to give their consent to police checks (para. 7.27, Vol. 3). They should receive some induction and training, particularly on local authority duties and responsibilities and the rights of children and their families. They will also need, and should be provided with, ongoing support, particularly if the child they visit has had a lot of broken relationships and moves in their life.

The appointment of someone as an independent visitor is a formal one, which can be terminated either by the visitor giving notice in writing of their resignation or by the authority giving notice in writing that they have terminated the appointment. The appointment must be terminated if the child objects to it continuing (para. 17(3) and (6), schedule 2, and para. 7.29, Vol. 3). Whether or not the appointment should continue is something that should be discussed at each review and the child's views on the matter will obviously be important.

Guidance stresses that:

> 'the local authority must act with the greatest care to avoid any suggestion that the termination of an independent visitor's appointment is a consequence of that visitor acting with appropriate independence and, for example, challenging the validity of the authority's care planning or standards of service in respect of a particular child.' (para. 7.30, Vol. 3)

If the local authority terminate an appointment, the independent visitor should be able to use the complaints and representations procedure as a person with a 'sufficient interest in the child's welfare' (s.26(3)(e)).

Someone who is no longer an official independent visitor for the child may well continue as a friend, and may, in that capacity, continue to have contact with the child and be involved in discussions and decisions concerning the child.

What do independent visitors do?

The Act requires an independent visitor to advise and befriend the child, and enables them to claim reasonable expenses in carrying out their duties (para. 17(2), schedule 2). Guidance goes into more detail about what the appointment entails (DOH 1991(3), Vol. 3, paras. 7.33 and 7.50). Independent visitors should visit the child concerned. As their relationship develops they may want to take the child out, or even have the child to stay. Care should be taken that any such arrangements are part of the overall plan for the child and don't raise expectations in the child which cannot be fulfilled. Where children are with foster carers it will be particularly important for the carers to be clear about the role of any independent visitor. If a child is placed in secure accommodation, the child's independent visitor must be involved in consultations about that (regs. 15 and 17, Secure Accommodation Regulations 1991).

Independent visitors have no formal right to inspect a child's files, but they will obviously need to be given information about the child's background. Local authorities will need to be flexible in their approach to giving information. Some cases will require more information to be given than others. The child should always be consulted first (DOH 1991(3), Vol. 3, paras. 7.23–7.24).

The independent visitor will be a relevant person to be consulted by the local authority and invited to contribute to reviews. They may contribute in writing or, if the child wishes, they should attend. The child may wish the independent person to speak on their behalf. Similarly, the child may want the independent visitor to help them make a complaint and be their representative at any complaints panel hearing. Independent visitors should be distinguished from the independent person involved in a complaints or representations procedure. Independent visitors should be given information about the law so that they can advise children on their rights to go to court, where appropriate. They should also know of sources of other independent representation and/or advocacy for children so they can direct children to that help if they need it.

When children leave accommodation or care they may wish to keep in touch with their independent visitor. In such circumstances, local authorities should always consider whether to go on meeting the expenses of the former visitor as part of their after-care provisions for the child.

8 Planning for children

Introduction

This chapter looks at the duties and responsibilities of local authorities towards children they are looking after, and towards the families of those children. Many of the duties and responsibilities apply also to voluntary organisations and the proprietors of registered children's homes. The term 'agency' is used in the chapter to refer to local authorities, voluntary organisations and registered children's homes.

The duties owed by local authorities are to children they are 'looking after'. With reference to local authorities this term has a specific legal meaning. Looked-after children are those children who are in care and those who are provided with accommodation on a voluntary basis for a continuous period of more than 24 hours (s.22(1) and (2)).

Children provided with accommodation include not only those specifically provided with accommodation under section 20 but also:

- children under an emergency protection order and removed from parents or carers;
- children under a child assessment order and removed and kept away from home;
- children under police protection;
- arrested juveniles not granted bail;
- juveniles on remand and refused bail;
- juveniles subject to a supervision order with a provision that they reside in local authority accommodation (s.21).

The prime duty owed to children

Agencies owe a general, overarching duty to children they are looking after, or proposing to look after, or to children placed in their establishments. This overarching duty has three major elements:

(1)   The duty to safeguard and promote the children's welfare;
(2)   The duty to consult with the children, their families and other relevant people before making any decision;
(3)   The duty to take into consideration the children's religion, race, culture and language when making any decision about them. (ss.22, 61, and 64)

The duty to safeguard and promote the child's welfare links with the duty owed by local authorities to children in need (s.17(1), see page 26). The other two elements of the overarching duty – to consult with children, their families and friends, and to take account of issues of race, culture, language and religion – both link with the key principle that agencies should work in partnership with families.

More specifically, from the duty to consult stem the duties to provide children and families with information, to involve them in planning and reviews, to make written agreements with them, and to provide them with a means of making complaints and representations. The duty to take into account issues of race, culture, language and religion is the basis for a positive approach to developing and maintaining anti-racist practice (see pages 27–9). This is backed up by baselines for good practice set out in guidance, which emphasise the importance of: involving the black and minority ethnic communities in consultation about services generally; recruiting staff, as well as day carers and foster carers from these communities; providing or ensuring access to representatives and interpreters, and translating written information.

It cannot be emphasised too often that the duties owed to looked-after children and their families are owed to children *in care* as well as those in accommodation. The principles of working in partnership apply:

'Although genuine partnership will be easier to achieve in the absence of compulsory measures, the same kind of approach should be taken in cases where a child is in the care of a local authority as a result of a court order.' (DOH 1991(3), Vol. 3, para. 2.12)

Even though local authorities acquire parental responsibility when a care order is made, they share this with the parents, although, of course, they have the right – if it is necessary to safeguard the child's welfare – to limit a parent's exercise of that parental responsibility (s.33). The continuance of parental responsibility under a care order should assist workers in seeing that, in the majority of cases, their work should be to assist parents in being able to meet their responsibility.

For children in accommodation it is only their parents or parent who have parental responsibility for them, and thus it is crucial that workers' approach to planning and monitoring is on the basis of an agreed service provision (see page 49).

Planning

Its importance acknowledged

For many years now the importance of planning for children has been stressed, yet, until recently, research studies showed that little effective planning could be found. So, the overview of research studies published by the DHSS in 1985 (DHSS 1985(2)) showed an increase in the use of compulsory measures linked with a belief that this led to better planning:

> 'The idea seems to be to "get control in order to plan and safeguard." Yet constructive planning seems all too often absent. There are suggestions in the research that control is being confused with planning and that in a laudable desire to manage risk, to improve decision-making, to avoid drift and be "firmer", controls are imposed at a time and in a manner that is unconstructive and often counter-productive.' (DHSS 1985(2), p.19)

The Government's second overview of research, published in 1991, concluded:

> 'Research findings indicate that considerable progress has been made in establishing the importance of planning for children and some success achieved in putting it into practice, although disturbing incidences of lack of plans are also mentioned in a number of the SSI and other reports . . .
>
> The problem now seems to be that of the quality rather than the quantity of planning. Sometimes rigid policies on "permanence" lead to rigid and unnecessarily painful confrontational plans for particular children.' (DOH 1991(1), p.64)

The Arrangements for Placement of Children Regulations 1991 now require agencies to make both immediate and long-term plans for looked-after children or children placed with them. Preferably, the plan should be devised *before* children are looked after or placed, but if that is not possible, for example in an emergency, then the plan should be made as soon as possible after the child has started to be looked after or has been placed (reg. 3(1) and (2)).

Guidance states that making individual plans for children 'will prevent drift and help to focus work with the family and child' (DOH 1991(3), Vol. 3, para. 2.20). The planning process should involve:

'(a)   assessing the child's needs;
(b)   determining what objectives have to be met to safeguard and promote the child's welfare;
(c)   consulting with parents, the child and others whom the local authority consider are relevant;
(d)   appraising fully the available options to meet those objectives;
(e)   making decisions only after full consultation with the child, his parents and other agencies and individuals with a legitimate interest;
(f)   identifying which individuals are to undertake which tasks; and
(g)   setting a timescale in which tasks must be achieved or reassessed.' (DOH 1991(3), Vol. 3, para. 2.20)

Recording individual plans

The plan for the child must be recorded in writing (reg. 3(5)) and copies sent to all those involved in the planning process – children; their parents; people with parental responsibility, and others whose views the agency considers to be relevant, who may be relatives, friends, and other professionals involved with the family (ss.22, 61 and 64, and reg. 5(3)). As well as sending a copy of the written plan to all concerned, social workers should always explain the details personally to children and parents (DOH 1991(3), Vol. 3, para. 2.70). In addition, the regulations require that others, who may not have been involved in the planning process, should be notified of a placement and given such (if any) details of the plan as are relevant to them. This group of people include the district health authority and the child's GP, the local education authority, the local authority (if the child concerned is not being looked after by the local authority), and anyone with a contact order under section 8 or section 34 of the Act (reg. 5).

The written record of the plan should be distinguished from a written agreement. Where there is such an agreement (see page 157) this will incorporate the plan, but even if no agreement exists, parents and others should receive written copies of the plan. Note that any reference to parents includes a non-married father, even if he has not acquired parental responsibility for the child.

The matters to be covered in the plan, and any written agreement, include issues arising from the legislation and specific matters referred to in the regulations (reg. 4, and schedules 1–4). They are summarised helpfully in the guidance as follows:

'• the child's identified needs (including needs arising from race, culture, religion or language, special educational or health needs);
• how those needs might be met;
• aim of plan and timescale;
• proposed placement (type and detail);
• other services to be provided to child and/or family either by the local authority or other agencies;
• arrangements for contact and reunification;
• support in the placement;
• likely duration of placement in the accommodation;
• contingency plan, if placement breaks down;
• arrangements for ending the placement (if made under voluntary arrangements);
• who is to be responsible for implementing the plan (specific tasks and overall plan);
• specific detail of the parent's role in day-to-day arrangements;
• the extent to which the wishes and views of the child, his parents and anyone else with a sufficient interest in the child (including representatives of other agencies) have been obtained and acted upon and the reasons supporting this or explanations of why wishes/views have been discounted;
• arrangements for input by parents, the child and others into the ongoing decision-making process;
• arrangements for notifying the responsible authority of disagreements or making representations;
• arrangements for health care (including consent to examination and treatment);
• arrangement for education; and
• dates of reviews.'

(DOH 1991(3), Vol. 3, para. 2.62)

The requirement in regulations that plans be made, and the detailed guidance about how to make them, are both informed by clear research evidence that good-quality planning requires the involvement of children and families and the setting of clear and achievable aims and objectives:

'Good planning requires specifying in writing what needs to be done, by whom, how and within what time span. General aims about providing a good standard of child care are insufficient. Long and short-term goals need to be agreed for each child and young person if planning is to be effective and there should always be a contingency plan at least to cover short-term crises.' (DOH 1991(1), p.75)

Since the implementation of the Act the Government have been investigating the possibility of introducing standardised forms for the making and reviewing of long-term plans for children. At the time of going to press this project is still in the process of piloting and developing forms. It is called the 'Looking after Children Project' and is based at Bristol University. It produces regular bulletins (Parker et al. 1991).

Involving children and families

Enabling children to be involved properly in discussions and decisions means making sure that they have information and explanations so that they are able to reach an informed view. The task for practitioners is a delicate one, for they must ensure that children feel they have been consulted without making them feel that 'the burden of decision making has fallen totally upon them' (DOH 1991(3), Vol. 3, para. 2.48).

In relation to consultation with families, the Act lists both parents and people with parental responsibility. Thus, non-married fathers without parental responsibility should be included in the consultation process. So should step-parents or other relatives or friends who have a residence order, in relation to children in accommodation, as they will also have parental responsibility for the child. The Act also provides that others whose views are relevant should form part of the decision-making process (s.22(4)(b)–(d)). The guidance makes it clear that this is an encouragement to involve the wider family and close family friends in planning for the child:

> 'The child's family, parents, grandparents and other relatives involved with the child should be invited to participate actively in planning and to make their views known . . . Such sharing of information and participation in decision making should be the norm subject only to the overriding best interests of the child.' (DOH 1991(3), Vol. 3, para. 2.49)

The legislation and the guidance both recognise that, for many children, 'family' means more than just one or two parents and brothers and sisters. It can mean step-parents, grandparents and other relatives, and god-parents and other non-related close friends. In some families a relative, rather than a parent, may have discharged the primary caring role, or it may have been shared between a number of adults. The importance of a flexible approach to families is now recognised. This is important for all children, but particularly those from black or other minority ethnic groups.

Guidance on the content of the plan (pages 154–5) recommends that specific details for the parents' role in the day-to-day arrangements for the child should be included in the child's plan. This should encourage the local authority to think about ways of helping parents to remain involved with their children and to meet their continuing responsibilities for them, even where the child is in care or where the placement is a long-term one.

Finally, the commitment in this legislation to consultation being a meaningful process is emphasised by the recommendation in the guidance that the plan should note precisely who has been consulted and, if those views or wishes have been discounted, should give specific reasons for that (see page 155).

Family members need adequate information too, if they are to be fully involved in planning and decision making. Guidance recommends that children and their families be given an information pack when a child first starts to be looked after (DOH 1991(3), Vol. 3, para. 10.16). This would include information about the review system and the complaints procedure, and could contain other information about the services available, and local authorities' duties in relation to the child and family, for example in relation to decision making or contact.

Plans for ending a placement

One of the matters to be covered in a child's plan (and any agreement, see page 155) is the ending of the placement. When a child is in care this will be decided either by the local authority or by a court, but the intentions for the future of the child should be included in the plan and any agreement. Where the child is accommodated by the local authority – in which case those with parental responsibility retain the right to remove the child at any time – it will be of particular importance to deal with the issue of the placement coming to an end, in both the plan and the written agreement. Both should include a notice period agreed by all concerned. This is particularly important where the placement is a long one. Such a notice period will not be legally enforceable, but it will serve as an important recognition by everyone of the need to prepare children for major changes in their life. Failure by any of the parties to take into consideration this notice period might well be an indication that some form of legal action needs to be taken (DOH 1991(3), Vol. 3, para. 2.66, and see section on **Provision of accommodation** in Chapter 3).

Written agreements

The use of written agreements is an effective way of ensuring that plans are specific, cover all the necessary points, and involve children, families and carers properly. Families welcome the use of written agreements because the openness that they require is preferable to their having to rely on the goodwill of professionals or their relationship with the social worker. If necessary, agreements can and should be recorded in ways other than, or in addition to, writing. For example, by using a videotape, audio cassette, braille or computer disk.

Whilst there is nothing in the Act itself about written agreements, regulations require them to be made with:

- people with parental responsibility (if none, the person caring for the child), when a child goes into accommodation (reg. 3(4), Arrangements for Placement of Children (General) Regulations);

- children of 16 and 17 going into accommodation, even where their parents object to this (reg. 3(3), Arrangements for Placement of Children (General) Regulations);
- foster carers, when a child is placed with them (reg. 5(6), schedule 3, Foster Placement (Children) Regulations);
- parents or people with parental responsibility when a child in care is placed back home with them (reg. 7, schedule 2, Placement of Children with Parents Regulations).

Guidance recommends that written agreements should also be used:

- with parents or people with parental responsibility where a child is receiving long-term services from the local authority (DOH 1991(3), Vol. 2, para. 2.10);
- with parents, and the child where old enough, when children are subject to child protection procedures (DOH 1991(2), para. 6.8; see also pages 72–3), and
- with parents or people with parental responsibility, and the child where old enough, when a child is in care: 'Although the regulations do not require a local authority to reach agreement on the planned arrangements for a child in their care, it is the intention so far as is practicable, and in the child's best interests that arrangements should be made in partnership with parents.' (DOH 1991(3), Vol. 3, para. 2.67).

When a child is in accommodation, or when a written agreement is used in relation to a child in care, it would be sensible to negotiate the agreement with all involved – parents or people with parental responsibility, and the foster carers or residential workers – rather than making one agreement with the family and another with the carers.

Where children have been provided with respite accommodation on a regular basis (see pages 52 and 55) these placements may be covered by just one plan and one written agreement, provided that the placements take place within one year, that no single placement is for more than four weeks, and that the total duration of the placements is not more than 90 days (reg. 13). A new plan and new agreement would have to be made each subsequent year. If the placements last longer than four weeks, or total more than 90 days, new plans and agreements have to be made, either for each placement or for each set of placements.

In those cases where a written agreement is required by regulations, there is no extra requirement that the parents sign it, and so the placement can go ahead without their signatures (DOH 1991(3), Vol. 3, para. 2.64). However, good practice would suggest that, whether or not a written agreement is required by regulations, it will be negotiated in such a way that all parties will usually be willing to sign it.

Practitioners tend to speak positively about written agreements and say they use them, but research evidence suggests that, in the past, they were used irregularly and often only with those clients that the agency wanted to control. 'Agreements' often amounted to stipulations that family members were required to agree to, rather than being the result of genuine negotiation. The regulations and accompanying guidance (DOH 1991(3), Vol. 3, paras. 2.63–2.67) encourage the development of a practice of open negotiation and partnership in the drawing up of agreements. Model agreement forms for a variety of different situations have been produced jointly by the Family Rights Group and the National Foster Care Association. Practitioners may find it helpful to follow the forms, one of which is included as *Annex A*, page 211 (FRG & NFCA 1991; FRG 1989(1)).

Using properly negotiated written agreements is one important way of putting partnership theory into practice. They may take more than one meeting to complete, and care should be taken not to let the process drag on too long. Equally, not everything needs to be tackled in one agreement, and particularly complex situations may well require a series of agreements. Breaking up objectives in this way, rather than trying to work on everything at once, is more likely to lead to overall success. If tasks are not completed, or goals not met, it may be that the tasks or goals were not the right ones and need renegotiating. This should not be seen as failure by the participants to the agreement.

In some situations, particularly child protection cases where children have had to be removed, the agreement may need to contain some stipulations. In those circumstances practitioners should be clear and honest about the implications if families do not comply with what is stipulated. The sanctions for failure must be set out clearly. It is worth noting here that people need to be rewarded, perhaps only by praise, when aims or objectives *are* achieved.

When copies of plans or written agreements are sent to family members, care should be taken to ensure that people also receive a translated copy if English is their second language. The fact that some people have poor literacy skills should not prevent practitioners from involving them in the process of devising a written agreement and, obviously, they should always receive copies of plans and agreements, as they will usually have someone to help them understand the documents. Where the negotiations have been considered with adults or children with a sensory impairment, consideration will need to be given to giving them the plan and agreement in braille or large print, or on a video, audio tape or computer disk.

In order to assist the process of negotiation, family members and young people may benefit from having supporters with them. Where English is a person's second language, interpreters should also be offered, even where people appear to be fluent in English. It is important that interpreters are provided if children or adults request that.

Even where a case arises as an emergency, practitioners should not be deterred from engaging in written agreements. Regulations and guidance make it clear that planning should occur in these circumstances, and much can be achieved once the immediate crisis has been responded to. Setting objectives is always important, even if the objectives can be short-term only.

Agency policies need to reflect the importance of practitioners having sufficient time at an early stage to make proper plans and agreements. Taking the time needed then to do this work well is likely to save time and misunderstandings later on. A positive approach is essential, too. Agencies and workers who see written agreements as primarily a tool for court evidence will severely limit their usefulness and their potential for working in partnership with families.

Reviews

An integral part of planning is reviewing and monitoring the plan and making changes where necessary. The Act provides for regulations to be made requiring each child's case to be reviewed (s.26(1), and the Review of Children's Cases Regulations 1991).

Timescales

The regulations apply to voluntary organisations and registered children's homes as well as local authorities. Children's cases must be reviewed within four weeks of the child first becoming looked after or placed with the agency. The second review must be carried out within three months of the first, and the third and each subsequent review must be held within six months of the previous one (reg. 3).

In some circumstances, for example respite accommodation arrangements, a series of short placements can be treated as one. Regulations allow this provided that:

- the placements are at the same place;
- all occur within the period of one year;
- no single placement lasts for longer than four weeks; and
- the total placement does not exceed 90 days (reg. 11).

The prescribed time-limits are minimum requirements and, in the initial period of a child being looked after or placed, it may be necessary to hold reviews more frequently. The timescales reflect the principle contained in the Act that delay is prejudicial to children. They also reflect research findings about the importance of the first few weeks spent in accommodation or care, and of the lack of planning at that critical stage:

'(1) Far less attention is given to what is to happen after admission than to whether or not to admit and if children stay long in care social work attention fades . . .

"This study has highlighted with considerable precision a situation that has long been known – that unless a child leaves care quickly, that is within six weeks – he or she has a very strong chance of being in care in two years time. Yet, the administrative arrangements within social services and social work practice often do not reflect this acutely short timescale. We find a time perspective entertained by social workers which is greatly at variance with the urgency experienced by the child and family or which, as this study demonstrates, is in their best interests." (Dartington)

"Once a child has come into care and the earlier pressure from other agencies and individuals to admit no longer applies, there is a consequent relaxation in the priority accorded to the case by the social worker as attention shifts to more pressing cases . . .

With a few notable exceptions, there is little evidence to suggest that planning becomes any more prominent an activity as time progresses." (National Children's Bureau)'

(DHSS 1985(2), p.9)

The timescales also mean that, where care and supervision proceedings are underway and an interim care order is made, the first, and possibly second, review will be held while those proceedings are continuing. This should encourage all those involved in the proceedings to continue to do some work together, rather than simply concentrating on preparing their case.

Review procedures

The definition of a review given in the guidance is wider than simply a meeting to review the case:

'The concept of review . . . is a continuous process of planning and reconsideration of the plan for the child. Review will include a number of components leading to meetings held to discuss the plan which has been drawn up for a child who is being looked after or accommodated by a responsible authority. This will require consultation and the gathering of information on an ongoing basis, discussing that information and making decisions to amend the plans as necessary.' (DOH 1991(3), Vol. 3, para. 8.3)

The regulations require, somewhat obliquely, that meetings of 'relevant personnel' of the agency and 'other relevant persons' be held where practicable (reg. 4, schedule 1).

Agencies are given a certain amount of discretion to devise their own review procedure but, having devised this, they must set out the procedure in writing and give details of it to children, parents, people with parental responsibility and relevant others (reg. 4). Guidance advises agencies that their review system should provide for:

'• the full participation of both children and parents in the decision-making process;
• a structured, co-ordinated approach to the planning of child care work in individual cases; and
• a monitoring system for checking the operation of the review process.'

(DOH 1991(3), Vol. 3, para. 8.8)

Before the review takes place the local authority must consult with the children concerned, their parents (including a non-married father without parental responsibility), other people with parental responsibility, and any relevant others – these may be relatives, friends, or other professionals (ss.22, 61, 64 and reg. 7). Parents and children should, where practicable, attend all or part of the review meeting (reg. 7(2)). Guidance makes it clear that there should be a presumption in favour of attendance throughout the meeting:

'Only in exceptional cases should a parent or child not be invited to a review meeting.' (DOH 1991(3), Vol. 3, para. 8.10)

and

'the attendance of the child and his parents at meetings to review the child's case will be the norm rather than the exception (subject to the reservations already expressed). It is expected that the parents and the child (if he is of sufficient understanding) will be present at the whole of the review, but this will depend on the circumstances of each individual case.' (DOH 1991(3), Vol. 3, para. 8.15)

and

'. . . the fears or inhibitions of professionals should not be the reason for excluding a child or his parent from a review.' (DOH 1991(3), Vol. 3, para. 8.16)

If it is decided that a parent or child, or both, should be excluded from all or part of the review they should be given a written explanation of why they have been excluded, and a copy of that must go on the child's record (DOH 1991(3), Vol. 3, para. 8.16).

Carers should also be invited to the review, and so should other people who have something to contribute to the discussions. These could be relatives or close family friends, or other professionals, such as the GP, health visitor, teacher or independent visitor. In relation to these others, their possible attendance should be discussed with the child concerned. It may be that their contributions will be given in writing instead (DOH 1991(3), Vol. 3, para. 8.17).

Guidance stresses the importance of choosing a venue for the review which is 'conducive to the relaxed participation of those attending', and recommends that the venue be discussed with the child concerned. It will also be helpful to seek the views of parents and carers. Parents may need help with the cost of travel, child care and other items (DOH 1991(3), Vol. 3, para. 8.18). If parents or carers have to take unpaid time off work, consideration should be given to reimbursing them. The money could be authorised under paragraph 16 of schedule 2, or under section 17(6).

As with initial planning and written agreement meetings, it will be important to check with children and family members to see if they wish to bring a supporter or representative with them. They may feel the need for this more at the start of their contact with the agency, or where there is a strong divergence of views over what should happen next, but it should be considered at each stage. Opportunities should be provided for children and family members to make a contribution in writing or by using a tape or video if they do not wish to attend the meeting, or have difficulty communicating their views. Interpreters should be available for those for whom English is a second language, and interpreters or other aids should be available for those with a sensory impairment.

'Parents should be expected and enabled to retain their responsibilities and to remain as closely involved as is consistent with their child's welfare, even if that child cannot live at home either temporarily or permanently . . . Parents should participate in decisions about their child and it should be exceptional for them not to be invited to reviews and case conferences. If they are not invited, the reasons for this should be explicit, justified and recorded. However, it must be recognised that attendance at such meetings can be daunting for parents, particularly if they will be the only black people present, if English is not their first language, or if they suffer from any form of disability. The presence of a friend, interpreter or advocate can provide useful support and facilitate communication.' (DOH 1989(1), p.9)

Schedule 2 to the regulations sets out the matters to be considered in a review, and the following extract from the guidance links these with other aspects of the legislation that require consideration. These are:

'• where the child is in the care of a local authority, whether or not the care order can be discharged or varied to a lesser order;
• whether the placement continues to be appropriate;

- the views of the child's carer;
- whether the plan makes necessary provision for the child's religious persuasion, racial origin and cultural and linguistic background;
- where a child is looked after, whether the plan takes account of the duty under Section 23(6) to enable the child to live with a parent, other person with parental responsibility, relative, friend; and where the child is in care, a person in whose favour a residence order was in force immediately before the care order was made, or other person with a legitimate interest in the child;
- the arrangements made for contact and where the child is looked after by a local authority with regard to the duty on the local authority in paragraph 15 of Schedule 2 to the Act to promote and maintain contact between the child and his family;
- where a child is looked after, the views of an independent visitor if one has been appointed, and if not whether to appoint one;
- whether the plan takes account of any particular needs the child may have, e.g. if the child has a disability;
- the arrangements made for the child's health (including consent to examination or treatment);
- the arrangements made for the child's education;
- the arrangements, if any, for financial support of the placement;
- where the child is provided with accommodation by voluntary agreement, whether or not the arrangements for the involvement of the parents in the child's life are appropriate; whether the social worker needs to encourage greater exercise of the parent's continuing responsibility to the child; whether or not there is still a need for accommodation or whether another sort of service would be more appropriate, or whether there is a need (for a local authority) to take care proceedings;
- reunification of the child with his parents and family;
- where a child has been in an agreed placement (not in care) for some time, whether the existing plan ensures that the child and the carer have an adequate sense of stability; whether the carer should seek a residence order, for example; and
- where appropriate, arrangements for after care.'

(DOH 1991(3), Vol. 3, para. 8.20)

Guidance stresses the importance of the review being chaired by a senior officer who can bring objectivity to the exercise. By referring to the fact that the field worker's supervisor will be in attendance, it suggests that supervisors should not chair meetings (DOH 1991(3), Vol. 3, para. 8.13). Minutes of the meeting should be kept on the child's file, with written reports attached, dissenting opinions recorded, and reasons given for decisions. The minutes should also note whether the child and parents were invited and attended, and if not, why not (DOH 1991(3), Vol. 3, para. 8.21). It will be helpful if all those who attend the meeting have the opportunity to check the minutes before they are placed on the file.

Children, parents, people with parental responsibility and relevant others should receive written information about the decisions of reviews (reg. 7(3)). Guidance refers to this being a summary of the main points from the minutes (DOH 1991(3), Vol. 3, para. 8.23). While this may be appropriate for relevant others, there would seem to be no reason why children, parents and carers should not be given the full minutes of the review meeting.

Agencies must monitor their review procedures for the purposes of quality assurance (reg. 9).

Complaints and representations

'The Children Act envisages a high degree of co-operation between parents and authorities in negotiating and agreeing what form of action will best meet a child's needs and promote his welfare. It also calls for the informal participation of the child and his parents in decision making about services for the child. Sometimes the required co-operation will not be achieved or will break down or delays will occur. The Act requires that responsible authorities establish a procedure which provides an accessible and effective means of representation or complaint where problems cannot be otherwise resolved.' (DOH 1991(3), Vol. 3, para. 10.3)

The guidance makes it clear that enabling children and families to challenge decisions made, or to complain about actions or inaction, is an essential element of partnership practice. The Act requires all local authorities to have a complaints and representations procedure, and the regulations extend this requirement to voluntary organisations and registered children's homes (ss.24(14) and 26(3), and reg. 1(2), Representations Procedure (Children) Regulations 1991).

The procedure should be available for use by children who are in need, looked after, provided with care by a voluntary organisation or registered children's home, or receiving or entitled to receive after-care services; by their parents; by their carers, and by anyone else who can show a reasonable interest in their welfare. The fact that children in need and their parents, as well as children looked after, can use the procedure means that increased participation in decisions about service delivery is extended to consumers of services generally. Guidance makes it clear that a decision that a child is not in need – which may involve denial of services – is also something that can be complained about (DOH 1991(3), Vol. 3, para. 10.8).

Guidance suggests that it would be sensible for local authorities to widen the range of people able to use the procedure. Examples given are foster carers who want to complain about their own dealings with the authority rather than issues connected with a particular child, and groups of children who want to complain about an issue that affects them all. Guidance also recommends using the procedure, or a linked procedure, for dealing with complaints about child protection issues (DOH 1991(3), Vol. 3, paras. 10.9–10.10).

As well as issuing guidance on complaints procedures under the guidance for the Children Act, the Government has also issued practice guidance on *how* to implement good practice which is applicable to both the Children Act and Community Care legislation (DOH & SSI 1991(4)).

The procedure

Complaints can be made in writing or orally. A complaint should be acknowledged in writing and details of the procedure sent to the complainant, together with an offer of help on how to use the procedure, or advice about where to go for such help. Where the complaint is oral, the complainant should also be sent a copy of a written version of what they have said, and an invitation to correct it if it is not accurate (reg. 4, DOH 1991(3), Vol. 3, paras. 10.37–10.38).

The written information sent to complainants should be clear and easy to understand. Local authorities will need to decide whether they will provide their own staff to help complainants through the procedure, or whether people will be referred to outside advisers. If outside advisers are chosen, workers will need to be told who they are.

If the person making the complaint comes into the category of 'any relevant person' (s.26(3)(e), and reg. 11), the agency has to decide whether they have 'a sufficient interest in the child's welfare'. Such a person might be a relative or family friend. Guidance encourages local authorities to have a flexible approach to such decisions so that people are not overlooked (DOH 1991(3), Vol. 3, para. 10.7). Agencies should consult with parents, children and carers before deciding whether or not to allow this sort of complaint to proceed. Their decision should be sent to the complainant in writing, together with the usual information (see above) if the complaint is to be dealt with (reg. 4(4), and DOH 1991(3), Vol, 3, paras. 10.39–10.40).

On receiving a complaint the agency must appoint an independent person to consider the complaint with them, and together they must respond within 28 days and send their written response to the complainant and any other relevant person (regs. 5 and 6). The independent person's considerations should be based on discussions with the agency and interviews with the child, parents, relevant professionals and other relevant people. They should also be allowed access to relevant parts of the case records (DOH 1991(3), Vol. 3, para. 10.41).

When the complainant receives the agency's response to the complaint they should be informed that, if they are still not satisfied, they can ask for the matter to be considered by a panel of three people, one of whom must be independent of the agency. This could be the same independent person as at the first stage of the procedure, or a different one. It would seem preferable to have a different person at the second stage, regardless of whether the independent person at the first stage has supported the agency's position (reg. 8(1)).

The complainant has 28 days to ask for the panel to deal with the case, and that request must be in writing. The panel must be held within 28 days of receiving the written request. Both the complainant and the agency can make written submissions before the panel meeting, and oral submissions during the meeting. So can the first independent person if they are not sitting on the panel. The complainant can bring a representative or supporter to the meeting to speak on their behalf, and should be informed of this entitlement in good time to organise that if they wish to. Guidance recommends that the meeting is conducted in as informal an atmosphere as possible. In addition, agencies are reminded to consider whether they need to arrange interpreters or provide special assistance in terms of both access and communication for people with disabilities (reg. 8(2)–(6), and DOH 1991(3), Vol. 3, paras. 10.43–10.46).

Within 24 hours of meeting, the panel must make recommendations to the agency, and give a copy of those recommendations to the complainant, to the first-stage independent person, and to anyone else who is relevant (reg. 9(1) and (2)). The agency must then decide what action, if any, should be taken in the light of the recommendations. The independent person will be involved in discussions with the agency about this. Within 28 days of the panel making its recommendations the agency must give its final decision with clear explanations (s.26(7), reg. 9(3), DOH 1991(3), Vol. 3, paras. 10.47–10.49).

It would be possible, theoretically, for a local authority to ignore the panel's recommendations, but such a response could well open the way to an application for judicial review of their decision (see page 173).

Publicity, consultation and monitoring

Local authorities are required to publicise their complaints procedure and, as with publicity about services (see Chapter 3), guidance makes it clear this information should be distributed widely to libraries, Citizens Advice Bureaux, health clinics and GP surgeries, and that it be available in different languages and accessible to people with a sensory disability (DOH 1991(3), Vol. 3, paras. 10.15–10.16). In addition, agencies need to prepare a booklet explaining their procedure, to be sent to complainants and also to be part of an information pack given to each child and their parents at the first review of the child's case. The booklet should be part of the information pack given to foster carers when they are first approved:

'The publicity should be framed in terms that make clear that the procedure is a part of the local authority's commitment to partnership and the informed participation of child and parents in the authority's decision making about provision of services to safeguard and promote the welfare of a child in need.' (DOH 1991(3), Vol. 3, para. 10.15)

Guidance recommends that agencies should not simply ensure that the procedure is publicised. They should involve staff, service users and the local community in consultation over how the procedure should be set up in the first place, 'so that the procedure reflects the needs of those who may need to use it'. It specifically points out that: 'adherence to the principles of the Race Relations Act 1976 and other equal opportunities legislation requires consultation with community groups reflecting the racial and cultural diversity of the local community' (DOH 1991(3), Vol. 3, para. 10.4).

Agencies are also required to monitor their complaints procedures by keeping details of each complaint and how it was dealt with, including whether or not the time-limits were kept to. In local authorities, annual reports on the operation of the procedure should be presented to the social services committee. Guidance recommends that the community groups and service users who were involved (hopefully) in the initial consultation should continue to be involved in the monitoring procedure, and be invited to comment on the effectiveness of the procedure itself (reg. 10, DOH 1991(3), Vol. 3, paras. 10.52–10.56).

Consultation with service users, community groups, voluntary organisations and other professionals is likely to be particularly helpful on the following matters:

(1) Who should be available to advise complainants about the procedure and help them through it, including representing them at the panel meeting?

If people are to make effective use of the agency's complaints and representations procedure it is important that they have easy access to independent and informed advice and representation. Consumers of services will find it difficult to rely on someone employed by the agency, although this might be less of a problem if the adviser were employed specifically to fulfil this sole function. If outside advisers are to be used, links need to be made by the local authority with existing local advice agencies, solicitors on the Children Panel and other local and national groups.

People should, of course, be free to choose for themselves where they go for advice and help, but having a pool of people suggested by the community will be helpful for many service users. It should mean that they have some choice about who to approach, and that advisers reflect the racial and cultural diversity within the community and include people with disabilities.

It will be particularly important for staff dealing with complaints to know who to suggest as a source of possible advice and help. In addition, agencies will need to think about how they might help complainants meet some or all of the possible costs incurred in seeking advice or representation (DOH 1991(3), Vol. 3, paras. 10.28–10.30).

(2) Who should be independent people, and should they be different at each stage of the procedure?

Queries have been raised about whether an internal complaints procedure can ensure accountability, so the inclusion of an independent element in the complaints procedure is very important. Independent people must not be a member or officer of the local authority; or an officer of the relevant voluntary organisation; or a person engaged in furthering the objects of that voluntary organisation; or a person involved in the management or operation of a relevant children's home or financially interested in the operation of that home (regs. 2(1) and 11). Guidance suggests that an independent person should not be a spouse or partner of a person listed above either.

If the independent element is to inspire confidence that complaints will be treated fairly, agencies should ensure that people chosen to be independent persons at either the first or second stage of the procedure are truly independent of the agency, reflect the racial and cultural diversity within a community, and include people from a wide range of age and ability.

Agencies can, perhaps, learn from the different types of independent people appointed to adoption panels. Some authorities worked hard to ensure that such appointees were of existing or future service users, representing both original and adoptive families, and ensuring that black and other minority ethnic groups were represented. In contrast, other authorities chose their 'independent' people from professional workers, and sometimes those with whom the authority had close links. The attitude conveyed here seemed to be more about paying lip service to the notion of independence than operating in the spirit of the legislation.

Local authorities should have a pool of independent people that is large enough for them to 'identify independent persons with particular skills or knowledge that may be required in a particular case'. Independent people should be given a letter of appointment that gives details of the procedure and their role. Agencies are encouraged to consider what training and legal advice they will offer to independent people (DOH 1991(3), Vol. 3, paras. 10.33–10.35).

(3)   What languages are needed for written information produced locally?

Consultation with the community and community groups will help indicate the answer to this question, and it might also suggest who would be able to do translation work or act as interpreters and/or supporters. Consultation might also produce ideas about the sort of aids to communication needed for people with disabilities and how those could be made available when needed.

If the complaints procedure is to be effective, it is important that *all* staff understand and accept the procedure and the need for it. Good consumer care begins with good staff care. Some staff members will feel threatened by having to deal with complaints, and they will need to be reassured that most complaints are about the organisation rather than an individual, no matter how they are expressed initially, and that it is part of their job to deal with complaints respectfully and constructively. They will not be able to do this unless they themselves feel supported.

Corporate attitudes, too, need to change to enable individual workers to be less defensive in their practice. Workers often have difficulties in reconciling the intellectual view that a client is a person with rights with the knowledge that the exercise of those rights may well result in disagreement and complaint.

During the last few years the need for *effective* complaints procedures has been acknowledged increasingly by many voluntary organisations, by the local authority associations, by the Association of Directors of Social Services, British Association of Social Workers (BASW), National Association of Local Government Officers (NALGO) and others. However, practice remains rudimentary and uncertain. The establishment of clear and relatively uniform procedures in all local authorities in England and Wales is long overdue.

Surveys prior to the implementation of the Act (NCC 1988, and Sheffield University 1987) showed that most local authorities did not have a formal complaints procedure and, although over 60 per cent of social services departments were said to have one, they generally did not cover all the department's services, and were not publicised. These findings are similar to the information the Family Rights Group collected in relation to the establishment of procedures to deal with complaints about access, as required by the Code of Practice on Access published in 1983. The group found only eight authorities who had complied fully with the code, while eleven had no procedure at all. Almost five years after the code was introduced most other authorities had procedures which did not comply with the guidance and they failed to give adequate or any information about the procedures to family or staff members (FRG 1989(2)).

It is to be hoped that the requirements in the Act and accompanying regulations and guidance are complied with positively and enthusiastically. The introduction of complaints procedures should be welcomed as another contribution to the attempts to create a more equal balance of power between personal social service-giving agencies and their consumers. Complaints procedures should also be used by agencies as a method of monitoring the delivery of services under the Act.

Other means of complaint

The complaints procedure provided by the Act will not be appropriate for some issues, and in other cases people will remain dissatisfied with an agency's response to their complaint. There are, of course, other possible avenues to explore.

Reference to the Secretary of State   Under section 84 of the Act a local authority which has failed, without reasonable excuse, to comply with one or more of its duties under the Act can be declared to be in default by the Secretary of State. If such a declaration is made, the Secretary of State can also give directions to the local authority to ensure that the duty is complied with in future. These directions can be enforced by a court order called 'mandamus'.

There is no formal procedure for referring cases to the Secretary of State. It is not yet clear what would be a 'reasonable excuse' for failing to comply with a duty and, in particular, whether lack of resources would be classed as unreasonable. It is unlikely that this procedure will be much use to challenge a failure by a local authority to provide services to an individual child or family, because most duties owed by the local authority are phrased fairly vaguely or hedged around with phrases like 'as appropriate' or 'as they consider appropriate'. It could, however, be used if a local authority failed to provide *any* day care for under-fives, or a very limited amount in relation to the number of children in need, or where it failed to publicise services or provide a complaints procedure. In other words, it might provide a useful remedy for general rather than particular issues: 'It may be necessary to use it . . . for example, where a local authority fails to make the requisite provision for a class of children' (*Hansard*, June 1989, col. 492).

The Commissioner for Local Administration   The basis for making a complaint to the Commissioner is that the complainant has suffered injustice caused by maladministration. Examples of maladministration include failure to follow an authority's agreed policies, rules or procedures; failure to have proper procedures; failure to tell people of their rights;

failure to provide advice or information when reasonably requested; or the provision of inaccurate or misleading advice.

The Commissioner will want to see evidence that the complainant has given the authority an opportunity to deal with the complaint by, for instance, pursuing the matter first through their local councillor (see below). If the matter is still not resolved, the complainant could then write to the Local Commissioner. The Commission's office issues information leaflets that contain a complaints form, and people should be advised to fill in the forms or to write a letter covering the points raised in the form.

The Local Commissioner will first check that the complaint is a matter that they are able to investigate and, if so, they will then send a copy of the complaint to the authority and ask for their comments. The Local Commissioner could not investigate something that could be resolved by court proceedings, or something that happened more than a year before they were asked to investigate it. On this last point, the Commissioner does have discretion to investigate if they think it reasonable, for example, the complainant did not know of the maladministration when it occurred but only discovered it later.

Sometimes the matter can be dealt with quickly by letter in this way, while other complaints require more detailed investigation by the Local Commissioner, including interviews with all the relevant people. When the investigation is completed, the Commissioner prepares a formal report which is available publicly. The names in the report are changed so people involved are not identifiable.

If the Local Commissioner finds that the complainant has been caused injustice as a result of maladministration, the authority will be required to tell the Local Commissioner what they intend to do as a result of the findings. Sometimes this will involve reconsidering the decision or action taken. At other times it will be impossible to change the situation, but the authority might offer the complainant a written apology and/or financial compensation. The Commission is not able to substitute its decision for the decision of the authority.

The fact that a person has taken a matter through the agency's complaints procedure does not prevent them from complaining subsequently to the Local Commissioner (DOH 1991(3), Vol. 3, para. 10.22).

Examples of cases where successful complaints have been made in child care cases are where a local authority has not set up a complaints procedure as it should have done in accordance with Government guidance (Complaint 88/H/1026, 4 September 1989); failed to inform people of their legal rights, or misled people as to their legal rights (Complaint 89/ C/2315, 11 September 1991), or where reduced fostering payments were made to the grandmother of a Down's syndrome child on the basis that she was a relative, despite the fact the child was being looked after by the local authority and was placed with her as a fostering placement (Complaint 88/C/1115, 11 December 1989).

Elected councillors   The existence of a complaints procedure does not prevent individuals or groups taking up an issue direct with their local councillor. As the guidance points out, officers and members will need to have clear guidelines about how complaints received by elected members can, if necessary, be transferred over into the complaints procedure.

Judicial review   This is a legal process dealt with by the High Court. The court can scrutinise a local authority's decision, action or failure to act. It can quash the decision that has been made (certiorari); it can order it to stop the action it is taking (prohibition); or to act or make a decision where it has wrongfully failed to do so (mandamus), but it cannot substitute its own decision for that of the authority. The other orders that the court can make are injunctions and a declaration that an action is unlawful.

The basis on which the court can make one of these orders is if it is satisfied that:

- The authority has acted outside of its legal powers.
- An error of law has been made which affects the outcome of the case.
- The authority has acted unfairly. This is referred to as 'acting against natural justice'. There are two elements to this, a duty to give unbiased decisions, and an obligation to allow all those directly affected by a decision to put their case.
- The authority has exercised its discretion unreasonably. Case law (*Associated Provincial Picture Houses Ltd* v. *Wednesbury Corporation* [1947] 2 All ER 680) has established that this means that it has failed to take into account factors which it should have considered, or has taken into account matters which are irrelevant, or has acted in a way that no objectively reasonable authority would have acted.

The court proceedings must be brought by someone who has a sufficient interest in the action, and the courts interpret this quite widely. Children, family members and foster carers affected by a particular decision would certainly be able to bring a case. Someone not themselves directly affected might still be able to bring a case, if they got the consent of the Attorney General. A local councillor used this process to challenge, successfully, her own council's policy of not providing help under section 1 of the Child Care Act 1980 (similar to s.17(6)) to families declared intentionally homeless by the housing department (*Attorney General (ex rel. Tilley)* v. *Wandsworth LBC* [1981] 1 All ER 1162). Legal Aid can be applied for, and may be granted, subject to a means and merits test.

It has been suggested that, as wardship is no longer available as a legal remedy where local authorities are concerned, judicial review will increasingly be used as a means of challenging local authority decisions. There are now a number of reported cases of judicial review relating to child care issues. These have made it clear that local authorities should not fetter their discretion by devising policies which prevent them from addressing particular circumstances in individual cases (*Attorney General (ex rel. Tilley*) v. *Wandsworth LBC* [1981] 1 All ER 1162); that they should always give people an opportunity to have their say, or answer allegations against them (*R* v. *Bedfordshire CC ex p. C; R* v. *Herts CC ex p. B* [1987] 1 FLR 239, and *R* v. *Hereford and Worcester CC ex p. D* [1992] FLR 448), and that they should take into account the wishes and feelings of children when deciding to close a children's home (*Liddle* v. *Sunderland BC* [1983] 13 Fam. Law 250; *R* v. *Solihull MBC ex p. C* [1984] FLR 365; *R* v. *Avon CC ex p. Katoula Koumis*, Legal Action, December 1984). Other cases have also made it clear that the processes and decisions of the Area Child Protection Committees can be judicially reviewed (*R* v. *Lewisham LBC ex p. P* [1991] 2 FLR 185; *R* v. *East Sussex CC ex p. R* [1991] 2 FLR 358; *R* v. *Devon CC ex p. L* [1991] 2 FLR 541).

The major problem with judicial review as a method of challenging local authorities is that the court is only looking at the *way* in which the decision has been made, and not at whether the decision *itself* is right or wrong. Thus, although a local authority may be required to take a decision again, or change a policy which fetters its discretion, that will not necessarily mean a different outcome for the families involved.

Court proceedings In some cases the dispute may ultimately be resolved only by an application to court under the Act, for example for a contact or residence order, or for the discharge of a care or supervision order.

9 Placement

Introduction

This chapter looks at the general principles that apply to placements; the different sorts of placement that are available for looked-after children, and the specific duties and powers that apply to the different types of placement. It also looks in some detail at the duties in relation to returning children to parents, relatives or friends (the most common outcome for children), and gives suggestions on good practice in such work. Finally it sets out the provisions relating to preparing young looked-after people for independent living, and the duties and powers in relation to after-care.

General issues

The options for the placement of children under the Children Act 1989 are as wide as they were under previous legislation. Children looked after by a local authority can be placed with relatives or friends, with foster carers, in a residential setting, in an independent living arrangement, or back at home (s.23).

Wherever a child is placed, there are certain specific requirements that a local authority must have regard to when making the placement. So far as is practicable, and providing it is consistent with their welfare, children should be placed near their homes and with their brothers and sisters (s.23(7)). For children with disabilities, and again so far as is practicable, the accommodation should not be unsuitable for their particular needs (s.23(8)).

In addition, of course, agencies must comply with their legal duties to consult with the children, their parents and other family members before making any decision on a placement, and to take into consideration the child's religion, race, culture and language:

> 'A child's need for continuity in life and care should be a constant factor in choice of placement. In most cases, this suggests a need for placement with a family of the same race, religion and culture in a neighbourhood within reach of family, school or day nursery, church, friends and leisure activities. Continuity also requires placement in a foster home which a child can find familiar and sympathetic and not remote from his own experience in social background, attitudes and expectations; a foster home in which he is most likely to be able to settle down and as far as possible feel "at home" and free from anxieties. This is equally if not more necessary where it is not possible to place a child near home or where there are special reasons for choosing a placement at a distance.' (DOH 1991(3), Vol. 3, para. 4.4)

Although the comments above are directed specifically at placements with relatives, friends or non-related foster carers, the points about continuity for children and about race, culture, language and religion are equally relevant to children placed in a children's home. Aiming for the best possible placement for children is important, even if, in reality, many placements – at least initially – might be a question of finding where there is a bed available. What should happen less frequently than in the past is to allow placements to continue which do not meet the legal requirements or the above guidance. That is to be welcomed, because such placements are not likely to be in the interests of the children concerned.

The legal requirement to place children near home and to keep sibling groups together links with the duty placed on local authorities to promote contact between children and their families (para. 15, schedule 2), the duty to reunite children with parents, relatives or friends (s.23(6)), and the duty to promote the upbringing of children by their families (s.17(1)). These legal requirements are all based on clear research evidence of the importance to children of maintaining links with family, friends and communities. In addition, there is growing evidence of the importance to children of being placed with their brothers and sisters when sibling groups come into care or accommodation together, as is frequently the case. Children in residential placements have been found to value being placed together with siblings, and to see their siblings 'as a source of support and protection'. If they were separated, 'a significant number struggled with feelings of loss, frustration and bewilderment, sometimes years after the separation took place' (Whitaker et al. 1985). In foster placements, children also value being placed together, referring to the benefit of having someone to talk to about their own family (Rowe et al. 1984). Berridge and Cleaver (1987) found a higher rate of disrupted placements when children were separated: 'in long, short, and intermediate fosterings alike, the separation of siblings between placements was found to be strongly linked with an unsettled care experience' (p.178).

The pain caused by separating children has often been underestimated:

'Me and my two brothers, both younger than me, got put into care five years ago when mum died. Dad didn't give a damn, he never has. To start with we got put in a children's home but after a while they said we were going to be fostered and it meant me going to one family and the two of them going somewhere else. I cried for days and I haven't seen them for two years. My social worker said they've got to be given the chance to have a fresh start. I've got nobody now. We used to fight and that but we've been through a lot together and we understood each other. I'll find them when I'm 18, nobody will be able to stop me then.' (Berridge & Cleaver 1987, p.82)

Children will find it easier to maintain contact with their families, and to return to them (as 80 per cent of children do eventually) if the family they are placed with is similar to their own. These issues are important for all children, but they are particularly important for black children and children from other minority ethnic groups, who have for so long been placed with families totally dissimilar to their own. As a result, many of these children have experienced severe problems in relation to their identity and self-esteem. For some children this results in them denying their identity, trying to become white, or believing that they *are* white (Ahmed et al. 1986). Other children feel cut off from their communities and deeply resent the fact that 'living only with white adults, they are unable to learn, from the first hand, day-to-day experience of others, how to develop and maintain their self esteem, identity and self respect in a racist society' (Macdonald 1991).

These issues are recognised in the Government's publication on the principles underlying the Act:

'If black children and those from ethnic minorities are placed in settings where issues of race are not acknowledged, they will be deprived of opportunities to discuss painful and confusing experiences of overt or covert racism and can become very insecure about their identity and self worth. Those of mixed parentage face particular problems. They are generally perceived by others as black yet need to integrate both strands of their heritage. Those who are brought up by their white parent or in a white family placement can find themselves experiencing an extra dimension to the normal problems and conflicts of adolescence. And if they have not had strong links with their community of origin, they may end up rejected by both groups.

Since discrimination of all kinds is an everyday reality in many children's lives, every effort must be made to ensure that agency services and practices do not reflect or reinforce it. Attention should be given to ways of equipping young people to cope with and resist the discrimination they experience. Ethnic minority children should be helped to be proud of their racial and cultural heritage. Those of minority religions need opportunities to understand, value and practice their faith.' (DOH 1989(1), p.11)

The Act, by encouraging the recruitment of foster carers from black and other minority ethnic groups (para. 11, schedule 2), and by requiring local authorities to consider issues of race, religion, culture and language before making any decision in relation to a child, provides a framework within which to develop the good practice of ensuring that children are placed with adults of a similar ethnic background. Guidance reinforces this:

'It may be taken as a guiding principle of good practice that, other things being equal and in the great majority of cases, placement with a family of similar ethnic origin and religion is most likely to meet a child's needs as fully as possible and to safeguard his or her welfare most effectively. Such a family is most likely to be able to provide a child with continuity in life and care and an environment which the child will find familiar and sympathetic and in which opportunities will naturally arise to share fully in the culture and way of life of the ethnic group to which he belongs. Where the aim of a placement is to reunite the child with his or her own family, contact and work with the family will in most cases be more comfortable for all and carry a greater chance of success if the foster parents are of similar ethnic origin. Families of similar ethnic origin are also usually best placed to prepare children for life as members of an ethnic minority group in a multi-racial society, where they may meet with racial prejudice and discrimination, and to help them with their development towards independent living in adult life.' (DOH 1991(3), Vol. 3, para. 2.40)

Guidance acknowledges that these issues are equally important for children living in children's homes:

'those responsible for recruiting staff to children's homes should seek to ensure that the composition of the staff group reflects the racial, cultural and linguistic background of the children being cared for. It is important that black children should have positive experience of being cared for by black care givers.' (DOH 1991(3), Vol. 4, para. 1.36)

If children cannot be placed in a foster or residential home that reflects their ethnic origins, workers should ensure that action is taken to encourage and enable children to continue to speak their family's first language, to continue to practise their religion, and to maintain and develop their sense of identity. This is most easily achieved by promoting contact between the child and their family, friends and community. In those rare cases where such links cannot be maintained and developed, the appointment of an independent visitor of the same ethnic, cultural or religious background as the child may help the child maintain a sense of continuity and identity (see Chapter 7 on contact).

Placements for looked-after children

Relatives and friends

'If young people cannot remain at home, placement with relatives or friends should be explored before other forms of placement are considered.' (DOH 1989(1), p.8). The recognition in this legislation of the importance to children of their wider family and friends is highlighted in section 23. Relatives are mentioned specifically as a possible placement for children (s.23(2)(a)), and local authorities are placed under a duty to enable children, unless it is not consistent with their welfare, to return to live with their parents or with relatives, friends or other people connected with them (s.23(6)). When children are unable to live with their parents or people with parental responsibility for them, practitioners should always look first to the extended family and to the family network to see whether there is someone who can offer the child, either immediately or in the long term, a home.

Once again, the encouragement in legislation to make use of relatives and friends as a resource for children is based on research findings of the benefits to children of such placements: 'To our considerable surprise, our data showed that children fostered by relatives seemed to be doing better in virtually all respects than those fostered by others' (Rowe et al. 1984). The researchers' surprise stemmed from the prevailing view in social work that placements with relatives tended to be unsuccessful, particularly where there was conflict in the family. This research study revealed that conflict was being handled well by the adults involved. It also included statistical evidence on the dwindling use of placements with relatives. Other research (Berridge & Cleaver 1987) found a low breakdown rate for placements with relatives.

Both UK and US research (Rowe et al. 1989; Link 1989) has shown that relatives are more willing than others to take on large sibling groups, and that they often have to deal with older children with more complex problems than those looked after by non-related carers. Even so, they tend to be more successful in achieving the aims of the placement. Placements with relatives and friends are most likely to provide the local, familiar setting recommended in guidance.

Relatives and friends may not be in evidence immediately when a placement is being sought for a child, particularly in an emergency. Some parents may seem isolated from their families and others may not get on well with them, but that does not necessarily mean that relatives and friends are not there, or are not willing to offer a home for the child or children, either short- or long-term. The duties on agencies to consult with all relevant people, and the duty on the guardian *ad litem* in court proceedings to seek out people who may wish to be parties to proceedings, should be a clear encouragement to practitioners to seek out relatives and friends.

Using relatives or friends in these circumstances is important for all children, but particularly for black children or children from other minority ethnic groups, especially in places where there are no, or an insufficient number of, foster carers from the same ethnic background. Placements with relatives and friends in these circumstances will ensure not only continuity for the child, but the best prospect of their developing a positive sense of identity and self-image.

Research has shown (Link 1989, Rowe et al. 1984) that placements with relatives and friends tend to be less well supported by social workers in terms of visits, advice, financial help and managing contact. It is important that the increase in placements with relatives and friends that should stem from the Children Act does not result in those children and carers receiving an inadequate level of support. Again, this is vitally important for black families, where assumptions about the role of the extended family and of women in particular can result in severely inadequate levels of material and other support. It is worrying to note that already many local authorities are adopting a three-tier structure for the payment and support of foster carers. In such a structure, foster carers who are not friends or relatives get the local authority's full allowance, plus support and training, friends of children get a slightly lower allowance and no training, whilst relatives simply get the income support rate for a child, no training, and very little support.

The possibilities for the legal status of a child living with relatives or friends is varied:

- Children could live with relatives or friends under a voluntary arrangement between them and the parents.

  If this was to be a long-term arrangement, the relatives or friends might want to consider applying for a residence order. Where a child lives with friends for any period longer than 28 days, this then becomes a private fostering arrangement (s.66). The local authority has a duty to monitor such placements (s.67), and both the child's parents and the carer have duties to notify the local authority of the arrangement (schedule 8). There is no system, in such circumstances, for paying relatives or friends who are looking after children, although they can claim child benefit for each child. If the children were in need, the local authority could make payments under section 17(6) to promote the welfare of the children and to promote their upbringing by their family. These payments can be made in 'exceptional circumstances'. This does not mean that the payment cannot be paid over a period of time, and many local authorities do use this provision to give financial support to relatives and friends caring for children.

- Children living with relatives or friends could be there as a looked-after child, either in accommodation or in care.

In either case the relatives or friends would be acting as foster carers for the local authority, and would need to be assessed and approved as such. All the duties owed by agencies to foster carers would apply (see pages 199–203). Foster carers can be approved to look after one named child or group of siblings (reg. 3(5), Foster Placement (Children) Regulations 1991), and this is obviously an important consideration when assessing relatives and friends in these circumstances, as they will probably not wish to become foster carers to any other child the local authority is looking after (DOH 1991(3), Vol. 3, paras. 3.33, 3.34 and 3.37). Once approved, the relatives or friends would be paid the relevant foster care allowance for the children.

If children *in accommodation* live with relatives or friends, the written agreement will specify the nature of the arrangement. If the children are to remain there long-term, they could stay in accommodation or the carers could apply for a residence order. Alternatively, it would be possible for the arrangement to become a purely voluntary one between parents and carers. Compliance with the Arrangement for Placement Regulations, particularly in terms of written plans and written agreements, provides a clear indication to everyone of the stage at which the placement ceases to be one of accommodation under section 20.

If children *in care* are living with relatives or friends and that arrangement was intended to be long-term, or become so, the local authority would need to consider carefully whether the care order needed to continue. It would be open to the local authority, or the child or parents, to apply to discharge the care order. Alternatively, the relatives or friends could apply for a residence order. A residence order made in such circumstances would discharge the care order (ss.8, 39, and 91(1)).

- Children could be living with relatives or friends under a residence order.

In such circumstances the carers would have parental responsibility for the child for so long as the order lasted. The parent or parents would still retain their parental responsibility, but they could not act in a way that would undermine the existence of the residence order (ss.2(8), 12(2) and (3)). Local authorities are able to pay an allowance to someone with a residence order (para. 15, schedule 1). It is important, if placements with relatives are to be encouraged, that local authorities do not develop policies that restrict such allowances to non-related foster carers only.

Non-related foster carers

Where a placement cannot be found within the family or with friends, or where such a placement would be contrary to the child's welfare, children may be placed with foster carers. The running of a fostering service and the placement of individual children with a particular carer are regulated by guidance (DOH 1991(3), Vol. 3) and the Foster Placement (Children) Regulations 1991.

Children cannot be placed with a foster carer unless the carer has been approved by a local authority or voluntary organisation. Foster carers are approved individually. Guidance recommends that each partner in a couple should be approved, and that where two people are to share the care of the child, then both of them should be approved, too (DOH 1991(3), Vol. 3, para. 3.13). Single people, living on their own or with others, can also be approved.

The regulations set out the specific matters that an agency must take into consideration when assessing whether someone should be approved as a foster carer (reg. 3(4)(b) and schedule 1, and DOH 1991(3), Vol. 3, paras. 3.12–3.32). Matters to be covered in the assessment include personal details, such as the age, sex, marital status and health of the person concerned and other adults in the household; details of the accommodation and who lives there; details of the carer's occupation, and details of any criminal convictions of the carer and other adult members of the household. In relation to this last point, all the adults concerned must give their consent for police checks to be carried out.

The other issues to be covered in an assessment are less specific, and relate to such matters as what the family is like – including matters like their standard of living, their leisure activities, their attitudes to discipline, and how they relate to one another.

Specific attention is directed to the family's religion and ethnic origin, and to their capacity to look after children from different religions and different ethnic origins. In addition, the family's capacity to work in partnership with the families and friends of children they are looking after is assessed, as is their ability to deal with contact between those children and their family and friends.

In assessing black families and families from other minority ethnic groups – whether or not they are related to specific children – care will need to be taken that those carrying out the assessment do not apply specifically Eurocentric beliefs and attitudes, particularly when looking at such matters as attitudes to, and capacities for, child rearing, and family functioning as a whole.

The information collected from the assessment is put into a report, and the agency must then decide whether or not to approve the relevant person or people as foster carers. Increasingly, agencies make use of panels to help them make this decision, and sometimes use foster carers from another area as panel members (DOH 1991(3), Vol. 3, paras. 3.37–3.43).

Foster carers can be approved to act as foster carers generally; or to care for a particular age range or type of child, such as children with disabilities; or to care for just one named child or sibling group. Where a person – usually a relative or friend – seeks approval to foster one particular child or family group, that will obviously mean a rather different type of assessment, although covering the same areas, than if the person wishes to apply to foster any child (reg. 3(5), DOH 1991(3), Vol. 3, paras. 3.33–3.34 and 3.37, and see page 181).

When approved, a foster carer is given a notice of approval which should specify the precise type of fostering for which they have been approved. Similarly, a refusal should specify the reasons for it. Agencies should have a representations procedure to enable people to seek a reconsideration of the decision to refuse approval, or to complain generally about the approval system (reg. 3, and DOH 1991(3), Vol. 3, para. 3.42). The National Foster Care Association recommends that this should be part of the general complaints procedure under section 26. Some local authorities are doing this, some have set up a separate appeals procedure which does not involve an independent element.

At least once a year, agencies must review whether or not a particular foster carer should continue to be approved. The review must take into account the views of the foster carer. The detail of the review and the decision taken should be recorded, and copies given to the foster carer (reg. 4, and DOH 1991(3), Vol. 3, paras. 3.44–3.51).

A person can be approved as a foster carer by only one local authority or voluntary organisation, but other agencies can place children with that carer providing they get the consent of both the approving authority and any other agency that has children placed with that carer (reg. 3(3), and DOH 1991(3), Vol. 3, para. 3.2).

On approval, the foster carer and agency must enter into a written agreement called 'the foster care agreement'. This sets out some general issues in relation to fostering, including details of the support and training to be given to the foster carer, details of the procedure for reviewing approval, and an undertaking by the foster carer not to use corporal punishment on any child placed with them, and to abide by the terms of any placement agreement (reg. 3(6) and schedule 2, see below).

The foster placement agreement (reg. 5(5) and schedule 3, and DOH 1991(3), Vol. 3, paras. 4.11–4.15) is used for the placement of an individual child. It sets out all relevant details about the child's history, religion, race, culture, language, education and health. It also includes details of the plan for the child, the objectives of the placement, the role of the child's parents, and the arrangements for contact between the child and their family and friends. Where the child is in accommodation, and where written agreements are used with parents of children in care, there is no reason why the process of negotiating the agreement should not be done jointly by parents, carers, children who are old enough, and agency workers. (See **Annex A** for an example of such an agreement.)

There is a limit on the number of children that any one person can foster. This is called the 'usual fostering limit', and is set at three. The limit does not apply where all the three or more children are siblings, or where carers have applied successfully to be exempt. If carers are not authorised to exceed the limit but do so, they must be treated as if they are running a children's home. The relevant regulations will then apply (paras. 2–4 schedule 7; and DOH 1991(3), Vol. 3, paras. 4.6–4.10, and the Children's Homes Regulations 1991).

Normally, before a child can be placed with any foster carers,

(1)   the carer must be formally approved;
(2)   the agency must be satisfied that the placement is the best way of safeguarding and promoting the child's welfare and that this particular placement is the most suitable one;
(3)   the foster carer must be of the same religion as the child, or undertake to bring the child up in her/his religion;
(4)   the carer and agency must have entered into a foster placement agreement (reg. 5).

There are two exceptions to these requirements:

(a)   In an emergency, a child can be placed for up to 24 hours with any approved foster carer, providing point (2) above is satisfied, and the carers enter into a short written agreement with the agency, to state simply that they will care for the child as if he or she were one of their own, and will allow the child to be visited by the agency and by family and friends, and removed if and when necessary.
(b)   A child can be placed for up to six weeks with a relative or friend who has not been approved as a foster carer if it is necessary to make an 'immediate placement' for the child. Again, point (2) above must be satisfied, and the shorter form of written agreement entered into. If it is likely that the child will remain in this placement beyond six weeks,

then the process of assessing the relatives or friends for approval should begin immediately.

(reg. 11, and DOH 1991(3), Vol. 3, paras. 4.24–4.26)

Guidance points out that these two exceptions should be used in 'unforeseen circumstances', but it makes the point that where no planning has been possible 'the powers may be used with benefit where it would clearly be advantageous to a child to be placed with or to remain in the care of a familiar figure in reassuring surroundings' (DOH 1991(3), Vol. 3, para. 4.26).

The regulations provide for respite accommodation by acknowledging that a series of pre-planned, short-term placements with the same carer can be treated as one placement for the purposes of the regulations. Thus, for example, only one written foster placement agreement would be required. This links with similar provisions in relation to planning and reviews (reg. 13, Arrangements for Placement of Children Regulations; reg. 11, Reviews of Children's Cases Regulations). The criteria for placements being treated as one are that:

- they are with the same carer; and
- they occur within a period of one year; and
- no individual placement exceeds four weeks; and
- the total length of the placements does not exceed 90 days.

(reg. 9, and DOH 1991(3), Vol. 3, paras. 4.27–4.30)

When a child is fostered, the agency must supervise and support the placement. The minimum number of visits by a social worker are once in the first week of the placement, once every six weeks in the first year, and once every three months after that. In an immediate or emergency placement, a visit should be made each week (reg. 6, and DOH 1991(3), Vol. 3, paras. 4.19–4.23). With respite arrangements, a visit should be made during the first placement and then, if the series continues beyond six months, there should be a second visit (reg. 9, and DOH 1991(3), Vol. 3, para. 4.27). The visits are to enable the supervisor to advise the foster carer and see the child. Whenever a visit takes place the child should be seen and, 'where appropriate', seen alone (reg. 6, and DOH 1991(3), Vol. 3, paras. 4.19–4.23).

Other aspects of support and supervision arise from the agency's general duty to safeguard and promote the child's welfare; to consult with children and all relevant people when making decisions; to take into consideration the child's religion, race, culture and language, and to make plans and review them (ss.22, 26, and relevant regs.).

The regulations and guidance in relation to the placement of individual children with foster carers provides a framework for good practice. The requirement that local authorities make a written placement agreement with foster carers should ensure that foster carers are provided with all the background information about the child that they need before the placement is made, or very soon after it occurs.

Wherever possible, carers and parents should meet before the placement is made, or, if this is impossible, the parents should be encouraged to take their child to the placement. In emergency child protection cases a meeting may need to be arranged after the placement has been made. Such a meeting is not only an opportunity for all those involved to discuss the plan for the child and negotiate the written agreement, it is also an opportunity for parents to pass on vital information about their child's routine, likes and dislikes, favourite toys, games and pastimes. It provides the carers with an early opportunity to meet and talk to the parents, instead of simply hearing the social worker's impression of them and the background details of the case. It also gives the parents the opportunity of first-hand experience of the people who will be caring for their child, rather than simply being given a name and address by the social worker (see DOH 1991(3), Vol. 3, paras. 4.16–4.17).

Recruitment of foster carers   'Publicity and recruitment campaigns should aim to reach all groups in the community, especially where there is or may be a need for foster parents from a particular racial, cultural or religious group' (DOH 1991(3), Vol. 3, para. 3.8). Local authorities now have a duty to consider the range of racial groups in their area when recruiting both day carers and foster carers (para. 11, schedule 2). In order to comply with this duty local authorities will need to introduce ethnic monitoring, if they have not done so already. It should cover children in need in the area; children receiving services; existing foster carers, residential workers and day carers, and the ethnic composition generally within the authority (for more information on ethnic monitoring see Macdonald 1991, and Ahmed et al. 1986).

Links with the local black and other minority ethnic communities need to be established to harness their resources as potential foster carers and to promote the authority's commitment to placing children with carers from the same ethnic background. Recruitment campaigns should be targeted clearly and positively at the particular groups being sought. The appropriate language or languages should be used, and direct contact should be made as well as using printed publicity and information through the media.

Recruitment drives should also aim to attract foster carers for specific types of provision, such as respite accommodation for children with disabilities and for children in need for other reasons. The job of caring for a particular child or children for a series of short placements over a period of time, and of building up close long-term contact with the family and the child, may well require different qualities than are needed for other sorts of arrangements.

Residential care

The range of placements for children still includes residential care – a placement in a children's home that is run by the local authority, or by a voluntary organisation, or privately. In recent years there has been a strong shift away from residential care towards foster care but, as the guidance points out:

> 'Residential care is a positive and desirable way of providing stability for some children which they themselves often prefer to other kinds of placements.' (DOH 1991(3), Vol. 4)

and

> 'Residential care remains a vital resource, but it is essential to see it as part of the overall network of services for children, used in a planned way and when it is in the best interest of the individual child.' (DOH 1991(3), Vol. 4, para. 1.2)

Research by Berridge and Cleaver (1987) into foster home breakdown led them to conclude:

> 'On the basis of this research, we would question the wisdom of restricting options for the placement of children in care . . . our results indicate that foster care is an appropriate intervention for some children in care but not for others; a range of different fostering styles is required; and residential care has an important role in the preparation for fostering, in dealing with the aftermath of unsuccessful family placements, and in sheltering – not necessarily indefinitely – children who cannot or will not live in another household.' (pp. 181–2)

Increasingly, children's homes now have a particular focus, such as providing a therapeutic community for abused children, preparing children for adulthood and leaving care, or for a move to a long-term placement. Children in children's homes tend to be an older group than before, and older than other looked-after children. Overly rigid policies about the use of children's homes, for example, excluding their use for children under the age of ten, may prevent a residential placement being used to ensure that siblings are placed together, with the result that they end up living separately. The choice of a residential placement for a child should be part of the overall plan, made in consultation with the child and family, and taking into consideration the need to promote the welfare of the child; the importance of race, culture, language and religion, and the duty to place children near home and together with brothers and sisters where possible.

All children's homes, whether run by a local authority, voluntary organisation or privately, and including independent schools with up to 50 boarders, are now covered by the Children's Homes Regulations 1991. In addition, the duties owed to looked-after children and to children placed by agencies apply, as do the regulations on planning, reviews and complaints.

Regulations cover such matters as the duty on local and central government to inspect homes (regs. 5, 22 and 28, and DOH 1991(3), Vol. 4, paras. 1.13–1.15 and 1.70), and the sort of accommodation and facilities that should be provided. There is an emphasis on ensuring that children in homes have some privacy, have access to a telephone, are able to do their own washing, cooking and shopping if they wish to, and that the home provides somewhere where children can meet in private with relatives, friends, independent visitors and legal advisers (regs. 6, 7, 9, 13 and 14, and DOH 1991(3), Vol. 4, paras. 1.54–1.81).

Regulations and guidance do not specify either the number of staff who should be employed or the qualifications needed, apart from stressing the importance of having sufficient staff for the type of home, and having staff who are properly trained for the work done. So, for example, a home should not say that it provides family therapy if the staff are not properly qualified to do that (reg. 5, and DOH 1991(3), Vol. 4, paras. 1.28–1.53).

Every home must produce a statement of the purpose and functions of the home, including the age, sex and number of children that can go there, and the particular work that the home offers. The statement should convey 'some idea of the "feel" of the home'. The statement should also give details of, among other matters, the number and qualifications of the staff, the admissions procedure, the measures used to discipline children, and the arrangements made for complaints and representations (reg. 4, schedule 1, and DOH 1991(3), Vol. 4, paras. 1.16–1.26).

The regulations set out clearly the methods of discipline which are not allowed. These include corporal punishment; deprivation of food or drink; restriction on any sort of contact (including letter and telephone contact) between the child and any parent, relative or friend, independent visitor, social worker, guardian *ad litem* or solicitor; being made to wear distinctive or inappropriate clothes, and being fined. Guidance expands on these prohibitions (reg. 8, and DOH 1991(3), Vol. 4, paras. 1.89–1.91).

Just as it is important to place children with foster carers with a similar ethnic background to the child, so those recruiting staff for children's homes should:

> 'ensure that the composition of the staff group reflects the racial, cultural and linguistic background of the children being cared for. It is usually possible to

invoke the genuine occupational qualification exemption to the Race Relations Act 1976 (Section 5(2)(d)), to recruit staff from a particular racial background.

Similarly there should be a proper balance of male and female staff and it may be appropriate to use the exemption in the Sex Discrimination Act 1975 (Section 7(2)(e)) to take positive steps in recruitment to ensure the appropriate balance, where it would be in the children's interest to do so.'

(DOH 1991(3), Vol. 4, paras. 1.36 and 1.37).

Ethnic monitoring of children in the home, or likely to be cared for in the home, will be necessary if staffing is to reflect the ethnic background of the children being cared for.

Where children with disabilities are in the home, staff may need additional training 'to instill a positive attitude and approach to dealing with particular disabilities', or to develop skills in communicating with children who have a visual or hearing impairment (DOH 1991(3), Vol. 4, paras. 1.32–1.33). Guidance is also given on the importance of ensuring that homes that accommodate children with disabilities have the necessary equipment, facilities and adaptations (DOH 1991(3), Vol. 4, paras. 1.71 and 1.78–1.81).

Residential provision for whole families   An important use that can be made of residential provision is to make accommodation available for whole families. There is an increasing range of such accommodation available, provided both by local authorities and the voluntary sector (FRG 1993), but there continues to be considerable unmet need for such provision. Placing the whole family in a residential setting is sometimes the only way of providing the necessary level of support and monitoring for that particular child and family, and is a very important resource to have and make use of in fulfilling the local authority's duty to work towards returning looked-after children to their families.

Secure accommodation

The sections in the Act that set out the circumstances in which children may be kept in secure accommodation apply not only to local authorities but also to health authorities and National Health Service Trusts, residential care homes, nursing homes or mental nursing homes and local education authorities (reg. 7, The Children (Secure Accommodation) Regulations 1991). The extension of the provisions of the Act to cover these other agencies is not intended to encourage their use of secure accommodation, but rather to ensure that children are locked up, or have their liberty otherwise restricted, only in the circumstances set out in the Act, and to give them access to legal redress and representation.

When children are living in accommodation provided by a health authority or local education authority, or in a residential care home, nursing home or mental nursing home for three months or more, or are likely to be there for three months or more, then those in charge of the home have to notify the local authority (ss.85 and 86). The local authority has to satisfy itself about the child's welfare and decide whether or not it needs to exercise any of its duties and powers in relation to such a child. Where there is a possibility of such children being placed in secure accommodation, the local authority should give particular consideration to the services it might be able to offer them.

Registered children's homes and homes run by voluntary organisations are not allowed to provide accommodation for the purposes of restricting the liberty of children (reg. 18). The only children covered by the regulations are those looked after by a local authority or living in a health or education residential establishment, but such children are *not* covered if they are:

- being assessed away from home under a child assessment order, and
- a young person of 16–21 who is provided with accommodation in a community home under section 20(5) (reg. 5(2)).

Accommodation for the purpose of restricting liberty has to be approved by the Secretary of State, and no child under 13 can be placed in secure accommodation without the prior approval of the Secretary of State (regs. 3 and 4, and DOH 1991(3), Vol. 4, para. 8.24).

A child may be placed in secure accommodation only if it appears:

'(a)   that –
   (i) he has a history of absconding and is likely to abscond from any other description of accommodation; and
   (ii) if he absconds, he is likely to suffer significant harm; or
(b)   that if he is kept in any other description of accommodation he is likely to injure himself or other persons.' (s.25(1))

Children who have been arrested and detained (s.38(6), PACE 1984) or remanded without bail (s.23, CYPA 1969) should be placed in local authority accommodation. The Secure Accommodation Regulations apply to them, but if the child concerned has been charged with or convicted of a violent or sexual offence, or an offence for which an adult could receive 14 years in prison or more, or has a history of absconding while remanded to local authority accommodation, and has been charged with or convicted of an offence while so remanded, then (ii) in the criteria above does not apply (reg. 6).

The maximum period during which a child can be kept in secure accommodation before the case is taken to court is a total period of 72 hours (consecutive or not) in a period of 28 consecutive days. There are provisions for exceeding this to cover Sundays or public holidays (reg. 10). Any decision to place a child in secure accommodation should be taken as part of the general plan for the child, and the duties on agencies to consult with children, parents and other relevant people apply (ss.22, 61 and 64). In addition, local authorities are under a specific duty to take steps to avoid the use of secure accommodation for children. This duty is owed to all children in the area (para. 7, schedule 2).

If a child in section 20 accommodation is placed in secure accommodation, that does not interfere with the right of those people with parental responsibility to remove that child at any time (s.20(8), and DOH 1991(3), Vol. 4, paras. 8.7–8.9).

Before the end of the 72-hour period, the relevant agency must apply to the family proceedings court if it wants to detain the child longer in secure accommodation. There must be sufficient evidence to satisfy the court that the criteria for placing a child in secure accommodation exist. If they do, the court must also regard the welfare of the child as its paramount consideration, and be satisfied that making the order will be better for the child than not making it, or making any other order instead (s.1).

Courts can authorise an initial period of detention of up to three months. If the case is brought back to court at the end of that period then a further period of up to six months can be authorised. Case law has established that the order should not be for longer than necessary, and that the court must give clear reasons for its decision (*Re W (A Minor)* [1993] 1 FLR 692). If the child concerned has been remanded to accommodation, the court cannot authorise detention for longer than the period of remand and, in any event, cannot authorise it for longer than 28 days at any one time (regs. 11–13). Children should be legally represented in court proceedings and a guardian *ad litem* should have been appointed before the hearing (s.25(6), and rule 2(2), FPC 1991). Case law has established that proceedings under section 25 are family proceedings, and therefore that hearsay evidence is admissible, although the weight to be given to it would always be a matter of judicial discretion (*R v. Oxfordshire CC* [1992] 1 FLR 648).

In addition to the general duty on agencies to consult with children and families, the regulations specifically require agencies to notify parents, independent visitors and other relevant people of a placement in secure accommodation, and of any intention to apply to the court for authorisation to keep the child there longer (reg. 14).

Once a child has been placed in secure accommodation the agency must appoint three people to review the placement. One person must be independent of the agency. The review must be held at least one month after the placement, and then once every three months. People reviewing the case have to consider whether the criteria still apply, whether the placement continues to be necessary, and whether any other sort of accommodation would be appropriate. In carrying out the review the panel should consult the child, the child's parents, other people who have cared for the child, and any independent visitor (regs. 15–17, and DOH 1991(3), Vol. 4, paras. 8.53–8.56). If the panel decides that child should no longer be in secure accommodation, the relevant agency must review the placement immediately.

Reunification

The Act places a specific duty on local authorities to work towards returning all looked-after children to their parents, relatives or friends (s.23(6)), unless that would not be consistent with the children's welfare. This specific duty underpins the general section 17 duty to promote the upbringing of children by their families. It is a duty that applies to all looked-after children. In addition, local authorities have similar duties towards children in need who are living away from their families but who are not looked after by the local authority (para. 10, schedule 2). It is important to remember that the duty is not just about returning children to *parents*. If that is not possible, local authorities should actively seek out and consider placements in the wider family or with friends (see pages 179–82).

In the Short Report in 1984 the House of Commons Select Committee on children in care expressed concern about the lack of attention given to the work of reuniting children with their families:

> 'If entry into care was used more as a natural part of sharing the care of a child, there might be a more positive attitude to rehabilitation.' (House of Commons 1984, para. 158)

and

> 'Within a generic framework, the growth of specialised units for finding foster parents or adopters has inevitably produced the intended concentration on that aspect of work for children. It may well be that a similar degree of concentration by a specific organisation on rehabilitation with the child's natural family would be of benefit.' (House of Commons 1984, para. 161)

In the past there has been an assumption that practitioners know how to return children home. The majority of children who come into care or accommodation do return home, but research indicates that this is often by default or as a result of pressure from children or their families, rather than as a result of positive planning. Research has found good practice in reunification work to be lamentably lacking. If agencies are really committed to permanency being pursued for children, they have often failed them because so little has been done to develop the skills needed to make permanent return home a realistic option. Consider, for example, the specialist teams and the special budgets, adoption allowances and limited caseloads of workers seeking new families for children. Given that it is still rare to find anything approaching similar provision made for placement back home, it is small wonder that return home for children in accommodation or care is fraught with difficulties, and that the incidence of breakdown is higher than for other sorts of placement.

Recent, and comprehensive, research on 'home on trial' placements was carried out by Farmer and Parker (1991). They studied placements of 321 children in the care of four local authorities. They found that the success of a placement home was influenced more by early and thorough planning than by reason for entry to care. They also found a breakdown rate in placements of almost 50 per cent. Compare this with the findings of a Barnardo's study (Trent 1989) where the success rate of the placements at home (80 per cent) equalled the success rate of placements in new families. This study was about children referred to Barnardo's by local authorities for placement with new families because the local authorities concerned had decided that the children could not return home. The Barnardo's staff used the same techniques of assessment, preparation and support for the placements back home that they had developed in their work of placing children in adoptive homes.

The above comparison provides a strong argument for the development of specialist skills in reunification work. It also emphasises the importance of giving this work status and resources so that adequate time can be given by skilled staff to enable children to return successfully to their families.

The most recent study on children returning home (Bullock et al. 1993) confirms the very high proportion of looked-after children who do return home, indicates that a long stay in care or accommodation may make return more complicated (but does not exclude it), and examines in detail the process of return. It is thus particularly helpful to practitioners in giving guidance on the issues to be considered and worked on in deciding whether children should return, and in enabling and supporting that process.

Legal issues If children in accommodation return to their parents or someone else with parental responsibility for them, they will simply cease to be in accommodation. This return should happen as part of the plan for the child; it should have been prepared for and included in the written agreement between parents, local authority and carers.

If a child in accommodation goes to live with relatives or friends, the placement will be a foster placement initially. Subsequently, the carers might wish to apply for a residence order, or the placement in accommodation might be brought to an end by agreement, possibly with the child remaining where they are in a private arrangement between the parents and carers.

If a child in care goes to live with relatives or friends, this placement, too, will be a foster placement and governed by the relevant regulations. At a later stage the parents, child or local authority might apply to discharge the care order or, if the relatives or friends applied for and were granted a residence order, that would automatically discharge the care order (s.91(1)).

If a child in care is placed with their parents, other people with parental responsibility, or someone who had a residence order in favour of the child immediately before the care order was made, that placement must be made in accordance with the Placement of Children with Parents, etc. Regulations 1991 (s.23(5)). These regulations apply only to children in *care*, not to those in accommodation or under an emergency protection order.

The reasoning behind the regulations is that, in the case of a child in care, a court would have been satisfied that the child was suffering, or was likely to suffer, significant harm attributable to the actions or inactions of their parents, and so the placement back with the parents should be monitored. There is, therefore, a clear element of monitoring and protection in the regulations, but they should not be seen as a hindrance to placing back home. They are not in contradiction to the duty to work towards reuniting children with their families, and they can and should be used as a tool for developing good practice in relation to returning children home. Similarly, they should not be viewed in isolation. If good practice is followed in relation to the planning, written agreements, reviews and consultation required and recommended in the Act and its regulations and guidance, many of the tasks required by these regulations will have been undertaken at an early stage, and compliance with the regulations should not hold up unduly the implementation of a planned return home.

Guidance points out that the first matter to be considered when a decision has been made to return a child is whether or not the care order is still necessary. If it is possible to organise a return that is suitably supported and supervised, then it may be sensible for an application to be made for the care order to be discharged first. The return of the child would not then need to be covered by the regulations (DOH 1991(3), Vol. 3, para. 5.2).

Before a child in care can be reunited with parents or other people who have/had parental responsibility, the following steps must be taken:

- A full assessment should be made of the parents, their household and other adults in the household. The investigation is very similar to the assessment carried out before approving foster carers. If the Arrangements for Placement Regulations and guidance have been complied with properly, most of the information required for the assessment should be on file already. The aim of the process is to 'identify all the factors which contribute to a general picture of the carer, his family and way of life' (DOH 1991(3), Vol. 3, para. 5.24). Police checks need to be carried out on the parents and other adults in the household, all of whom must give their consent to this (reg. 3, schedule 1 and DOH 1991(3), Vol. 3, paras. 5.23–5.29).

- In addition, the local authority must comply with its duty to consult widely before making any decision in relation to a looked-after child. The children themselves, parents, others with parental responsibility and other relevant people should be informed and consulted (s.22(4) and (5)). The 'other relevant people' will include the wider family and other professionals. Where the child is on the child protection register, the issue should be considered at a child protection conference (DOH 1991(3), Vol. 3, paras. 5.30–5.34). The placement must be in accordance with the child's welfare (reg. 4, s.22(3)), and the local authority must consider the child's religion, race, culture and language in deciding whether or not the placement will be appropriate (s.22(5)). This latter point is particularly relevant if a child of mixed parentage is to return to one parent only, or where there are religious differences in the family and the child is to live with one parent only.
- The local authority and the parent or parents must enter into a written agreement (reg. 7). Once again (see section on written agreements, pages 157–60), this should be the outcome of a process of negotiation. However, in these particular circumstances it may be necessary for the local authority to include some stipulations in the agreement. The agreement should set out the plans for the child and the objectives of the placement. It should also detail how the local authority is going to support and visit the placement. The arrangements for contact between the child and any other parent or relatives and friends should be set out, and details included about health and education. The agreement should be clear, and it should specify the extent to which the local authority will continue to limit the parents' exercise of their parental responsibility while the care order is in force. If the child is being placed with a non-married father who does not have parental responsibility, this particular issue will not arise; the agreement will specify instead the extent to which parental responsibility has been delegated to him (ss.33(3) (2) (5), 2, and 3(5), and DOH 1991(3), Vol. 3, paras. 5.16–5.18). As with all written

agreements, the aims and objectives should be clear, specific and achievable.

- The decision to go ahead with the placement should be made by the Director of Social Services or their nominee/s. More than one officer can be nominated to take these decisions, but guidance recommends that the nominees be at area director or area manager level, and that they should have a good knowledge of child care practice (reg. 5, and DOH 1991(3), Vol. 3, para. 4.50). If this process of decision making is not to interfere with a child's welfare by delaying an agreed return home, it is obviously important that more than one person in an authority is designated to take the decision to authorise placement.

Guidance reminds practitioners that children subject to these regulations will have had very different histories. Some may have spent a long time in care, others only a very short time; some may have been abused and be returning to the abuser, others not; some may be returning permanently, others just for visits. The particular circumstances of the child's case must affect the way in which the work required by the regulations is carried out (DOH 1991(3), Vol. 3, paras. 5.21, 5.24, and 5.32).

Any placement of a child in care with the relevant group of people is covered by these regulations if it lasts for more than 24 hours. Thus, any contact that involves overnight, weekend or school holiday stays is covered by these regulations even if it is not intended that the child should return permanently to their parents. Regulations do provide for a series of short-term placements to be treated as one, so that the above steps need be taken only once a year. A series of placements will be treated as one if:

- they occur within a period of a year; and
- no single placement is for more than four weeks; and
- the total length of the placements does not exceed 90 days.

(reg. 13, and DOH 1991(3). Vol. 3, paras. 5.12–5.13)

The regulations (reg. 2(5)) make it clear that where contact has been ordered by the court (under s.34 or in accordance with any directions given prior to the implementation of the Act), these regulations do not apply in so far as they are incompatible with the order or directions for contact. Thus, the requirement that the decision to place be made by a director or nominated officer would not apply (reg. 5). It would also seem to be the case that failure to comply with all the regulations should not prevent contact going ahead as ordered by the court.

There are other exceptions to the rule that all the steps set out above must be carried out before the placement is made. They are:

- For 16- and 17-year-olds, the only parts of the regulations that apply are that the placement must be in accordance with the child's welfare and be terminated if not, and that the director or nominated officer must make the decision to go ahead with the placement. None of the provisions in relation to assessment, agreements, notification or supervision of the placement apply (reg. 2(2) – i.e. only regs. 4, 5, 10, 11 and 13 apply).
- If a care order is made on a child who has remained living at home, or if the child is returned home after a very short period away from home, then all the enquiries, consultation and the making of a written agreement can be carried out while the child remains at home (reg. 2(4)). Thus, if a child spends a short period of time away from home under an emergency protection order, but it is intended that he or she should return home under an interim care order, it would be possible to argue that this provision should apply. The child could return home immediately and the assessment process then be carried out (DOH 1991(3), Vol. 3, para. 5.10).
- An immediate placement of the child can be made without all the steps above being completed, if that would be in the interests of the child's welfare. The decision to place must be taken by the nominated officer and, before the placement is made, the local authority should interview the parent or parents and obtain as much of the information required for an assessment as possible in relation to that parent, their household and the other adults in it (reg. 6). Guidance suggests that such placements should occur only in an emergency, although 'immediate' is not defined in the regulations. Guidance also recommends that the enquiries and consultation required by the regulations should be carried out within six weeks (DOH 1991(3), Vol. 3, para. 5.11).

Once the decision to go ahead with the placement has been taken, all those involved in the consultation process should receive written notice of the decision and details of the child's address. In addition, this written notice should be sent to other professionals, such as the district health authority, the child's GP, the local education authority and the child's current carers (reg. 8).

While the child remains in care all the duties of the local authority in relation to looked-after children apply, particularly those about the child's welfare, consultation, planning and reviews. In addition, the Placement with Parents Regulations and guidance emphasise the support that should be given to children and their families when children return home after a period in care. The regulations require the local authority to give advice and assistance to the parents. They must also visit the child – in the first week of the placement, then every six weeks for the first year, and every three months after that. This is the minimum level of visits required. The social worker should make arrangements to see the child alone on each visit, as well as ensuring that the child is seen with their parents in the family setting. Written reports on all visits should be recorded on the file (reg. 9).

The guidance emphasises the importance of proper preparation for a return home, particularly if the child has been away for any length of time:

'A period of gradual reintroduction may be needed, depending on the length of time the child has been away from the family and the changes which have occurred there. Children may return to different addresses, new babies in the family, new stepparents and stepbrothers and sisters. Sometimes a child must change schools (though this should be avoided if possible) and leave behind friends and interests acquired. Contacts with friends and previous carers should be maintained if this is in the child's best interests. Parents, too, need to be prepared for changes in the child's habits, interests and routines; and for the possibility of disturbed behaviour while the child is settling in. The local authority should assess the support needed to achieve a successful placement and should provide any assistance or services they consider appropriate.' (DOH 1991(3), Vol. 3, para. 5.45)

The support required by the family should be a matter for discussion between the local authority and the family, and will vary in each case. Guidance draws on the findings from research about the kinds of support that might be most useful.

'In some cases it may be necessary for the carer to be allocated a social worker; or in other cases a family aide or links with the family centre might be alternatives which can provide the carer with support at a time when the placement is under stress. Other examples of support include an emergency telephone number, respite care arrangements, babysitting or childminding to provide a break and financial help. The power to make such provision for the child's family or any member of that family is provided by Section 17(3) of the Act.' (DOH 1991(3), Vol. 3, para. 5.48)

Guidance also stresses the importance of the supervisor giving feedback to the child and family about their perceptions of how the placement is going and how far the aims and achievements of the agreement are being reached (DOH 1991(3), Vol. 3, paras. 5.53 and 5.54). These are issues to be discussed on an ongoing basis, and also at reviews. Some aims and objectives may need to be changed as circumstances change. Guidance points out that:

'the supervising social worker will need to be aware of the delicate balance to be achieved in recognising and supporting the needs of the carer, without undermining ability to cope . . . the child and carer should have a sense of stability and security to allow them to build up trust in each other. Thorough and perceptive social work supervision and monitoring will help to develop this, but it should avoid undermining parenting skills and the authority of the carers.' (DOH 1991(3), Vol. 3, paras. 4.49 and 5.54)

What if the placement goes wrong and a decision is made that the child's welfare requires that she or he be removed? Where possible, this should be planned for and, also where possible, an alternative placement should be found within the family. Everyone should be given a clear explanation of why the child cannot remain in the placement (DOH 1991(3), Vol. 3, paras. 5.58 and 5.59).

There will be circumstances where the local authority does not agree that a child in care should return to their parents, or go to live with relatives or friends, but where a court dealing with the parents' application to discharge the order (s.39) or an application by relatives and friends for a residence order (s.8) disagrees with the local authority's decision. In such cases, children still need preparation for the return home, and both children and the family need support once return has taken place. Sadly, some workers in such circumstances are unwilling to do this important work of preparation and support. Sometimes it may be possible to negotiate for a new social worker to be involved, or for a voluntary organisation, such as a Family Service Unit or the NSPCC, to provide a link worker to prepare the child and family and provide support. Where the local authority is unco-operative and the court is reluctant to authorise the immediate return of the child by discharging the care order or making a residence order, it could make a very detailed contact order, increasing the extent and duration of contact over a period of time, or alternatively it could make a time-limited residence order (s.11(7)) in favour of foster carers who were sympathetic to the child returning to family or friends. What the court cannot do, regrettably, is direct a local authority to do the necessary work of preparation and support for return home as, while the care order remains in force, the local authority has discretion as to how to exercise its parental responsibility for the child.

Checklist for good practice

The following checklist should help ensure that good practice is followed in reunification work.

The legal framework for reunification

- Have you considered the wide range of placements available for this work (s.23)?
- Do you consider you have sufficient knowledge of, and sensitivity to, matters of race, culture, religion and language (s.22, and para. 11, schedule 2)?

- Are you familiar with the legal provisions concerning contact (ss.8 and 34, and paras. 10, 15 and 16, schedule 2)?
- What are your local procedures for reviews of children being looked after (s.26)?
- Are you familiar with:
  - The Arrangements for Placement of Children (General) Regulations 1991 and related guidance (Vol. 3)
  - The Foster Placement (Children) Regulations 1991, and related guidance (Vol. 3)
  - The Children's Homes Regulations 1991, and related guidance (Vol. 4)
  - The Placement of Children with Parents, etc. Regulations 1991, and related guidance (Vol. 3)
  - The Contact with Children Regulations 1991, and related guidance (Vol. 3)
  - requirements and recommendations about written agreements (Vol. 3)?

Using the placement that best supports the plan

- Have you thought about all placement possibilities – including relatives, friends, others connected with the child, non-related foster carers, residential units?
- Do you need to move the child to assist successful reunification?
- Do the carers have the right attitudes/skills/knowledge to help the child return home?
- Do the carers have the right attitudes/skills/knowledge to help the parents?
- Are the carers getting the financial support they need?
- What other support have you provided for the carers?

Anti-racist practice

- Who constitutes family for the child?
- How do you know what constitutes family for the child?
- Do the parents and child see role models in the staff they deal with?
- Are the child and parents encouraged and enabled to use their family's first language?
- Are all written agreements negotiated and given to the family in their first language? Are letters, information and other written material also translated?
- Are the parents in contact with any support groups?
- Are you using the race and culture of the parents in a positive way?
- Are you using the parents' religious faith in a positive way?

- Does the child's placement, and do the carers, promote the racial and cultural identity of the child and parents? If not, what will you do about this?
- Do you have access to support and information about the racial and cultural needs of the family?

Assessing and preparing children

- What means have you used to enable the child to understand you?
- What means have you used to help you understand the child?
- How do the contact arrangements (including overnight stays and non-visiting contact) help the child prepare to return home?
- Have the parents contributed to, and seen, the child's life-story work?
- What supports (financial, material, personal) have you been able to arrange for the parents?
- Have you identified the parents' strengths?
- Have you identified the parents' weaknesses?
- How can you show that the parents know what they have to do before their child is returned home?
- What work has been done to help the parents prepare for the emotional upheaval of their child's return home?
- What work has been done to help the parents plan for managing the re-entry problems that are likely to crop up for family members?

Participation in decision making

- Do the parents have detailed information about the child's placement, and about their current likes and dislikes, progress at school, friends and other day-to-day matters?
- Does the child have appropriate detailed information about the circumstances of their parents and family?
- Do you have clear written records of the views and wishes of parents and child at each stage of work?
- Can you identify when the parents and child have *participated*, rather than just been involved, in discussions and decision making? How do you make this distinction?
- Are the tasks to be undertaken negotiated/assigned fairly and realistically to parents and workers, and are they appropriate culturally?
- How do you know that the child and parents have correct information about the law and child care practice relevant to their particular situation?
- What degree of access to their records have you given the parents and child?
- Do you use shared-recording methods with parents and children?

- What information do the parents have about how they can challenge decisions or make representations or complaints?

Timing

- Is your timetable realistic for the tasks involved?
- Have you started overnight contact early enough for parents, children and yourself to get enough good-quality opportunities to identify people's strengths and any problems that many need attention?
- Have you ensured that your timescale for full-time return is not so long that parents and child will get too used to the interim stage before the return home takes place?
- Have you planned the full-time return home so that it represents a point along the reunification line, rather than the end of it?
- Have you started work on the requirements of the Placement with Parents, etc. Regulations early enough to avoid overnight contact or full-time return being delayed because the necessary information is not available?

Financial assistance

- What have you done, at each stage of reunification, to ensure that the parents receive their proper entitlement to social security, housing and other benefits?
- Should the child make a claim for criminal injuries compensation?
- What financial help is needed from social services:
  - to promote the contact plan
  - to enable the parents to meet any requirement of the reunification plan before full-time return
  - to enable the parents to provide well enough materially for the child after full-time return?
- What, if any, help do the parents need with budgeting?

Support after full-time return home

- Do you know what support the parents would like after the child returns home?
- What financial assistance do you need to build into this stage of the plan?
- What plans have you made to enable parents and children to discuss any difficulties in a way that sees their openness as a strength rather than their difficulties as a weakness?
- Are the parents in contact with a family support group?
- What provision have you made for the parents to have 24-hour access to workers they know and have confidence in?

- Are the previous carers willing to maintain contact with the parents and child?
- What arrangements have been made to provide parents with alternative child care, such as respite accommodation and day care?
- Have you updated the written agreement?

Independent living and after-care

The majority of children leave care or accommodation by returning to their families or communities, although some children leave through being adopted, and a significant number leave for independent living. It has been accepted for some time now that local authorities, voluntary organisations and private children's homes should not just cut off looked-after young people when they reach 18, whether or not they are returning to their families or moving on to an independent life. This is particularly important for young people who have no or few links with family or friends. The duties placed on agencies by the Act should ensure that young people are prepared properly for moving on to independence, and are given some continuing support into early adulthood.

Local authorities are under a duty to advise, assist and befriend children they are looking after, with a view to promoting their welfare when they cease to be looked after. In other words, they are under a duty to prepare children properly, both materially and in other ways, for independence. Voluntary organisations and those running registered children's homes are under a similar duty (ss.24(1), 61(1), and 64(1)). Guidance enlarges on this duty by setting out the following underlying principles that should inform practice when preparing young people for leaving accommodation or care:

- Services for young people must take account of the lengthy process of transition from childhood to adulthood, to reflect the gradual transition of a young person from dependence to independence. The support provided should be, broadly, the support that a good parent might be expected to give.
- Young people should be fully involved in discussions and plans for their future. Well before a young person leaves care, a continuing care plan should be formulated with him. This should specify the type of help the young person will be receiving and from whom. This plan should incorporate contingency arrangements in the event of a breakdown in a young person's living arrangements after he has left care since such breakdowns in arrangements are not uncommon. Such arrangements might include, for example, the possibility of a return to a community home, or to foster care.

- Parents should be invited to help formulate the plan (if they are not estranged from the young person). So too, should foster parents if the young person is leaving a foster placement (whether local authority or private).
- Preparation for leaving care should help develop a young person's capacity to make satisfactory relationships, develop his self-esteem and enable him to acquire the necessary practical skills for independent living.
- In helping young people to develop socially and culturally, carers must be prepared to take some risks and to take responsibility for doing so; to let young people take some risks, e.g. in attempting relationships that do not work; and to take responsibility for supporting young people through breakdowns in relationships.
- All preparation for leaving care and provision of aftercare must take account of the religious persuasion, racial origin, cultural and linguistic background and other needs of a young person (s.22(5)(c)).
- Preparation for leaving care and the provision of aftercare must be planned in conjunction with all other interested agencies, e.g. education and housing authorities, health authorities and, where appropriate, other local authorities. These agencies should be invited to contribute to a young person's continuing care plan.'

(DOH 1991(3), Vol. 3, para. 9.12)

In addition, guidance sets out the three broad areas that should form part of a young person's preparation for leaving care:

- Enabling young people to build and maintain relationships (both general and sexual) with others

  This includes helping young people keep in touch with their families and friends; helping them make friends while they are being looked after; encouraging foster carers to keep in touch, and helping young people make friends with adults, such as independent visitors. Guidance stresses the importance of young people from minority ethnic groups being enabled to develop and maintain links with their particular community. Children with disabilities should be encouraged to maintain and develop links with groups and voluntary organisations that will help them make contacts and obtain services. Advice on sexual relationships should include information about practical matters, such as contraception and AIDS, as well as the emotional aspects of sexuality (DOH 1991(3), Vol. 3, paras. 9.46–9.50).

- Enabling young people to develop self-esteem

  Information about their background and why they are where they are is obviously important here. Particularly helpful in this respect can be ensuring continuity of links with family, friends and community. Children with disabilities may need particular help in developing self-esteem. Young people from black and other minority ethnic groups may need help to develop pride in their background and culture if these issues have been ignored in the past because they have been in a trans-racial or residential placement where they either faced direct racism or were not encouraged and enabled to develop a positive sense of identity (DOH 1991(3), Vol. 3, paras. 9.51–9.54).

* Teaching practical and financial skills and knowledge

   This needs to include matters as how to budget, shop, cook, find a flat, get a job or apply for benefits, etc. (DOH 1991(3), Vol. 3, paras. 9.55–9.56).

As well as sharing with agencies the duty to prepare young people for independence, local authorities are under an additional duty in some cases, and have a power in others, to provide advice and befriending for young people who have left accommodation or care, or other sorts of residential provision. A young person qualifies for this help if:

* they live in the local authority area, and
* they are under 21, and
* at any time between the ages of 16 and 17 they were:
   – looked after by a local authority; or
   – accommodated by or on behalf of a voluntary organisation; or
   – accommodated in a registered children's home; or
   – accommodated by any health authority or local education authority or in any residential care home, nursing home or mental nursing home for a consecutive period of at least three months; or
   – privately fostered. (s.24(2))

Young people cease to be privately fostered when they reach 16, unless they have disabilities, in which case they remain privately fostered until aged 18 (s.66). Thus, this condition about private fostering applies only to children with disabilities.

If it appears to the local authority that any young person who comes into the above categories is in need of advice and befriending, they have a *duty* to provide these services if the young person was looked after by a local authority or voluntary organisation, and a *power* to provide them in any other case. In all such cases local authorities have an additional *power* to provide assistance, which may be in kind or, in exceptional circumstances, in cash. If assistance is given, the person can be means-tested first, and all or part of the assistance can be in the form of a loan (s.24(4)–(7) and (10)).

Young people who qualify for help by virtue of having been looked after by a local authority may also be given contributions to help them live near their employment or training, or to obtain further educational training. This help can continue beyond 21 if the education they are receiving does so. Any help given in these circumstances cannot be given as a loan (s.24(8)).

As guidance rightly points out, provision of adequate after-care services will involve liaison with other departments of the local authority, particularly housing, and liaison with other agencies also. Local authorities may need to have recourse to their powers under section 27 to ask a specific authority for help in carrying out their duties (DOH 1991(3), Vol. 3, paras. 9.7–9.8 and 9.75–9.96).

Local authorities must publish details of the after-care services they provide, and this information should include a statement of the authority's practice and philosophy on the preparation of young people for leaving care, and on the provision of after-care services. The statement must take into account the different sorts of needs of the young people concerned, including those with disabilities, those from black or other minority ethnic backgrounds, and those who are young mothers or fathers. This statement should be revised at least every three years (DOH 1991(3), Vol. 3, para. 9.20).

Research carried out into the views of consumers of after-care services found that the young people consulted wanted, in this order of preference:

(1)   money and somewhere to live;
(2)   a programme of training and educational support;
(3)   access to advice, information and counselling (Stone 1990).

Most parents or carers give financial help to their offspring as they reach adulthood and move into independence. Guidance makes it clear that local authorities should not hold back from providing financial help, and that they should be clear that such help can be provided up to the age of 21: 'the presumption should be that such assistance should be provided where this is necessary to protect the young person's welfare and it cannot be made available by any other agency' (DOH 1991(3), Vol. 3, para. 9.71). Details about financial help should be set out in the written information on policies and services (see above). It will not be regarded as part of the young person's income or capital when their entitlement to benefits is being calculated (DOH 1991(3), Vol. 3, para. 9.102).

In relation to housing, the guidance points out that young people who have left care or accommodation are over-represented among the young homeless. It is, therefore, very important that there is close liaison between housing departments and social services departments. Guidance recommends that housing department policy on priority provision for young people leaving care or accommodation is included in the department's information and statement on after-care services (DOH 1991(3), Vol. 3, paras. 9.80–9.86). Local authorities can accommodate 16–20-year-olds in children's homes able to take that age range (s.20), and the voluntary sector may also be able to help with the provision of accommodation (DOH 1991(3), Vol. 3, paras. 9.75–9.78).

Annex A

Foster or residential placement agreement

FOSTER OR RESIDENTIAL PLACEMENT AGREEMENT

This agreement is for use when children are being looked after by a local authority and are placed in a foster home or residential placement.

Each participant should be given a copy of the completed agreement. This form conforms with requirements for written agreements in Regulation 4 of the Arrangements for Placement of Children (General) Regulations 1991 and Regulation 5 of the Foster Placement (Children) Regulations 1991.

CHILD'S NAME

DATE OF BIRTH   RELIGION

ETHNICITY   FIRST LANGUAGE

LEGAL STATUS OF PLACEMENT: Accommodation/care order (*please delete*)

AGENCY

NAME(S) OF FOSTER CARER(S)

ADDRESS

TELEPHONE NUMBER

Date from when the placement is to start

1

This must include people with parental responsibility, the foster carers and the local authority. Where possible children should also participate. Apart from the foster carers and local authority workers, there should be a minimum number of professionals participating – only those actively involved in carrying out the agreement.

Where a young person is 16 or over and they are being provided with accommodation against the wishes of the person/s with parental responsibility for them they, and not those with parental responsibility, must participate.

NAMES AND ROLES OF PARTICIPANTS to agreement

211

2

What problems led to the placement being necessary and the child not being able to live at home?

These should be specific.

WRITE THIS IN SIMPLE CLEAR TERMS.

Note if different participants have different opinion.

PRESENT SITUATION ie. why child cannot live at home

3

When was this statement (sch.3, no 1, Foster Placement Regulations) covering the general plan, the child's personal history, involving details of religion, race, culture and language, health and educational needs, provided to the foster carers? Will it be provided to parents, others with parental responsibility and to the child?

STATEMENT FOR FOSTER CARERS

4

State who, apart from those present at this meeting, has been consulted, and how, in advance of the making of this agreement. This may include children, their families and/or professional workers.

CONSULTATION

5

What objectives will everyone work towards?

The objectives must be ones that the participants agree can BE ACHIEVED and where progress can be measured. Keep them few, simple and clear and give a priority to them. Tasks to reach the objectives are detailed in number 9.

OBJECTIVES ie. what is needed

6

When are the objectives above to be achieved?

OBJECTIVES' TIME LIMIT/REVIEW

7 How long is the placement to last?

PLACEMENT TIME LIMIT

8 Full details of contact (visits as well as other forms of contact – who, when, where, how and why), and of the help to be given. In relation to 'who', remember the duty to promote contact with parents, others with parental responsibility, relatives, friends and others who have a connection with the child.

CONTACT between child and family

9 If there are any obstacles to contact how are they going to be overcome?

OBSTACLES TO CONTACT

10

Brief details of who, what, when and why are needed here. Check to see if there is a necessary order for doing tasks, and check to see that no one thinks there are particular obstacles in the way of completing them. Include any steps which will be taken to enhance the child's sense of identity and self-esteem. As before try and keep things simple and clear.

Include arrangements for:

• health
• child's development
• child's race and culture
• education
• employment (where appropriate)

In some situations the child's family and the local authority may do work together which is confidential to them. If so, this will be recorded elsewhere.

WORK TO BE DONE ie. who will do what to achieve the objectives

a) for agency and social worker

b) for foster carers

c) for child

continued

10 continued

WORK TO BE DONE ie. who will do what to achieve the objectives

d) for those with parental responsibility

---

11 Those with parental responsibility before the child came into accommodation keep it but may delegate some or all of it to someone else. Will any be delegated here and to whom?

Think particularly about medical treatment (emergency or routine), schooling issues, haircuts, overseas travel. Do the current carers need a medical consent card?

* *meaning any non-local authority person with parental responsibility*

DELEGATION OR SHARING OF PARENTAL RESPONSIBILITY

a) remaining with parent *

b) to parent (without parental responsibility) or other adult

c) to foster carers

d) to Agency

---

12 Are there any circumstances in which local authority permission is needed for the child to have overnight stays with school friends, the foster carers' relatives etc, and are any restrictions needed?

PERMISSION NEEDED TO STAY ELSEWHERE

13 Any additional work to be carried out by other agencies over and above normal arrangements.

Each agency should be named and if there are any special arrangements these should be stated. It will be assumed that the placement carers are responsible for ensuring that the services are provided, unless the contrary is stated.

WORK TO BE CARRIED OUT BY OTHER AGENCIES

a) education

b) employment

c) health

d) other

14 Are finances available and agreed for parents, others with parental responsibility, children and others to make plans work? Please describe the provision to be made.

FINANCES FOR PARENTS AND CHILDREN

Parents   YES/NO

Child   YES/NO

Others   YES/NO

15 Have arrangements for the financial support of this child and the objectives of this agreement been made between the foster carers and the local authority?

FINANCES FOR FOSTER CARERS

16 Who will visit whom, when and why? The minimum allowed for a local authority is within 1 week of the placement, then every 6 weeks for the first year and every 3 months after that.

FREQUENCY AND PURPOSE OF SOCIAL WORK AND OTHER AGENCY CONTACT

17 When and how will progress towards the objectives be reviewed?

Will there be a number of reviews before the time limit noted in 6? How will this fit in with the statutory review requirements in s26? Note date, time, venue.

REVIEW OF PROGRESS

18 What are the arrangements for ending the placement?

ENDING THE PLACEMENT

19 What further help will be needed when the objectives of the placement have been achieved?

FURTHER HELP

20 What are the means of dealing with dissatisfactions of any participant, or for changing this agreement? How are parents, children, others with parental responsibility, relatives, friends or others named in this agreement to be informed of any changes to it?

Note the name(s) of the social worker(s) who will arrange any necessary meetings to discuss dissatisfactions or proposed changes. Give time limit for contact.

DISSATISFACTIONS AND CHANGES

21 What are the plans for the child if the objectives are not achievable?

Give a broad indication of a contingency plan and/or state clearly that changes to this agreement will not be made before full discussion with at least the participants to this agreement.

CONTINGENCIES

a) Prime responsibility for work with foster family during this placement will rest with

b) Prime responsibility for work with the child/child's family during this placement will rest with

NAME

WORKPLACE ADDRESS

TELEPHONE NUMBER

SOCIAL WORK SUPERVISOR

The foster carers agree to co-operate with this agreement and to the terms and conditions of the Foster Care Agreement. Parents and other participants to this agreement may like to see a general statement about the areas covered in the Foster Care Agreement.

List the participants to the making of this agreement together with a note of any dissensions and by whom.

NAMES   SIGNATURES

DATE

© FRG and NFCA. Reproduced by agreement with FRG and NFCA.

Further copies of this agreement may be obtained from:

Family Rights Group	National Foster Care Association
The Print House	Francis House
18 Ashwin Street	Francis Street
London E8 3DL	London SQ1P 1DE
Tel: 071 923 2628	Tel: 071 828 6266

Annex B

Useful organisations

Family Rights Group
The Print House
18 Ashwin Street
London
E8 3DL

Tel: 071 923 2628

Advice Line: Monday–Friday 1.30–3.30 pm
               Tel: 071 249 0008

Children's Legal Centre
20 Compton Terrace
London
N1 2NU

Tel: 071 359 6251

National Foster Care Association
Francis House
Francis Street
London
SW1P 1DE

Tel: 071 828 6266

British Agencies for Adoption and Fostering
11 Southwark Street
London
SE1 1RQ

Tel: 071 407 8800

Grandparents's Federation
Room 3
Moot House
The Stow
Harlow
Essex
CM20 3AG

Tel: 0279 437145

PAIN (Parents Against Injustice)
11 Riverside Business Park
Stansted

Essex
CM24 8PL

Tel: 0279 647171

Parentline – OPUS (Organisation for Parents Under Stress)
Head Office
Rayton House
57 Hart Road
Thundersley
Essex, SS7 3PD

Tel: 0268 757077

Interights (International centre for
   the legal protection of human rights)
Kingsway Chambers
46 Kingsway
London
WC2B 6EN

ASC (Advocacy Service for Children)
1 Sickle Street
Manchester
M60 2AA

Tel: 061 839 8442

Home-start Consultancy
2 Salisbury Road
Leicester
LE1 7QR

Tel: 0533 554988

NEWPIN Development Programme
Sutherland House
35 Sutherland Square
Walworth
London
SE17 3EE

Tel: 071 703 6326

References

Ahmed, S, Cheetham, J and Small, J (eds) (1986) *Social Work with Black Children and their Families*, Batsford.

Aldgate, J, Pratt, R and Duggan, J (1989) 'Using Care Away from Home to Prevent Family Breakdown' in *Adoption and Fostering*, Vol. 13, no. 2, British Agencies for Adoption and Fostering.

Barn, R (1990) 'Black Children in Local Authority Care: Admission Patterns', in *New Community*, Vol. 16, no. 2, Commission for Racial Equality.

Bebbington, A and Miles, J (1989) 'The Background of Children who enter Local Authority Care', in *British Journal of Social Work*, Vol. 19, no. 5.

Becker, S and MacPherson, S (1986) *Poor Clients: The Extent and Nature of Financial Poverty Amongst Consumers of Social Work Services*, Nottingham University, Benefits Research Unit.

Berridge, D (1985) *Children's Homes*, Blackwell.

Berridge, D, and Cleaver, H (1987) *Foster Home Breakdown*, Blackwell.

Bonnerjea, L (1990) *Leaving Care in London*, London Boroughs Children's Regional Planning Committee.

Bowlby, J (1952) *Maternal Care and Mental Health*, World Health Organisation.

Bradshaw, J (1990) *Child Poverty and Deprivation in the UK*, National Children's Bureau.

Brent (1985) *A Child in Trust: The Report of the Panel of Inquiry into the Circumstances surrounding the death of Jasmine Beckford*, London Borough of Brent.

Bullock, R, Little, M and Millham, S (1993) *Going Home: The Return of Children Separated from their Families*, Dartmouth.

Conway, J (1988) *Prescription for Poor Health*, Shelter, SHAC, London Food Commission and Maternity Alliance.

223

Derbyshire et al. (1990) *Inquiry into Giselle*, Derbyshire and Nottingham-shire County Councils and Area Child Protection Committees.

DHSS (1985(1)) *Review of Child Care Law: Report to Ministers of an Interdepartmental Working Party*, HMSO.

DHSS (1985(2)) *Social Work Decisions in Child Care – recent research findings and their implications*, HMSO.

DHSS (1987(1)) *The Law on Child Care and Family Services*, White Paper, HMSO.

DHSS (1987(2)) *Report of the Inquiry into Child Abuse in Cleveland*, HMSO.

DOE (1992) *Households Found Accommodation under the Homeless Provisions of the 1985 Housing Act*, HMSO.

DOH (1988) *Protecting Children: A Guide for Social Workers undertaking a Comprehensive Assessment* (The 'Orange Book'), HMSO.

DOH (1989(1)) *The Care of Children: Principles and Practice in Regulations and Guidance*, HMSO.

DOH (1989(2)) *An Introduction to the Children Act*, HMSO.

DOH (1990) *Children in Care of Local Authorities: Year Ending 31.3.1990*, HMSO.

DOH (1991(1)) *Patterns and Outcomes in Child Placement: Messages from Current Research and their Implications*, HMSO.

DOH (1991(2)) *Working Together under the Children Act 1989: A Guide to Arrangements for Inter-agency Co-operation for the Protection of Children from Abuse*, HMSO.

DOH (1991(3)) *The Children Act: Guidance and Regulations*, Vols 1–10, HMSO.

DOH (1992) *The Timetabling of Care Proceedings before the implementation of the Children Act 1989: Evaluation of a pilot project in a Magistrates Court*, HMSO.

DOH and SSI (1991(4)) *The Right to Complain: Practice Guidance on Complaints Procedures in Social Services Departments*, HMSO.

DOH and Welsh Office (1993) *Children Act Report 1992*, HMSO.

Fanshel, D and Shinn, EB (1978) *Children in Foster Care – A Longitudinal Study*, Columbia University.

Farmer, E and Parker, R (1991) *Trials and Tribulations*, HMSO.

FRG (1989(1)) *Using Written Agreements with Children and Families*, Family Rights Group.

FRG (1989(2)) *FRG Bulletin*, Spring.

FRG (1993) *Residential Resources for Families*, Family Rights Group.

FRG and NFCA (1991) *Children Act 1989 – Written Agreement Forms for Work with Children, Families and Carers*, Family Rights Group/National Foster Care Association.

FRG and NSPCC (1992) *Child Protection Procedures – what they mean for your family*, Family Rights Group/National Society for the Prevention of Cruelty to Children.

Fruin, D and Vernon, J (1985) *In Care – A Study of Social Work Decision Making*, National Children's Bureau.
Gardner, R (1992) *Supporting Families: Preventive Social Work in Practice*, National Children's Bureau.
Gibbons, J (ed.) (1992) *The Children Act 1989 and Family Support: Principles into Practice*, HMSO.
Gibbons, J (forthcoming).
Greenwich (1987) *A Child in Mind: Protection of Children in a Responsible Society* (The Kimberley Carlile Report), London Borough of Greenwich.
Home Office (1948) Circular no. 160/1948.
House of Commons (1960) *Report of the Committee on Children and Young Persons* (The Ingleby Report), HMSO.
House of Commons (1984) *Children in Care: Second Report from the Social Services Committee* (The Short Report), HMSO.
In Need Implementation Group (1991) *The Children Act and Children's Needs: Make it the answer and not the problem*, National Council of Voluntary Child Care Organisations and Family Rights Group.
Lambeth et al. (1989) *The Doreen Aston Report*, London Boroughs of Lambeth, Lewisham and Southwark Area Review Committee.
Law Commission (1988) *Review of Child Law, Guardianship and Custody*, Law Commission 172, HMSO.
Link, MJ (1989) *Kinship Foster Care: The Double-edged Dilemma*, Task Force for Permanency Planning for Foster Children Inc. (16 North Goodman Street, Rochester, N.Y. 14607, USA).
Macdonald, S (1991) *All Equal Under the Act? – A Practical Guide to the Children Act 1989 for Social Workers*, Race Equality Unit at National Institute of Social Work.
Maluccio, A and Sinanoglu, P (1981) *The Challenge of Partnership: Working with Parents in Foster Care and Parents of Children in Placement: Perspectives and Programmes*, Child Welfare League of America, New York.
Millham, S, Bullock, R, Hosie, K and Haak, M (1986) *Lost in Care: the problems of maintaining links between Children in Care and their Families*, Gower.
Millham, S, Bullock, R, Hosie, K and Little, M (1989) *Access Disputes in Child Care*, Gower.
NCC (1988) *Open to Complaints*, National Consumer Council and National Institute of Social Work.
OPCS (1989) *Disabled Children: Services, Transport and Education*, Office of Population and Census Surveys, HMSO.
Oppenheim, C (1990) *Poverty: the Facts*, Child Poverty Action Group.
Packman, J, Randall, J and Jacques, N (1986) *Who Needs Care? Social Work Decisions about Children*, Blackwell.
Parker, R Ward, H, Jackson, S, Aldgate, J and Wedge, P (eds) (1991)

Looking After Children: Assessing Outcomes in Child Care, HMSO. See also *Looking After Children*, bulletins, Dartington Social Research Unit.

Rowe, J, Cain, H, Handleby, M and Keane, A (1984) *Long-Term Foster Care*, Batsford.

Rowe, J, Hundleby, M and Garnett, L (1989) *Child Care Now*, Research Services 6, British Agencies for Adoption and Fostering.

Rutter, M (1972) *Maternal Deprivation Re-assessed,* Penguin.

Secretary of State for Social Services (1974) *Report of the Committee of Inquiry into the Care and Supervision Provided in Relation to Maria Colwell*, HMSO.

Sheffield University (1987) *Complaints Procedure in Local Government*, Vol. 1, 3.5.2., Centre for Socio-Legal and Criminological Studies.

SSI (1990) *Inspection of Child Protection Services in Rochdale*, Department of Health.

Stone, M (1990) *Young People Leaving Care: A Study of Management Systems, Service Delivery and User Evaluations*, Royal Philanthropic Society.

Thoburn, J (1988) *Child Placement: Principles and Practice*, Wildwood House.

Thoburn, J (ed.) (1992) *Participation in Practice – Involving Families in Child Protection*, University of East Anglia, Social Work Development Unit.

Trent, J (1989) *Homeward Bound: the Rehabilitation of Children to their Birth Parents*, Barnardo's.

Welsh Office (1992) *Children in Care or under Supervision Orders in Wales: Year Ended 31/3/91*, HMSO.

Welsh Office (1993) *Welsh Housing Statistics No. 13*, Welsh Office.

Whitaker, D et al. (1985) *The Experience of Residential Care from the Perspectives of Children, Parents and Care Givers*, York University, Department of Administration and Social Work.

Index

CHILD PLACEMENT:
PRINCIPLES AND PRACTICE
SECOND EDITION
June Thoburn

"...will be warmly welcomed by social work practitioners, teachers and students alike... promises to become a popular and well-thumbed text.'
Dr Jean Packman, Dartington Social Research Unit

This is the second edition of a practice handbook which has proved popular with those who work with children and families or who are training to do so. It offers guidance to social workers about how to plan for, and work with, children who are looked after by local authorities, including children who have been abused or neglected.

The book emphasizes the importance of balancing the duty to safeguard the child's welfare with the duty to enhance the ability of parents to fulfil their parental responsibilities. It endorses the partnership philosophy of the Children Act 1989, and provides practical guidance on how this principle can be put into practice, whether the child remains at home, lives in residential care, or moves to a permanent foster or adoptive family. The text combines research findings, case material, social work values and practice wisdom to provide a coherent base from which to practice.

June Thoburn is Senior Lecturer in Social Work at the University of East Anglia. She is an acknowledged expert of international standing on child protection and family placement.

1994   189 pages   1 85742 119 1   £9.95

Price subject to change without notification

arena

the **ABC** of
Child Protection

JEAN MOORE

"...an excellent source of information on the subject. If you buy this for your own reference shelf, you will take it down again and again to help you make sense of the child protection cases which all too often come your way.' **The Magistrate**

The ABC of Child Protection examines four faces of abuse in detail: physical abuse, children caught up in marital violence, the much neglected subject of neglect, and sexual abuse.

The painful stresses experienced by the worker are not forgotten and emphasis is put upon the specific skills required in child protection work. There is a lively chapter on face-to-face work with abused children and the complexities of child protection conferences are helpfully analysed with particular reference to the attendance of parents and children.

The black perspective is given prominence with contributions from Emmanuel Okine and David Divine. A chapter by Caroline Ball describes the contents and implications of the 1989 Children Act. Issues relating to racism, sexism, classism, ageism and disabilityism are honestly tackled.

Jean Moore is a child abuse consultant and freelance trainer.

1992   **224 pages**   1 85742 027 6   **£8.95**

Price subject to change without notification

arena

The Police and Social Workers

Second Edition

Terry Thomas

Social workers and police officers are in daily contact with one another in various areas of their work. This book offers a clear guide to that inter-agency work and critically examines how it is carried out in practice.

This second edition of the book has been substantially revised to take account of changes in the law, policy and procedures affecting both police and social workers. In particular the Children Act 1989, The Criminal Justice Act 1991 and the findings of the Royal Commission on Criminal Justice 1993. The opportunity has also been taken to revise parts of the original text to ensure as clear a light as possible is thrown on police-social work collaboration – illustrating both the positive and the negative.

Terry Thomas is Senior Lecturer in Social Work at Leeds Metropolitan University.

1994   346 pages   1 85742 157 4

— *The* —
LEGAL RIGHTS
Manual

A guide for social workers and advice centres

SECOND EDITION

Jeremy Cooper

This book is a practical manual dealing with a wide range of typical legal problems facing clients of those engaged in social work. It will be an invaluable source of reference to social workers and assistants, to those working in the medical and paramedical professions, and to those involved in training in these areas, whether as students or as teachers.

Written by a lawyer with considerable practical and teaching experience in this field, the book adopts a straightforward, non-technical style to explain the legal rights of the public in many important areas of daily concern: general consumer problems and how to complain about them; welfare benefits; in the workplace; the rights of consumers of council services; the rights of older people, and of physically or mentally disabled people; civil rights and the police; finding and keeping a home; and using legal rights to improve a home.

Jeremy Cooper is a barrister and Professor of Law and Head of the Law Division at the Southampton Institute

1994   319 pages   1 85742 136 1

arena